INDIA BRIEFING

The Asia Society

The Asia Society is a nonprofit, nonpartisan public education organization dedicated to increasing American understanding of Asia and broadening the dialogue between Americans and Asians. Through its programs in contemporary affairs, the fine and performing arts, and elementary and secondary education, the Society reaches audiences across the United States and works closely with colleagues in Asia.

The Society's Center for India-U.S. Education, under whose auspices this volume was published, was established in 1991 as a resource for policymakers and analysts in both the public and private sectors. Through its public programs, conferences, and working groups, the Center provides an independent source of information and analysis and a forum for dialogue.

The views expressed in this publication are those of the individual contributors.

INDIA BRIEFING

Staying the Course

Philip Oldenburg, Editor

Published in Cooperation with The Asia Society
Deborah Field Washburn, Series Editor

An East Gate Book

M.E. Sharpe
Armonk, New York
London, England

An East Gate Book

Library of Congress ISSN: 0894-5136
ISBN 1-56324-609-0 (hardcover)
ISBN 1-56324-610-4 (softcover)

Printed in the United States of America

The paper used in this publication meets the minimum requirements of American National Standard for Information Sciences— Permanence of Paper for Printed Library Materials, ANSI Z 39.48-1984.

∞

BM (c) 10 9 8 7 6 5 4 3 2 1
BM (p) 10 9 8 7 6 5 4 3 2 1

Contents

Preface

India Briefing: Staying the Course is the eighth volume in the *India Briefing* series, picking up where *India Briefing, 1993* left off. The authors bring fresh perspectives to the analysis of contemporary India, with special focus on the state level of government and the importance of grass-roots forces. Chapters on Gujarat as a laboratory for events with national implications, India's canny chief ministers, the course of economic reform since 1991, and the neglected informal sector of the labor movement all illuminate recent developments by providing incisive, original analysis in historical context. As editor Philip Oldenburg points out in his introduction, this is not the India that American audiences encounter in the media. The background to a rounded appreciation of India today is deepened by the comprehensive, annotated reading lists supplied in the book's final chapter and the two-year chronology of key events in Indian affairs.

This volume launches a copublishing relationship between The Asia Society and M.E. Sharpe, which will include planned volumes in the *China Briefing* and *Korea Briefing* series. We wish to thank Douglas Merwin and his colleagues at M.E. Sharpe for their encouragement and support.

Thanks also are due to Dr. Gowher Rizvi, whose enthusiasm for the series has sustained its momentum; to Deborah Field Washburn, whose careful attention to this and earlier *Briefings* has been a key ingredient in their high quality; to Karen Fein, who skillfully prepared the manuscript and made valuable editorial suggestions; to Amit Bose and Bettina Buss, who provided first-rate research assistance; and especially to Philip Oldenburg and the fine team of authors he assembled. The dedication of each of these individuals is reflected in the pages that follow.

Marshall M. Bouton
Executive Vice President
The Asia Society

June 1995

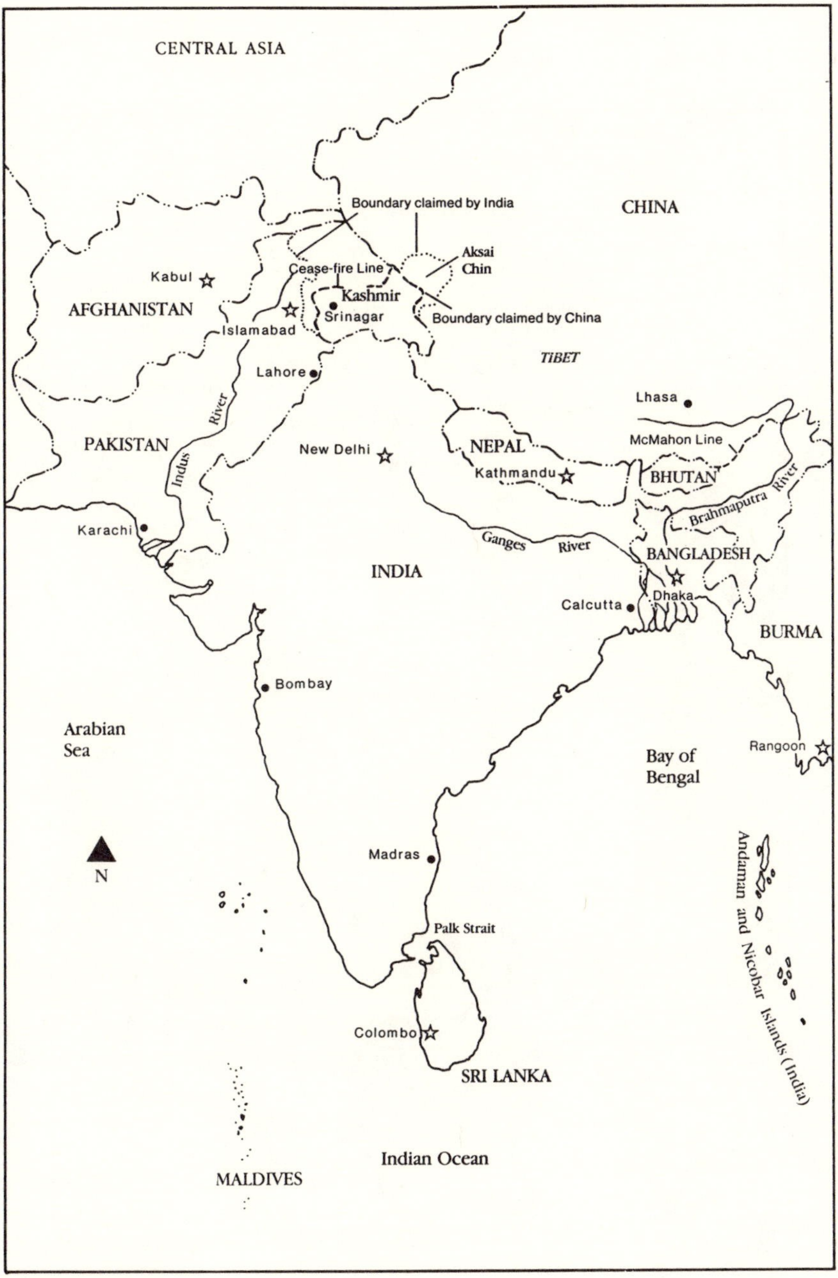
CENTRAL ASIA
CHINA
Boundary claimed by India
Aksai Chin
Cease-fire Line
Kashmir
Srinagar
Boundary claimed by China
Kabul
AFGHANISTAN
Islamabad
TIBET
Lahore
Lhasa
Indus River
PAKISTAN
NEPAL
McMahon Line
New Delhi
Kathmandu
BHUTAN
Brahmaputra River
Karachi
Ganges River
BANGLADESH
INDIA
Dhaka
Calcutta
BURMA
Bombay
Arabian Sea
Rangoon
Bay of Bengal
N
Madras
Andaman and Nicobar Islands (India)
Palk Strait
Colombo
SRI LANKA
Indian Ocean
MALDIVES

South Asia

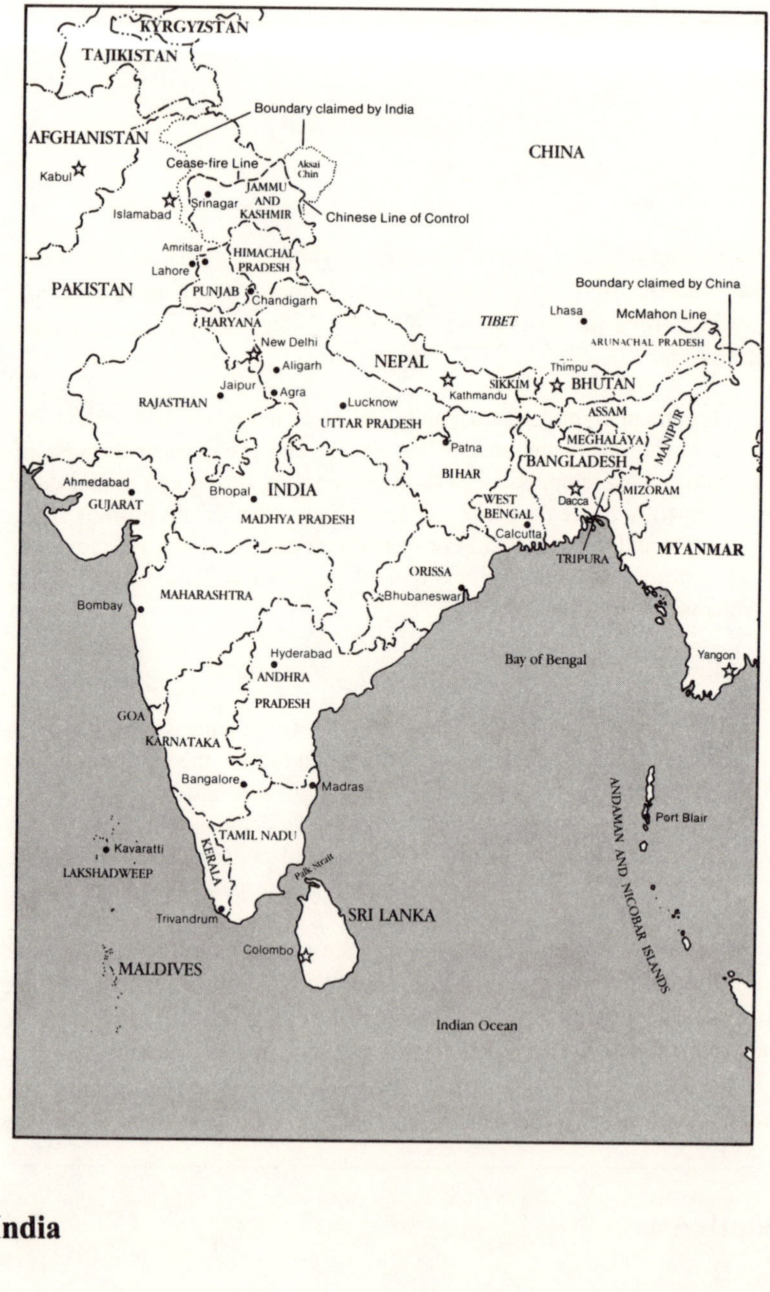
KYRGYZSTAN
TAJIKISTAN
Boundary claimed by India
AFGHANISTAN
CHINA
Kabul
Cease-fire Line
Aksai Chin
JAMMU AND KASHMIR
Srinagar
Islamabad
Chinese Line of Control
Amritsar
HIMACHAL PRADESH
Lahore
PAKISTAN
PUNJAB
Chandigarh
Boundary claimed by China
HARYANA
TIBET
Lhasa
McMahon Line
New Delhi
ARUNACHAL PRADESH
NEPAL
Aligarh
Thimpu
Jaipur
SIKKIM
BHUTAN
Agra
Kathmandu
RAJASTHAN
Lucknow
ASSAM
UTTAR PRADESH
MANIPUR
MEGHALAYA
Patna
BANGLADESH
Ahmedabad
BIHAR
Bhopal
INDIA
MIZORAM
GUJARAT
WEST BENGAL
Dacca
MADHYA PRADESH
Calcutta
TRIPURA
MYANMAR
ORISSA
Bhubaneswar
MAHARASHTRA
Bombay
Hyderabad
Bay of Bengal
Yangon
ANDHRA PRADESH
GOA
KARNATAKA
Bangalore
Madras
ANDAMAN AND NICOBAR ISLANDS
Port Blair
TAMIL NADU
Kavaratti
KERALA
LAKSHADWEEP
Palk Strait
SRI LANKA
Trivandrum
Colombo
MALDIVES
Indian Ocean

India

Introduction

Philip Oldenburg

India is "staying the course" toward wished-for goals. In his famous "tryst with destiny" speech, made to parliament "at the midnight hour" of India's freedom on August 14, 1947, Nehru set out those goals in these words:

> A moment comes, which comes but rarely in history, when we step out from the old to the new, when an age ends, and when the soul of a nation, long suppressed, finds utterance. It is fitting that at this solemn moment we take the pledge of dedication to the service of India and her people and to the still larger cause of humanity. . . . The service of India . . . means the ending of poverty and ignorance and disease and inequality of opportunity.

Or, in the expanded version of that day's press note:

> The future beckons to us. Whither do we go and what shall be our endeavor? To bring freedom and opportunity to the common man, to the peasants and workers of India; to fight and end poverty and ignorance and disease; to build up a prosperous, democratic and progressive nation, and to create social, economic and political institutions which will ensure justice and fullness of life to every man and woman.[1]

In the broadest terms the goals were retaining and enhancing a proud independence won by a nationalist struggle; eradicating poverty through industrialization; and removing social and cultural injustice. The means to those ends, and an end in itself, was democracy.

In the decades since independence, India has come a long way toward those goals, and that progress is not the less because a great

1. Jawaharlal Nehru, *Speeches*, Vol. 1: September 1946–May 1949 (New Delhi: Publications Division, Government of India, 1958), pp. 24–28.

deal more needs to be done. Chapters in previous *India Briefing* volumes have outlined accomplishments and failures on a number of fronts—poverty, justice, and population control—as well as in the larger fields of foreign affairs, economic growth, and political development.[2] Indian analysts have taken to referring to the Indian "elephant"—in contrast to the "tigers" to the east—to suggest economic size and power, but it is worth underscoring something Rudyard Kipling wrote: "Elephants do not gallop. They move from spots at varying rates of speed. If an elephant wished to catch an express train he could not gallop, but he could catch the train."[3] India's ponderous movement has been deceptive.

Nowhere has this been more true than in the political system. It is not simply that India has preserved its democracy, but also that democracy has put down deep roots, which penetrate into the local arenas of villages and city neighborhoods. For most of India's history, "local" politics has meant politics of the (now 25) states; with the passage of legislation that gives life to the recent constitutional amendments on city and village self-government, that may change.

The chapters by John R. Wood and James Manor focus on the state level of Indian politics. Wood notes that some of the major issues that have shaken the national government in recent years—Hindu-Muslim antagonism and violence, the criminalization of politics, the advancement of "backward" castes, the environment and development—have been at the core of the politics of the western state of Gujarat for some time. As Wood suggests, while Gujarat is literally on the edge of India and on the margin of the "heartland" areas of the interior and the Gangetic plain, the state has played a role in political change that is central: what Gujarat deals with today, it appears, India may have to confront tomorrow.

Gujarat may be special because of its history and location, but it is

2. Inter alia. Granville Austin, "The Constitution, Society, and Law," in *India Briefing, 1993,* ed. Philip Oldenburg (Boulder, Colo.: Westview, 1993); Holly Sims, "Malthusian Nightmare or Richest in Human Resources?" in *India Briefing, 1992,* ed. Leonard A. Gordon and Philip Oldenburg (Boulder, Colo.: Westview, 1992); Stephen Philip Cohen, "India as a Great Power: Perceptions and Prospects," in *India Briefing, 1991,* ed. Philip Oldenburg (Boulder, Colo.: Westview, 1991); Eleanor Zelliot, "Dalit: New Perspectives on India's Untouchables," in ibid.; Alan Heston, "Poverty in India: Some Recent Policies," in *India Briefing, 1990,* ed. Marshall M. Bouton and Philip Oldenburg (Boulder, Colo.: Westview, 1990).

3. Rudyard Kipling, "Moti Guj—Mutineer," in *Kipling: A Selection of His Stories and Poems,* Vol. 2 (Garden City, N.Y.: Doubleday & Co., 1956), p. 273.

important to evaluate how India is governed by focusing far more than we have on how state governments work. James Manor looks carefully at the strategies and tactics that state-level leaders, the chief ministers, have employed. He suggests that they almost never act as selfless, farseeing statesmen (most have been men), yet the numbers who are thoroughly corrupt or totally incompetent are equally small. As Manor concludes, "[India] is less ungovernable than many have suggested. Enough has been achieved there to warrant appreciation for the practical utility of Indian democracy, and to discourage despair about its prospects."

If the view presented here about the stability of India's governance is more favorable than the conventional wisdom would have it, then the view of where the Indian economy is headed is more cautious than the excited talk of India as a "Big Emerging Market" might imply.[4] Few doubts have been expressed about the overall thrust of the economic reforms initiated in 1991, though some have severely criticized certain aspects of reform; but many are not convinced that the political system can sustain the new direction. As Meghnad Desai argues in the conclusion of his chapter, "Economic policy requires a medium-term perspective to be effective. As of now, the political system cannot guarantee such a perspective." One touchstone of "political will" is how the prerogatives of organized labor, analyzed by E.A. Ramaswamy in his chapter, will be dealt with, as pressures build to step up the pace of privatization and implement an "exit" policy (one that allows management far greater freedom to hire and fire). Certainly the continued momentum of the economic liberalization program and thus the prospects for sustained economic improvement are open to question.

A few important political and economic developments aside, the major items of news of India reported abroad after March 1993 (when a series of bombs in Bombay killed some 200 people, shattering the Bombay Stock Exchange, but *not* triggering riots like those of January 1993) were the earthquake of September 30, 1993, and the pneumonic plague that hit the western Indian city of Surat a year later. While the preponderance of attention to "disaster" in India underlines a core

---

4. See particularly the 20-page *Financial Times Survey* (London), November 8, 1994; "The Tiger Steps Out," *Economist* (a 30-page survey), January 21, 1995; and T.N. Ninan, "Do We Need Rao for Reform?" *Seminar 425: India 1994* (January 1995).

image of the country, the nature of the disasters portrayed is suggestive: the disasters that did not occur included major riots (like those in Bombay in January 1993); elections severely marred by violence, including assassinations; and wars with neighbors. Politics and economic policy initiatives did not cause upheavals; the Indian elephant lumbered along.

Comprehending India

Still, our picture of what India "is" contains many distortions, built up by what we have read and seen. What the newspapers print is both cause and effect of that portrait: editors choose to publish largely what readers want to read about, which in turn reinforces those readers' images. Ainslie Embree's chapter, "Reading India," represents an escape from that pernicious circle. He lists and annotates works we can read to bring all of India's complexity into focus and to achieve "a sense of intimacy and a depth of understanding with a world that is not our own but in which we feel welcome."

A comparison of coverage of the disasters of earthquake and plague with that of other important stories is indicative of how India's image is formed outside the country. The plague story was most heavily covered: from the first outbreak around September 24, 1994, and continuing up to November 15, 1994, the story was told in some 35,000 words in three American newspapers with full-time South Asia correspondents *(New York Times*, *Washington Post*, and *Los Angeles Times*).[5] The story of the earthquake, in which about 10,000 people died, took about 20,000 words to tell. Compare this with the coverage of the major state elections of November 1993, and those of November 1994 and February–March 1995, which taken together took about 18,000 words to report. And all the articles on the economy (including the topics of economic reform, trade, and business) totaled just over 40,000 words, in coverage stretching from January 1, 1993, to March 15, 1995.

This is hardly a new pattern. Christopher Thomas of the *Times* of London bitingly lists the things "people want to know about":

> When Mahatma Gandhi was assassinated, foreign journalists said the Indian union would never last. Generations of reporters have come here

5. The data here come from a NEXIS citation search of headlines and lead paragraphs in those newspapers.

> since then to cover subsequent crises and to write stories on the same theme. There has been plenty of ammunition—language riots, caste riots, communal bloodshed, the assassinations of Indira Gandhi and Rajiv Gandhi, wars with Pakistan and China, secessionism in Punjab, an uprising in Kashmir, bloodshed in Assam, anti-Hindi movements in the south, starvation, corruption, pollution, environmental catastrophe, disparities of wealth and poverty, caste prejudice, burning brides, *sati*, killing girl babies, bonded labor, child labor, criminalization of politics, discrimination against women, human rights abuses—there is a torrent of wretchedness from which emerge the most heartrending stories.[6]

The reasons for this negative coverage are both general and particular:

> It is the stuff of newspapers to be negative: news is about what goes wrong, about the abnormal and the outrageous, not about what goes right. This leads to an excess of gloomy reportage, particularly in the case of India, which teaches the world how to regard it through the columns of its own overly pessimistic press and the utterances of its doom-obsessed politicians.[7]

And part of it is lack of knowledge and experience. Thomas forthrightly admits, "Most of us are hampered by the language barrier and lack of knowledge about the intricacies and complexities of the country, so we gorge off the dying news in the morning newspapers."[8] Further, "I have become less apocalyptic about India the longer I have stayed. In my first year I thought it was in a constant state of decay, with props and patches all over it and that one day it would give a groan and keel over. Four years have taught me about the endurance of India."[9]

It is hardly surprising, then, that one of the most significant distortions of India's reality lies in the misunderstanding of the stability and genuineness of India's democracy. The editorial in the *New York Times* titled "India's Shallow Democracy" illustrates the point well.[10] It begins:

6. Christopher Thomas, "Perceptions of India in the Foreign Press," *India International Centre Quarterly*, Vol. 20, nos. 1–2 (Spring–Summer 1993), p. 266.

7. Ibid., p. 267.

8. Ibid., pp. 272–73.

9. Ibid., p. 271.

10. January 29, 1995.

> India boasts, accurately, of being the world's biggest democracy. But India's democracy can be as superficial as it is big. Multiparty elections are regularly held, opposition parties occasionally win and when Indira Gandhi attempted to establish an outright dictatorship in the 1970s, India's people drove her from power.[11]

The editorial goes on to detail the features of Indian politics that make the country's democracy "shallow." It says that "India's elections, particularly at the state level, are notoriously corrupt and violence-prone," and it notes that India has been dominated by one party—the Congress. But half the editorial is devoted to India's human rights record, in Punjab, Kashmir, and elsewhere; it asserts that the facts of arbitrary arrests and torture, the deaths of "terrorists" in encounters with the police and army, and the rapes and wanton killings by those forces puncture all India's claims to be a democracy.

These views, often expressed in the American press, represent an unbalanced appraisal. Even in the "positives," the editorial misleads. Since the 1971 national elections and the 1972 state elections, won overwhelmingly by the Congress Party, the opposition has won two of the five national elections and 41 of the 72 assembly elections held in the 16 major states, which is hardly winning "occasionally." The people not only drove Indira Gandhi from power, but they did so in an election called by Mrs. Gandhi, whose Emergency was not a dictatorship of the viciously oppressive type so sadly familiar all over the world. That 1977 election, moreover, was not the sort dictators call. It was in fact free and fair, in part because, in all probability, Mrs. Gandhi had a paradoxical commitment to democratic procedures. More important, it was free and fair because a bold press defied the government and because the people's angry mood of opposition to the government became fully evident only just before the poll date, thus lulling the government into believing it would win easily.[12]

---

11. These characteristics are set out, in about the same pattern, in John Burns's analytical article of the previous week: John Burns, "Democracy in India: Now You See It . . . ," *New York Times*, January 22, 1995, Section 4.

12. See Ashis Nandy, "Indira Gandhi and the Culture of Indian Politics," in his *At the Edge of Psychology* (Delhi: Oxford University Press, 1980); Myron Weiner, *India at the Polls: The Parliamentary Elections of 1977* (Washington, D.C.: American Enterprise Institute, 1978); and L.P. Singh, *Electoral Reform* (New Delhi: Uppal Publishing House, 1986), p. 12, on the integrity of election commissioners.

One other factor that kept the election fair was the institution of an independent election commission, headed by a chief election commissioner of integrity. Indeed, the election commission has since independence striven to ensure genuine elections, with one major device being the countermanding of voting in polling stations (precincts) and even whole constituencies where there is evidence of severe disruption, with "booth capturing," violence, and fraud. Repolls are routinely conducted. Thus despite corruption and significant violence, no political scientist has argued that elections to national and major state legislatures are perversions.[13]

The present chief election commissioner, T.N. Seshan, has emerged as a major political figure.[14] Seshan, who had served as cabinet secretary, the seniormost position in the civil service hierarchy, has attempted to enforce the strict code of election practice. He has appointed observers to check that candidates do not spend more than the legal limit and attempted to put a stop to the practice of plastering political posters and stenciled political slogans seemingly on every available wall, among other things. More important, he has arranged election schedules so that he can deploy massive police forces to prevent violence and booth capturing, and, indeed, in the elections to state assemblies that have occurred under his direction, there has been far less violence than in previous elections. In the Uttar Pradesh elections of November 1993, for example, there were only two murders, compared to more than 190 in the 1991 elections.[15]

---

13. Burns writes, "Politicians have assured themselves of election by vote-buying, ballot-stuffing, and driving unwanted voters from the polls at gunpoint." As Paul Brass (saying that "for the most part, elections in India since independence have been free, fair, and competitive") notes, "In the 1984 elections, the election commission reported incidents of disruption or attempted rigging in 53 parliamentary constituencies [of 540], but these officially recognized incidents occurred in only 264 of the country's nearly half a million polling stations." Paul Brass, "Political Parties and Electoral Politics," in *India Briefing, 1989,* ed. Marshall M. Bouton and Philip Oldenburg (Boulder, Colo.: Westview, 1989), p. 62. These incidents have tended to occur in a few geographic areas, including parts of Bihar, western Uttar Pradesh, and Haryana. Most Indian politicians win for reasons similar to those in other democracies: their stands on issues; their personal and ethnic or class characteristics; their political party; and, far from least, the amount of government money they have arranged to have spent to benefit their constituents. And many win because they have money, either their own or raised from business leaders and the like.

14. See Vir Sanghvi, "Rage Cannot Wither Him," *Seminar 425: India 1994* (January 1995); John-Thor Dahlburg, "Election Umpire Calls Them as He Sees Them," *Los Angeles Times,* January 25, 1994.

15. Dahlburg, "Election Umpire Calls Them as He Sees Them."

The other major step Seshan has enforced is to require photo identification cards for voters, as a way of preventing fraudulent voting—as in many American cities not long ago, the absent or the dead are frequently found to have voted. Although Seshan was forced to postpone the deadline for their issuance in states where elections were scheduled in early 1995, photo identification cards were in fact used in Maharashtra, Gujarat, and Orissa, though not in Bihar. These steps have been widely welcomed in the press.

A number of the chief election commissioner's other initiatives and his style and method of getting his policies accepted, however, have been strongly criticized by both politicians and journalists. Seshan has tried to remove those members of the Rajya Sabha, Finance Minister Manmohan Singh among them, who are not in fact residents of the state from which they are elected, as the law requires. (A time-honored practice has been for party leaders to direct members of the state legislatures to vote in ministers serving in the national government, who must be members of parliament.[16])

Far more controversial was Seshan's "request"—it had the tone of an order, which he admitted he could not issue—that the finance minister not present the 1995–96 budget at its scheduled time in February 1995, just as the elections in Gujarat, Maharashtra, Orissa, and Bihar were to be held, on the grounds that it was possible that policies designed to attract votes would be announced. This request was not honored. But Seshan successfully prevented Doordarshan (the government television network) from airing discussion of the election results from Gujarat, Maharashtra, and Orissa, on the grounds that commentary would influence voters in Bihar who were about to go to the polls.

Some of the chief election commissioner's orders and policies have been challenged in the courts. On April 4, 1994, the Supreme Court enjoined the chief election commissioner from unilaterally enforcing a nonstatutory "model code of conduct" for elections and criticized him for attempting to "usurp" the powers of other state bodies, ordering him to mend his ways. The court asked Seshan's counsel to "advise your client that he is talking too much and behaving in a manner

16. Members of the Rajya Sabha are elected by state legislature, and when party discipline is enforced, the results mirror the strength of the various parties in the legislature. This enables a national party to get candidates elected who are not, strictly speaking, politicians.

unbecoming of a high constitutional functionary. . . . If necessary, this court will summon him here and set him right. This person seems to have lost his balance."[17]

The Congress government attempted to bring Seshan to heel by introducing a bill that would amend the constitution to increase the power of the two additional election commissioners they had appointed so the commission could make decisions by majority rule; Seshan simply had ignored their existence. But the government suffered an ignominious defeat when the Communist Party of India, joining the Bharatiya Janata Party (BJP), refused to contribute to the necessary two-thirds vote in parliament. Indeed, the government withdrew the bill rather than lose the vote.[18]

Seshan "won" because of the enormous support he enjoys, particularly among the urban middle class. According to the editor Vir Sanghvi, "No nonpolitician [in India] has ever had anything like the kind of power that Seshan now commands."[19] In an *India Today* poll conducted just before the constitutional amendment bill was to be introduced, some 90 percent of both urban and rural respondents who had heard of Seshan and the bill rated his overall performance as "good" or "very good"; 71 percent of the urban sample said he "has the right approach"; and 78 percent thought Seshan's motive was to "root out corruption," rather than to "look for personal glory" (14 percent).[20] Sanghvi, referring to Seshan as the "middle-class messiah" of the day, describes both how much he is disliked by politicians and journalists and how limited some of his initiatives have proved to be. "Yes," Sanghvi writes,

---

17. *Times of India* (Bombay), April 5, 1994, p. 1. See also Manoj Mitta, "T.N. Seshan: Reined In," *India Today* (North America), April 30, 1994, pp. 26–27.

18. Although it was clear that this bill was introduced because Seshan had flaunted the power of the chief election commissioner, it should be noted that the proposal to enlarge the election commission has a long history:

> The Joint Committee on Amendments to Election Law . . . unanimously recommended in its report (1972) that the election commission should be a multimember body. . . . Three successive chief election commissioners whose views are available have, it is true, been opposed to the enlargement of the Commission for no convincing reason that one can see. (L.P. Singh, *Electoral Reform*, p. 13.)

19. Sanghvi, "Rage Cannot Wither Him," p. 43.

20. *India Today* (North America), July 15, 1994, p. 29. Only 30 percent of the rural sample (and 67 percent of the urban) had heard of Seshan, and far fewer were aware of the constitutional amendment bill.

> [Seshan] is a publicity hound who has made tactical decisions on who to attack and who to let off. Yes, he has overplayed his role. But he is making an attempt to do something that is long overdue. . . . And even if he can't cleanse the system, there is no doubt that he has halted the decline.[21]

Sanghvi interprets the middle class's devotion to Seshan as the result of its anger at its "lack of empowerment"; thus, "every time [Seshan] kicks around some hapless politician, he is striking a blow for middle-class rights."[22] If Seshan's initiatives survive—and India's huge middle class is a formidable force—then one crucial foundation pillar of democracy in India will be strengthened.

In the area of human rights India's democracy is found severely wanting, by American journalists and American politicians alike.[23] Human rights (and the closely allied problem of the Kashmir dispute) have indeed been a major irritant in U.S.-India relations, in a period when these two countries have moved closer, based largely on shared economic interests.

The most recent U.S. Department of State annual human rights report on India, released in February 1995, provides detailed descriptions of a wide range of human rights problems in India, but its opening paragraph states forthrightly, "India is a longstanding parliamentary democracy." There are indeed far too many cases of police torture, extrajudicial killings, and injustice even when the courts are reached, but there is very little evidence that these abuses extend much beyond being shameful blemishes on the democratic polity. That a rich variety of organized groups can forcefully challenge the government's policies and actions—and survive and flourish—suggests that human rights violations do not outweigh India's democratic practices.[24]

Human rights issues have been pursued in India by the press and a

---

21. Sanghvi, "Rage Cannot Wither Him," p. 45.

22. Ibid.

23. Also in this group is Freedom House, whose 1993–94 *Freedom in the World* (New York: Freedom House, 1994) classifies India as "partly free," apparently because of insurgencies in Kashmir (where democracy certainly is severely crippled) and the northeast, and civil liberties violations. One's confidence in their judgment is undermined by gross errors of fact (e.g., the following statements: India received its independence in February 1947; the assassination of Rajiv Gandhi "[threw] the country into chaos" [pp. 304–5]).

24. See Smitu Kothari, "Social Movements and the Redefinition of Democracy," in *India Briefing, 1993*.

number of civil liberties and human rights organizations. Most encouraging has been the emergence of the National Human Rights Commission (NHRC). Many thought this was established by the government as a gesture to deflect criticism from international human rights groups such as Amnesty International, but the commission, according to the State Department report, "began to establish a record as an effective advocate for human rights." It notes, "Indian human rights groups criticized the legislation creating the NHRC; they remain skeptical, but have indicated that thus far most of their concerns appear to be unfounded."[25] At the end of February 1995, the chairman of the NHRC, Justice Ranganath Misra, wrote to all members of parliament, urging them to vote against extending the Terrorist and Disruptive Activities (Prevention) Act (TADA), which has been widely abused.[26] In May 1995, the government replaced TADA with a less sweeping law.

Other severe problems trouble the functioning of India's polity. For one, there is evidence that in some areas of India, most notably in parts of the state of Bihar, the local political system has become significantly affected by violence and criminalization. John R. Wood in his chapter points out that "India is no longer witnessing simply 'crime from below,' which is small-scale and localized (if increasingly violent), but also 'crime from above,' in which much larger stakes, organized professionals, and international transactions are involved." But that is a far cry from saying that violence and criminalization threaten to dominate the system, even in those areas, let alone in the whole of India.

The insurgencies in Kashmir and the northeastern states remain confined, and revolutionary activity—that of the Peoples' War Group of Andhra Pradesh is the most significant—hardly constitutes a serious threat to India's stability. The central government continues to claim that it is aiming to bring about a political settlement in Kashmir; trial balloons on the holding of elections are regularly floated. Certainly, the way the crisis of the occupation of the Hazratbal shrine in Srinagar by Kashmiri militants in October–November 1993 was handled—with

25. U.S. Department of State, *India Human Rights Practices, 1994* (February 1995), Introduction, Section 4.

26. Intended to be used in places like Punjab where terrorism makes the ordinary functioning of courts impossible (witnesses prepared to testify publicly cannot be found, for example), this law—under which, among other things, the person arrested must prove his or her innocence—has been most widely used in places like Gujarat, where there are no terrorists. See Harinder Baweja, "TADA: An Act of Terror," *India Today* (North America), September 15, 1994, for an overview.

patience and firmness—is a good sign. So too was the release from jail of several leaders who favor "self-determination" for Kashmiris—meaning the independence of Kashmir. Nonetheless, killings and kidnappings by a wide spectrum of guerrilla groups continue, as do killings (sometimes under questionable circumstances) by the security forces.

When a democracy can ensure that a wide range of political opinion can be disseminated; that political parties of a startling variety can compete in free and fair elections; that the government cannot tame an independent election commissioner; that an institution like the National Human Rights Commission that immediately exerts an embarrassing autonomy can be allowed to exist; then it is hardly "shallow" and about to disappear.

This should not surprise us. Since independence, the Indian elephant's political movement has been slow and erratic, but it has in fact survived crises the like of which have ripped apart other Third World countries. Those crises have been mainly dealt with not by decisive action, but by attrition: rearranging political institutions and actors (by appointing commissions, amending laws, holding elections, and creating parties and movements), temporizing, and waiting for the crisis to subside. (The one apparent exception, Indira Gandhi's declaration of a state of Emergency in 1975, was in fact the result of a shallow political crisis—the challenge to Mrs. Gandhi's personal position—and produced rather than solved the deeper political crisis.) Comprehending India requires the sort of long-term perspective toward which Embree's recommended readings point us.

The Polity

The effective functioning of democratic institutions indeed helps us understand the post–January 1993 weakening, if not reversal, of the Hindu nationalist upsurge.[27] There has been no significant revival of direct action by militant members of the Vishwa Hindu Parishad since the destruction of the Babri mosque in December 1992. The terrible Hindu-Muslim riots that followed that event have not recurred, and even minor disturbances are few and far between. The partial defeat of

27. Shekhar Gupta, "The Gathering Storm," in *India Briefing, 1990*; Ashutosh Varshney, "Battling the Past, Forging a Future? Ayodhya and Beyond," in *India Briefing, 1993*.

the BJP in the November 1993 elections—and the way it fought that campaign, significantly toning down its inflammatory rhetoric on the Ayodhya issue—suggested that Hindu nationalism had lost a good deal of its value as a mobilizing ideal.[28] The state elections in early 1995 in which the Hindu nationalist parties did very well in Gujarat and Maharashtra did not necessarily contradict this trend, since those elections were clearly fought primarily on issues of corruption and leadership.[29]

This has not been the result of inspired leadership by the prime minister or his government, unless P.V. Narasimha Rao's inactivity and retreat from decision making is, as some have interpreted it, a conscious and shrewd strategy. A more plausible interpretation focuses on the workings of Indian democracy. As Ashutosh Varshney argues:

> What has pulled India back from the brink [of ungovernability and escalation of violence in 1993 and 1994]? [It is] the self-correcting mechanisms of Indian democracy. . . . The system punishes politicians or political parties that go to an excess, violating democratic norms flagrantly, or pushing the system to ideological extremes of right or left. In other words, *political and ideological excesses are checked; routine political misconduct, on the whole, is not.*[30]

This point is well illustrated here by John R. Wood, in his discussion of the 1995 Gujarat election results, and by James Manor, who writes, "Over the past two decades, India's voters have become . . . more aware of their collective strength and self-interest, more insistent in demanding responses from politicians, and more willing on election days to punish those who fail to respond."

We can see this "self-correcting" mechanism in four major developments of the recent past: the Supreme Court decision on Ayodhya; the decisions on the Narmada dam project; the Harshad Mehta bribe accu-

---

28. See *India Today* (North America), November 30, 1993, pp. 26–28. The BJP lost considerable ground in Karnataka, the southern state in which it is strongest, in the November 1994 state elections, compared to its 1991 showing in the parliamentary elections, but Ayodhya was not much of an issue there.

29. The article on the Gujarat results in *India Today* is titled "Gujarat: Cashing In on Corruption." *India Today* (North America), March 31, 1995. John R. Wood in his chapter notes that the explanation for the BJP victory in Gujarat "cited most often is voter impatience with corruption and criminality, long associated in many Gujarati minds with the ruling party."

30. Ashutosh Varshney, "The Self-Correcting Mechanisms of Indian Democracy," *Seminar 425: India 1994* (January 1995), p. 38; emphasis in the original.

sations; and the so-called sugar scam. Before the Babri mosque was destroyed, the Supreme Court had issued orders that the existing structure was not to be touched and no construction was to be allowed, and had received assurances from the chief minister, Kalyan Singh, that its directive would be honored. It had also been asked to resolve the archaeological issues of whether a Hindu temple had existed at the site of the mosque. On October 24, 1994, almost two years after the destruction of the mosque, the Supreme Court declined to rule on the latter point and allowed the central government to acquire the disputed land pending judgment on the court cases contesting title. It also convicted Kalyan Singh for contempt of court and sentenced him to one day's symbolic imprisonment and a fine of Rs.2,000. Although the BJP rallied in support of Kalyan Singh, the significant feature of this outcome was that it essentially settled the matter. No one seriously argued with the sentence, the decision on the land, or the Supreme Court's unwillingness to settle the archaeological dispute. The routine and deliberate judicial process produced an acceptable result, thus underlining the wisdom of diverting those explosive issues into the judicial system in the first place.

The central government attempted to curb the BJP's activities. The BJP tried to stage a massive rally in Delhi at the end of February 1993 to demand the dissolution of the Lok Sabha and a new election, among other things; the government responded by banning the rally and arresting many who planned to attend. Those BJP leaders who did defy the massive deployment of security forces were drenched by water cannons.[31] In July 1993 the government proposed a bill to "delink" religion and politics by not allowing parties deemed religious in nature to contest elections, going beyond existing legislation that forbids the use of religious symbols in election campaigns. This was clearly aimed at the BJP, but the Congress Party could not muster a two-thirds majority and was forced to withdraw the bill. The defeat of the BJP in the November 1993 elections in Uttar Pradesh and Madhya Pradesh, however, seemed to suggest that the Hindutva "wave" had receded; the legislation on religion and politics was not reintroduced.[32]

31. *India Today* (North America), March 15, 1993.

32. When asked in an opinion poll conducted in mid-July 1993 by the market research firm MARG for *India Today,* "What are the major problems that the country faces?" 37 percent of the respondents chose "inflation," while only 14 percent chose "Ayodhya" (23 percent chose "corruption"). *India Today* (North America), August 15, 1993, p. 32.

At the end of March 1993, the government asked the World Bank to cancel the remaining $170 million of the $450 million loan sanctioned for the Narmada dam project. John R. Wood describes in his chapter the array of forces that brought this about, and the consequences. The BJP government elected in Gujarat in March 1995 has, if anything, been even stronger in its support of the project than the Congress government it replaced. It is probable that the interplay of activists putting pressure on the central government and the Congress-run Madhya Pradesh government with the BJP–Shiv Sena government in Maharashtra (and a strong BJP presence in Madhya Pradesh) will produce compromise solutions on environmental protection measures and the rehabilitation of villagers whose homes are being inundated.

Financial scandals livened up the political landscape but did not cause any major disruption. In June 1993 the claim by stockbroker Harshad Mehta, who had been at the heart of the stockmarket scandal of 1992,[33] that he had bribed the prime minister with a suitcase filled with Rs.1 crore in cash (about $300,000) was fairly quickly rejected—here a careful press investigation rather than political maneuvering had the greater impact. The echoes of the stock market scandal, however, continued to sound, as the Joint Parliamentary Committee issued first a draft report (June 1993) and then a final report that criticized the Finance Ministry for inadequate supervision of the financial system. Three days after the final report was tabled on December 21, 1993, Manmohan Singh submitted his resignation—former minister for petroleum and natural gas B. Shankaranand, who was specifically criticized in the report, felt no need to do so—but it was rejected by the prime minister. A full year later, after several incidents of parliamentary uproar on what the opposition saw as a weak "action-taken report" (i.e., action taken on the recommendations of the Joint Parliamentary Committee), the prime minister dropped Shankaranand from the cabinet.

In the meantime, in June 1994 another scandal had broken, this one on the delayed decision to import sugar, a delay that cost the government some Rs.650 crores ($200 million).[34] Yet another inquiry report—this one not made public, but made available to all members of parliament in mid-December 1994, after yet more opposition pres-

33. See Jay Dehejia, "Economic Reforms: Birth of an 'Asian Tiger,' " in *India Briefing, 1993*, pp. 85–86.

34. See "The Great Sugar Scandal," *India Today* (North America), June 30, 1994, cover story.

sure—put most of the blame on the food minister, Kalpanath Rai, who was also dropped from the cabinet.

In all these cases, ranging from scandals to crises that reached deep into the social force of Hindu nationalism, the political system proved to be resilient. Ministers were fired, court decisions were sought and obeyed, and opposition demands were met in part. While each crisis in different ways could be viewed as calling into question the genuineness of Indian democracy, their resolution seems to reaffirm the notion that India's democracy is indeed self-correcting.

Foreign Relations

The outline of India's international position has not changed much since the major shifts caused by the collapse of the Soviet Union in 1990 and the opening to the global economy brought on by the 1991 economic crisis.[35] Relations with Pakistan deteriorated even further, mainly over Kashmir, but those with China were marked by a major agreement. Prime Minister Rao's visit to the United States in May 1994 underlined the continued improvement, though not without hiccoughs, in India-U.S. ties. India continued to pursue a foreign policy centered on its economic rather than security interests.

With the end of the cold war and the continued use of the army for internal low-intensity conflict (again, mainly in Kashmir), India's national security concerns have changed, and the place of the defense establishment has changed with them.[36] Defense expenditure as a percentage of GDP has continued to decline, falling below the 2.5 percent level that some argue is the bare minimum needed.[37] Development of various missile systems has continued—which has also caused friction with the United States—but there is little indication that they are being put into a central place in military strategy. With the cutoff of cheap military hardware from the Soviet Union, procurement of foreign weaponry has slowed. Yet with some 1.5 million men under arms, India remains clearly capable of protecting its borders. It has also

---

35. See Paul Kreisberg, "Foreign Policy in 1992: Building Credibility," in *India Briefing, 1993* for a detailed account. More recent developments are superbly analyzed in Shekhar Gupta, *India Redefines Its Role*, Adelphi Paper 293 (London: Oxford University Press for The International Institute for Strategic Studies, 1995).

36. The best discussion of this is by Gupta, *India Redefines Its Role*, pp. 34–49.

37. Ibid., pp. 38–39.

continued to contribute personnel to UN peacekeeping forces; as of May 31, 1994, India had some 6,000 peacekeepers, the third largest number (after Pakistan and France).[38]

A major milestone in India's relations with China was passed in September 1993, when the prime minister visited Beijing. An agreement was signed that "marked the end of military tension on the Sino-Indian borders. No territory was given or lost as the long-term settlement on the border was effectively put in cold storage."[39] Regular diplomatic meetings continued along with the expansion of economic relations, and China did not support Pakistan's efforts to have India condemned for human rights violations in Kashmir at the UN Human Rights Commission meeting in March 1994. It is probably indicative of the Indian view of China that in a late 1994 public opinion survey of members of the Indian educated elite, only 20 percent of those who advocated India's acquisition of nuclear weapons (who were some 33 percent of the sample) gave "threats from China" as a reason for India developing nuclear weapons (57 percent listed "threats from nuclear Pakistan").[40]

India-Pakistan relations, though not descending to threats of war in recent years, continue to be bitter. India accuses Pakistan's Inter-Services Intelligence agency of complicity in the Bombay blasts of March 1993; Pakistan counters by seeing India's hand in the disturbances in Karachi (where thousands have been killed in riots and reprisals). Pakistan closed its consulate in Bombay in March 1994 and forced the closure of India's Karachi consulate in December 1994. Charges and countercharges over Kashmir are almost a daily occurrence. India scored a "victory" when Pakistan was forced to withdraw its resolution condemning India for human rights violations in Kashmir at the March 1994 session of the UN Human Rights Commission in Geneva.[41] One

---

38. *South Asia and the United States After the Cold War* (New York: The Asia Society, 1994), p. 45.

39. Shekhar Gupta, with Sudeep Chakravarti, "Sino-Indian Relations: Vital Breakthrough)," *India Today* (North America), September 30, 1993, pp. 22.

40. *A Study of India's Nuclear Choices* (Notre Dame, Ind.: Joan B. Kroc Institute for International Peace Studies at the University of Notre Dame; and Goshen, Ind.: Fourth Freedom Forum, November/December 1994), p. 15.

41. See "India-Pakistan Relations: A Short Fuse," *India Today* (North America), March 15, 1994, cover story, and "Human Rights Commission: How the Vote Was Won," *India Today* (North America), March 31, 1994, cover story. See also Shekhar Gupta, "A Hawk's Agenda," *Seminar 425: India 1994* (January 1995) for a critique of India's preoccupation with Pakistan's efforts to "internationalize" the Kashmir dispute.

hopeful sign was a gathering of Indian and Pakistani nongovernmental activists and intellectuals in Delhi in February 1995, sponsored by the "Pakistan-India People's Forum for Peace and Democracy." About 100 people attended from Pakistan, and the Pakistani government, surprised that India would give them all visas, apparently saw this attempt at dialogue as harming Pakistan's interests.[42]

Despite a flap over remarks by Assistant Secretary of State Robin Raphel on Kashmir in February 1994, India's relations with the United States have continued to improve, marked particularly by the prime minister's May 1994 visit to Washington, where he addressed a joint session of Congress.[43] Discussion of the human rights situation in Kashmir and elsewhere was apparently kept out of conversations with visiting American cabinet members (Energy Secretary Hazel O'Leary in mid-1994 and February 1995, Defense Secretary William Perry and Commerce Secretary Ron Brown in January 1995, and Treasury Secretary Robert Rubin in April 1995). Particularly at the time of Secretary Brown's visit, this subjected the Clinton administration to severe criticism by human rights activists.[44]

The nuclear issue, of course, continues to pose a threat to U.S.-India understanding; with the renewal of the Nuclear Nonproliferation Treaty and the rise of what some in Washington call nonproliferation fundamentalism, relations are likely to become even more strained.[45] India will continue to keep its nuclear options open, clearly supported by public opinion: 57 percent of the elite sample surveyed in the fall of 1994 believe that India should maintain its official position on nuclear issues; only 8 percent believe that India should renounce nuclear weapons.[46] Efforts by the United States—including (unannounced) talks in London in May 1994—to get India to stop developing its nuclear option have not been successful.

When Prime Minister Rao met with President Bill Clinton in Washington in May 1994, there was apparently an agreement to focus en-

42. *Times of India* (Bombay), February 27, 1995.

43. See *Seminar 422: The U.S. and Us* (October 1994).

44. Patricia Gossman, "U.S. Proves Once Again That It's Business, Not Human Rights, That Matters," *Boston Globe*, January 23, 1995; "India's Shallow Democracy," *New York Times*, January 29, 1995, editorial page. Compare *South Asia and the United States After the Cold War*, pp. 37–38.

45. See The Asia Society report *Preventing Nuclear Proliferation in South Asia* (New York: The Asia Society, 1995) and Gupta, *India Redefines Its Role*, pp. 44–45.

46. *A Study of India's Nuclear Choices*, p. 8.

tirely on positive aspects of the relationship, most significantly India's placing its new economic policies at the center of its foreign policy efforts. With agreements on intellectual property rights, textile exports to the United States, and trade in financial services more or less in place, some major irritants in India-U.S. relations have indeed been removed. The pace of U.S. investment in India has picked up, with the active encouragement of the Clinton administration, which is giving India special attention as one of ten "Big Emerging Markets" of the new global economy.

The Economy

In the mid-1990s, India has seemingly established an economic reform program of real momentum, initiated and sustained by a skilled yet quiet political leadership. The finance minister, Dr. Manmohan Singh, has survived politically because he is considered indispensable for the continued credibility of the reforms.[47] In an *India Today* poll conducted two years into the reforms, 47 percent of the voters felt that economic liberalization had been "beneficial," compared to 28 percent who thought it "harmful."[48] Swaminathan S. Anklesaria Aiyar, analyzing the increase in the numbers of poor people and the slightly increased income inequality since the reforms began, argues convincingly that "voters had the maturity to see that the economic mess had been created by three preceding prime ministers . . . and that it was silly to blame the Rao regime, which was trying to clear up the mess."[49]

As both the *India Today* poll and Anklesaria Aiyar suggest, the voters' concern is with inflation. Meghnad Desai notes in his chapter that out-of-control inflation has brought about major political crises several times. If the government can bring inflation back down to the single-digit level voters seem to demand, as it proposed to do in the 1995–96 budget presented to parliament on March 15, 1995 (when inflation had reached an 11 percent annual rate), then the chances for the reforms foundering on the rocks of popular disapproval will be considerably lessened.

But as Desai argues in his chapter, effective economic reform requires

47. One of India's most respected economic journalists, T.N. Ninan, believes that reform will survive even if Manmohan Singh and Narasimha Rao leave office; see his "Do We Need Rao for Reform?"

48. *India Today* (North America), August 15, 1993, p. 32.

49. Swaminathan S. Anklesaria Aiyar, "Does Poverty Influence Elections?" *Times of India* (Bombay), January 29, 1995.

a "powerful governing coalition" that persists for a significant length of time. Aside from the issue of inflation, the major determinants of electoral success seem not to be directly linked to economic policy. Still, electoral pressures from farmers unwilling to give up fertilizer subsidies, business people still unsure of their ability to compete in a global marketplace, and a labor movement that has been wedded to the inefficient public sector and government protection of its rights clearly have slowed the reforms down.

E.A. Ramaswamy, in his chapter on organized labor (which, as he notes, has a membership of less than 10 percent of the workforce), shows why unions, particularly those affiliated to the political parties, have "not made it easy for government to resolve [the complex problems of economic reform]." Thus, "little has changed so far on the labor front." The political federations, which see no need to change policies that virtually guarantee their members will not be fired and give them enormous advantages in confronting the government, owing in part to their control of critical public sector industries such as banking, have not been expanding their reach. Rather, new unions organizing particular enterprises and independent of political parties, and the third strand of the labor movement, voluntary organizations such as the Self Employed Women's Association, may break with them as liberalization proceeds.

India's economic program has been quietly and solidly enhanced by its foreign economic policy. Nonetheless, as Meghnad Desai notes, while India signed and ratified the new world trade arrangements (formalized in the treaty that ended the Uruguay Round of GATT negotiations, in which India had helped negotiate favorable provisions), this was done without the government forcefully presenting its case for the value of the treaty. Still, protests over the signing of the treaty had a marginal political impact. The government has acted to improve its position in the global marketplace, with an "entry policy" that has shown progress in attracting foreign investment, most notably from the United States.[50]

But staying on the economic course India has chosen, as Desai points out, will require a politics that eschews electoral advantage and simple interest-group jockeying for benefits. The signs are difficult to read. On the one hand, we have the Congress Party defeated decisively in Andhra Pradesh in November 1994 because the winning Telugu Desam party promised highly subsidized rice and the prohibition of

50. See "India Shakes Off Its Shackles," *Business Week*, January 30, 1995.

alcohol (which will lose the state a major item of tax revenue). This is, it would seem, a formula for increased deficits and a populist competition among parties, each trying to be more "pro-poor" than the next, that would make the problem even worse. On the other hand, the Communist Party of India–Marxist government of West Bengal has been vigorously wooing industry, and the chief minister of the newly elected BJP–Shiv Sena government in Maharashtra quickly made his commitment to continuing the state's policies of supporting economic reform and welcoming foreign investment.[51]

Desai does not believe that a reformed political system that will undergird the new economic policies is in the offing, and Ramaswamy is not sanguine about the possibility of a positive contribution from labor, which will be needed as the reforms move forward. Both imply that the crises that will inevitably come as a result of the economic slowdown they foresee may produce another lurch forward in government policy, but neither suggests that the *direction* of the economy will change. In that sense the reforms are "irreversible," though they may slow to the point where they are meaningless.

It is ironic that the popular image of India now is that of a country with a vibrant economy, destined to develop at a pace that will make comparisons with the "Asian tigers" meaningful, and a political system mired in corruption and violence, with the dangers of religious nationalism simmering. Yet the academic view, to the extent that it is represented in this volume, suggests a polity more resilient and balanced and an economic reform program less dynamic than the image would have it. Still, we are not, taken together, presenting a portrait of an India either stagnating or heading for some sort of fundamental political or economic crisis—common images in the past; rather, we see a stable polity of weight and vitality. India is moving, perhaps ponderously, toward goals set many years ago. We would be wise to avoid writing off its chances of reaching them.

Suggested Reading

Robert Repetto, *The "Second India" Revisited: Population, Poverty, and Environmental Stress over Two Decades* (Washington, D.C.: World Resources Institute, 1994).

51. Reuters report, March 22, 1995.

On the Periphery but in the Thick of It: Some Recent Indian Political Crises Viewed from Gujarat

John R. Wood

Indian politics in the past few years has often presented a complex and turbulent picture that bedevils analysis, let alone prediction. Observers have struggled to explain crises and paradoxes including impressive ascents to leadership and falls from power, surprising tactical moves, and rapid shifts in party or factional advantage. Some might argue that this is all "business as usual" for India and that beyond any day's startling headlines Indian political life is quite routine. Many would admit, however, that during the first half of the 1990s they were frequently uncertain about where and how the next dramatic developments would occur.

Recent events provide many illustrations. Since it took office in 1991, the government of P.V. Narasimha Rao has had to cope with numerous crises, many involving issues of profound consequence for Indian society. This chapter focuses on religious tensions, crime and corruption, caste politics, the environment, and finally, the spring 1995 state elections. For an in-depth look at how these crises developed, I investigate their manifestations in Gujarat, a state on the western periphery of India.

Gujarat received new attention in March 1995 with its resounding rejection of Rao's Congress Party in a momentous state election. Along with other state election setbacks, this has weakened the prospects of Rao's party in India's next general election, which must be

I would like to acknowledge the support of the Shastri Indo-Canadian Institute and of a University of British Columbia Humanities and Social Sciences grant for travel and research respectively, and to thank Siobhan Hurley for her expert and dedicated research assistance.

held by June 1996. My objective here is not to analyze these elections but rather, by examining the impact of certain all-India crises and issues on Gujarat and vice versa, to explore the interaction between national and state levels and derive lessons about the initiation and spread of political change in India. Paradoxically, Gujarat often appears to be on the margin of change in India, but also "in the thick of it." Can both be true, and if so, how?

The View from the Periphery: Gujarat as Harbinger

Historically, Gujarat has played an important part in the shaping of India. Three pre–twentieth-century instances reveal its role. Archaeologists such as S.R. Rao and Gregory Possehl have discovered, through extensive digs in Gujarat's Saurashtra and Kutch regions, that the latter formed a vital part of the Harappan civilization, hitherto associated mainly with Mohenjo Daro in Pakistan. Possehl described the area around the ancient port of Lothal near Cambay as a gateway to India, not only because of evidence of trade with the Persian Gulf as early as 2000 B.C., but also because it linked the entrepreneurial and agricultural Harappans and the hunting-gathering peoples of the hinterland.[1] Many of India's immigrating and indigenous peoples met in Gurjara Desa, home to a plurality of religions and cultural traditions.

More than 3,000 years later, in 1026 A.D., Mahmud of Ghazni looted and sacked the famous temple of Somnath located near Veraval on the Arabian Sea coast. His depredations are bitterly embedded in Gujarati folkloric memory and still live in the propaganda of Hindu militants in Gujarat today.[2] But the shattering impact of Islam in India, symbolized by Somnath's destruction, gave way in Gujarat to a gentler synthesis of Islamic ideas and innovations over the next seven and a half centuries. Gujarat gained not only a sizable Muslim minority, but also contributions to its political economy, art, architecture, and overall cultural development that remain visible today.

In 1608 Captain William Hawkins sailed the East India Company's

1. Gregory L. Possehl, "Lothal: A Gateway Settlement of the Harappan Civilization," in *Ancient Cities of the Indus,* ed. Gregory L. Possehl (New Delhi: Vikas Publishing, 1979), pp. 212–18.

2. See Satish C. Misra, *The Rise of Muslim Power in Gujarat* (Bombay: Asia Publishing House, 1963).

ship, the *Hector*, into Surat harbor and began more than three centuries of British involvement in India. Gujarat was never so strategic to company concerns that it had to be ruled directly like Bengal, Madras, or the Punjab. Only one-fifth of present-day Gujarat was ruled by the British; the rest was left to maharajas and nawabs.[3] But many Gujaratis learned early how to use imperial opportunities for business purposes, not only in India, but under the Union Jack in the Middle East, Africa, the Indian Ocean, and the South Pacific. The effects of this diaspora (including its more recent North American and European branches) on commercial linkages, capital formation, and many other cosmopolitanizing influences have continued to benefit Gujarat to the present day.

The best-known illustration of feedback from Gujarati experiences abroad is the career of Gujarat's most famous politician, Mohandas K. Gandhi. Indian nationalism may have traced earlier roots elsewhere in the subcontinent, but Gandhi's choice of Ahmedabad as the hub of his anti-imperial campaign after returning from South Africa in 1915 soon placed Gujarat in the forefront of the struggle. Several significant *satyagrahas*, each a turning point in nationalist mobilization, were fought on Gujarati soil. These events and Gandhi's leadership socialized a whole generation of Gujaratis into a habit of political activism and constructive social work. The habit continues long after Gandhi's demise and keeps Gujaratis in the vanguard of all-India social, economic, and political change.

Gujarat's role as harbinger in Indian development has never been systematically examined. The state ranks only seventh in terms of size and tenth in population. However, its geographical location on the western side of India, its maritime exposure, and its natural resources (save the most precious, water) have been significant factors. Gujarat's relative linguistic homogeneity, its lesser penetration by colonialism, the cosmopolitanizing effects of its diaspora, and, especially, the entrepreneurial approach Gujaratis have taken to economic opportunities also further the explanation.

Gujarat is one of India's more developed states. Currently, it ranks third among the major states in urbanization, fourth in literacy, and

3. For the political consequences of this distribution, see John R. Wood, "British Versus Princely Legacies and the Political Integration of Gujarat," *Journal of Asian Studies,* Vol. 44, no. 1 (November 1984), pp. 65–99.

third according to the Physical Quality of Life Index.[4] In 1991–92, Gujarat ranked fourth in per capita state domestic product.[5] It is one of the more industrialized states, with a concentration in chemicals, fertilizers, textiles, and dairy products.[6] Gujarat has often had a food deficit because of periodic drought and lack of sufficient irrigation; but where irrigation is adequate, as in its southern districts, Gujarat has achieved yields as high as Punjab's. In cash crops like cotton, tobacco, and groundnuts it leads the country in production.[7]

Several notable features of Gujarati politics reveal the pragmatism inherent in Gujarati economic activity. First, Gujarati politics has never been ideological or separatist. Since independence, Gujarat's election of only Congress Party and Janata Dal governments demonstrates its electorate's pragmatic preferences. The same may be said of the election of a Bharatiya Janata Party (BJP) government in the March 1995 Gujarat state election. There have been no strong regional parties in Gujarat, moreover, like the Akali Dal in Punjab or the Telegu Desam in Andhra Pradesh. The Mahagujarat Janata Parishad, which agitated between 1956 and 1960 for the creation of a separate Gujarat, disappeared soon after Maharashtra and Gujarat were carved out of Bombay state in 1960. Gujaratis identify strongly with all-India politics and usually seek to influence, not oppose, New Delhi. Clearly, their stake in India's economic development is instrumental here. Despite a lack of powerful representation in New Delhi, the post–World War I habit of Gujarati involvement in national politics continues.

A second feature of Gujarat's polity has been the rapid restratification of political participation whereby new groups, usually castes placed low in the Hindu social hierarchy, have risen to political power. This process reflects rapid socioeconomic modernization, along with the spread of what is often called the Bania ethic. The phrase refers to the hardworking, frugal habits of Gujarat's Vaishya (Bania) castes as well as their shrewdness in business. Skillful political entrepreneurship—in mobilization, coalition formation, and patronage dispensation—has been evident at all societal levels.

---

4. See "Social Indicators of Development for India—II: Inter-State Disparities," *Economic and Political Weekly,* Vol. 29, no. 21 (May 21, 1994), pp. 1303, 1307, and *A Social and Economic Atlas of India* (Delhi: Oxford University Press, 1987), p. 20.

5. "Social Indicators," p. 1307.

6. *A Social and Economic Atlas,* pp. 178–89.

7. Ibid., pp. 158, 162, 168.

High-caste Banias and Brahmans predominated in the Congress Party governments formed after the first four general elections. Enterprising middle peasant castes, such as the Patidars, had also become highly mobilized before independence, thanks to early ruralization of the nationalist movement in Gujarat and formidable leaders such as Sardar Vallabhbhai Patel. After Gujarat's creation as a separate state in 1960, however, a process combining the mobilization of lower castes and the recruitment of lower-caste politicians by both Congress and opposition parties led to greater assertiveness on the part of the hitherto politically deprived.

When the Congress Party split in 1969 and Indira Gandhi began her populist *garibi hatao* (get rid of poverty) campaigns in the 1970s, the Gujarati restratification process produced what seemed like a class confrontation. By 1980 lower castes, ex-untouchables, tribals, and the Muslim minority gained prominence in the Congress Party in what was known as the KHAM coalition.[8] They were opposed by the higher and middle castes of the Janata coalition, which wrested power from the Congress and governed Gujarat in the late 1970s. Thus social change in Gujarat produced an early political restratification that animated virtually all levels of the society. The peaceful Gandhian style of Gujarati politics turned tense and turbulent; what is remarkable, however, is that the restratification was real and rapid.

A third feature of Gujarat's pattern of political change is the extraordinary vigor of voluntary activism. Its roots lie in the tradition of resistance to state tyranny, in the assertiveness of the private sector, and in the Gujarati penchant for organization. Gandhi harnessed these in his political campaigns and also developed a model of social activism that carried into postindependence Gujarat. Currently, the voluntarism of grassroots organizations of a dozen kinds—environmental, human rights, and feminist, among others—accomplishes in practical ways much that government cannot and also provides an outlet for nongovernmental (and periodically, anti-government) energies.

Most Gujarati intellectuals would regard the foregoing as an overly optimistic view of their state's polity, and it must be said that along

8. KHAM stood for Kshatriyas (often lower castes claiming Kshatriya status), Harijans (ex-untouchables), Adivasis (tribals), and Muslims. See John R. Wood, "Congress Restored? The 'KHAM' Strategy and Congress(I) Recruitment in Gujarat," in *State Politics in Contemporary India: Crisis or Continuity?* ed. John R. Wood (Boulder, Colo.: Westview, 1984), pp. 197–227.

with its rapid changes have come several worrisome features. The rise in political participation has meant not only more turbulent politics but also cutthroat competition, creating new lows in political morality. Corruption, criminality, and violence, including political murder, are now regular features of the political struggle. The big cities—Ahmedabad, Vadodara, and Surat, in particular—have become arenas where politics and crime go hand in hand. When the politics of communalism and caste are added—and recently, of new migrant groups from other parts of India attracted by Gujarat's wealth and job opportunities—the result is a periodically deadly mix. While none of it approaches the degree of oppositional violence or state repression found in Punjab, for example, the riots of the 1980s and 1990s in Gujarat have revealed a disturbing viciousness of conflict and deterioration of governance.

With some of these features of the Gujarat political arena in mind, let us now turn to an examination of some national crises and issues, both in their all-India manifestations and as they developed in Gujarat. In the process, we shall investigate the links and interactions between the two levels, and probe further the question of how change in Indian politics is initiated and spread.

The following descriptions of five recent crises suggest some of the intensity and uncertainty of contemporary Indian politics, but only hint at the underlying causes of conflict. They cannot do justice to the complexity of each issue, either for all-India politics or for India's 25 distinctive state polities. Rather than try to embrace that totality, I will concentrate on the perspective to be gained on each crisis from the vantage point of one state. The issues have by no means been resolved in Gujarat, and their ramifications are inevitably different in other state and local contexts. But Gujarat has often been a harbinger of change in India and the battleground on which issues are first tested.

The Communal Cauldron

The most serious issue Rao's government has yet faced arose from the communal bloodletting that followed the December 6, 1992, demolition by Hindu extremists of the 16th-century Babri mosque in

Ayodhya, Uttar Pradesh.[9] This brazen act of vandalism set off Hindu-Muslim rioting and killing in numerous cities and towns of northern India, reducing governance to its most inept level since before independence. The carnage and disarray continued into 1993 and extended well beyond northern India. The crisis reflected the intensifying struggle for power between Rao's Congress Party and the opposition BJP. Initially, the Rao government pinned blame for the communal disaster on the BJP and its associated Hindu militant organizations and imposed President's Rule on four BJP-ruled states: Uttar Pradesh, Madhya Pradesh, Himachal Pradesh, and Rajasthan. Eventually, moderates within the BJP regained control of the party and by late 1993 began to win back lost political momentum with election victories in Rajasthan and Delhi. By late 1994, the BJP showed new strength in the Karnataka state election, and by March 1995 it came to power in the Gujarat and Maharashtra elections.[10] Meanwhile, Hindu militants threatened further Ayodhya-type actions at mosque-temple complexes in Varanasi and Mathura.

The Ayodhya incident drove a deep wedge into the Indian collective consciousness, dividing believers in Hindutva nationalism (espoused by the BJP's right wing) and believers in a secular-pluralist India (with which religious minorities, comprising 17 percent of the population, could identify). Beyond intensifying hatred and politicizing religion, the incident also severely, if not fatally, compromised government's ability to govern. In the final analysis, the loss of institutional integrity by governing agencies and the lack of political will to uphold the law may well be seen as the prime cause and the most pernicious consequence of Ayodhya-related events.

Communal slaughter raged across northern India, but the savagery was worst in Bombay and Gujarat. Although news of the Babri mosque's demolition triggered riots there, local factors shaped and prolonged the bloodbaths that followed. In Bombay, the temple-mosque issue in a town 1,200 kilometers away explains far less about

9. For an account of the buildup to the crisis, see Ashutosh Varshney, "Battling the Past, Forging a Future? Ayodhya and Beyond," in *India Briefing, 1993,* ed. Philip Oldenburg (Boulder, Colo.: Westview, 1993), pp. 9–42, and "Contested Meanings: India's National Identity, Hindu Nationalism, and the Politics of Anxiety," *Daedalus,* Vol. 122, no. 3 (Summer I993), pp. 227–61.

10. In Maharashtra, it was the junior partner in a coalition with the Shiv Sena.

the rioting than do contextual features of the metropolis: the tensions of its slums, the anomie created by its staggering unemployment, and, especially, the omissions and commissions of its politicians.

The Bombay riots occurred in two stages. After the Ayodhya incident, primal passions unleashed in a Muslim *bandh* called to protest the Babri mosque's destruction were met by those of Hindu mobs egged on by Shiv Sena extremists. According to one estimate, 227 people died in these spontaneous clashes.[11] After a lull, riots broke out again on January 5, 1993, and continued into early February; in these, the killing was more systematic and widespread. Out of a total of 557 deaths approximately two-thirds were Muslim. And this time, the "cleansing" of various areas was being undertaken not only by Shiv Sena fanatics, but by the goons of land developers hoping to cash in on Muslim removal.

Politicians' failure to act prolonged the terror. Maharashtra's chief minister, Suddhakarrao Naik, in particular was blamed for inaction, and beyond him Prime Minister Rao, who did not remove Naik until mid-February. Secularists within the Congress Party were attacking Rao and his attempts to find a compromise on the Ayodhya issue. He faced an overt challenge to his leadership from Arjun Singh, the second most powerful man in the cabinet. If Rao took too anti-Hindu a stand, however, he would play into the hands of the BJP or the Shiv Sena. The factional rivalry between the two most important Maharashtrians in his cabinet—Sharad Pawar, the defense minister, and S.B. Chavan, the home minister—also made choices difficult for Rao. It was widely believed that Naik, as an opponent of Pawar, the dominant Congress Party figure in Bombay, had been too accommodative of Bal Thackeray, the leader of the Shiv Sena. Eventually, after sacking Naik, Rao sent Pawar back to his old job as chief minister of Maharashtra, ostensibly because only he was thought capable of restoring order.[12] By then, however, most of the communal damage in Bombay had been done.

The post-Ayodhya communal violence in Gujarat was equally disastrous; in fact, the number of deaths in Gujarat's towns was proportionately higher than anywhere else in India. But as in Bombay, Ayodhya

11. See Dileep Padgaonkar, ed., *When Bombay Burned* (New Delhi: UBS Publishers' Distributors, 1993), p. xvi.

12. See "Machiavellian Politics: Maharashtra Congress in a Bad Way," *Times of India* (Ahmedabad), March 4, 1993.

was more a pretext than a cause, for the roots of communal conflict in Gujarat run deep. In 1969 Ahmedabad had been the scene of the first large-scale Hindu-Muslim conflict in contemporary India, when more than 1,000 people, mostly Muslims, were killed in an orgy of violence lasting three days and ending only when the army intervened. The initial causes of the 1969 violence lay in local tensions and isolated incidents.[13] The escalation into a major conflagration, however, was caused by government inaction, irresponsible press coverage, and active manipulation by politicians. The bloodshed left festering anger, particularly among the Muslims, who bore the brunt of the violence.

Over the next decade and a half, numerous smaller incidents of communal trouble occurred in various parts of Gujarat. But the 1985 riots that engulfed Ahmedabad for nearly half a year and erupted again in 1986 were the direct forerunner of the heightened communalism of the 1990s. These began as an agitation against the Congress government of Madhavsinh Solanki because of its policy decision to raise the quota of reservations for backward castes.[14] The 1985 riots also turned communal in part, allegedly because the Solanki government had included Muslims in its coalition and was seen as "pampering" Muslims in appointments and other forms of patronage.[15]

After 1985 communal polarization intensified in Gujarat. A new Beirut-style division of Ahmedabad into exclusively Hindu and Muslim neighborhoods began, as families and businesses moved for the sake of protection. New and more overt badges of communal self-identification appeared, in forms of dress, in increased ostentation of places of worship (and obtrusiveness of the worship itself), and especially in the growth of fundamentalist religiosity. There was even a move by Hindus to rename Ahmedabad "Karnavati," after the original Hindu village on the banks of the Sabarmati.

---

13. See Ghanshyam Shah, "Communal Problem in Gujarat: Report of a Preliminary Investigation," *Economic and Political Weekly,* Vol. 3, nos. 4 and 5 (January 1970), pp. 187–200, and Chairman Jaganmohan Reddy, *Report of the Inquiry into the Communal Disturbances at Ahmedabad and Other Places in Gujarat on and after 18th September 1969* (Gandhinagar: Government Central Press, 1970).

14. See John R. Wood, "Reservations in Doubt: The Backlash Against Affirmative Action in Gujarat, India," *Pacific Affairs,* Vol. 60, no. 3 (Fall 1987), pp. 408–30.

15. For an insightful analysis highlighting Ahmedabad's changing urban ecology and the erosion of civic structures that had managed conflict resolution in the past, see Howard Spodek, "From Gandhi to Violence: Ahmedabad's 1985 Riots in Historical Perspective," *Modern Asian Studies,* Vol. 23, no. 4 (1989), pp. 765–95.

Again, one needs to observe the political context of these changes. Just as the Janata Dal/National Front led by V.P. Singh defeated Congress in the parliamentary elections of 1989, so too in Gujarat the Janata Dal led by Chimanbhai Patel defeated Congress in the state elections of 1990. In order to govern, both Singh and Patel had to rely on the support of the BJP, which in both cases was eager to topple the government. In 1990–91, following the breakup of the Janata Dal and the parliamentary defeat of first V.P. Singh and then Chandra Shekhar, Patel's party, now named Janata Dal (Gujarat) (JD[G]), clung to power more tenuously. In the 1989 election, the BJP had won 12 Lok Sabha seats in Gujarat; in 1991 it won 20. The BJP opposed Patel's JD(G) in the Gujarat assembly, but public support for the BJP was rising so rapidly by early 1992 that in June Patel merged his JD(G) with the Congress Party.[16]

Most Gujaratis viewed Chimanbhai Patel as the wiliest of politicians, who had managed to remain in power through clever manipulation of patronage and a multiplicity of shadier practices.[17] There was a strong feeling in 1992–93 that if a state election were held, his government would be defeated by the BJP. But Chimanbhai ignored such talk and hung on to power until his untimely death in February 1994.

In this atmosphere of political illegitimacy the Ayodhya crisis made its impact on Gujarat. Gujaratis had shared in the BJP-sponsored events and mobilizational fervor of the campaign leading to the destruction of the mosque. For example, in 1990 BJP leader L.K. Advani's famous Toyota *rathyatra* (pilgrimage by chariot) had commenced at Somnath in Gujarat with ringing denunciations of the Muslim conquest of India. But again, local factors mostly shaped the violence in Gujarat.

Within hours of the Ayodhya news's arrival, rioting broke out in virtually every town of northern, central, and southern Gujarat. Total curfew was widely imposed; in Ahmedabad, Vadodara, and Surat the army was quickly deployed. Perhaps even worse casualties might otherwise have occurred; nonetheless, the records show a disastrous toll of over 400 deaths (with unofficial estimates even higher).

Surat accounted for half the deaths, remarkably, because it had ex-

16. "Yeh Hi Hai Dubious Choice, Baby," *Times of India* (Ahmedabad), June 8, 1992.

17. For a brief biography, see ibid. Patel was also called the Chote Sardar (Little Sardar) after Sardar Vallabhbhai Patel.

perienced little communal tension since the 1920s and was widely regarded as a "bastion of communal amity."[18] The horrific accounts of several observers reveal an unprecedented level of brutality and sadism, most of it visited upon Muslims. In Surat, moreover, there was clear evidence of preplanning in what amounted to a pogrom. BJP party workers had previously collected information about Muslim families while ostensibly helping to renew their ration cards. During the riots, trucks with loudspeakers directed Hindu mobs toward Muslim homes and shops. Another shocking feature was the fact that while "lumpen" elements from slum and migrant worker colonies did most of the killing, middle-class people participated in the rioting and looting.[19] But it was the disease developing since 1969 that was most to blame: the police, hand in hand with local politicians, had become infected with the communal virus to the extent that their effectiveness as upholders of the law was nullified.

Crime and Little Punishment

Following hard upon the Ayodhya events, another crisis erupted on March 12, 1993, with the sudden sequential detonation of ten bombs in Bombay, killing 317 people and throwing India's commercial capital into panic and terror.[20] Four days later, a massive explosion in Calcutta killed 60 people and demolished four buildings.[21] Rumors ran rampant, of Muslim retaliation against the earlier communal killing, of a Pakistani attempt to destabilize the economy, and of a plot by underworld criminals to intimidate the government. As investigations proceeded, attention focused on the underworld crime factor. In Bombay the culprits were not, apparently, the kind of petty racketeers long notorious in the city, but operators of a larger crime empire, centered in the Persian Gulf and dealing in drugs, gold, and sophisticated weaponry.

The Bombay bombings not only brought a new realization of societal vulnerability to organized criminal terrorism but also evoked fresh questions about the nexus between criminals and politicians in India.

18. Asghar Ali Engineer, "Bastion of Communal Amity Crumbles," *Economic and Political Weekly,* Vol. 28, no. 7 (February 13, 1993), p. 262.

19. Jan Breman, "Anti-Muslim Pogrom in Surat," *Economic and Political Weekly,* Vol. 28, no. 10 (April 17, 1993), p. 738.

20. "Terror in Bombay," *India Today* (North America), March 31, 1993, pp. 42–53; see also Padgaonkar, ed., *When Bombay Burned.*

21. "60 Die as Blast Rips Calcutta," *Times of India* (Ahmedabad), March 18, 1993.

One Bombay blast had demolished the trading floor of the Bombay Stock Exchange, and theories developed about a criminal attempt to thwart the government's economic liberalization strategy. When no significant arrests were made, accusations of political protection for the guilty followed.

The connection between crime and politics had already reached crisis proportions for the Rao government because of the infamous "scam" that shocked the Bombay money markets in April 1992.[22] The revelation that a Bombay broker, Harshad Mehta, and other members of a "bear cartel" had swindled more than Rs.4,500 crores (about $1.5 billion) in fraudulent transactions led to a major investigation by a Joint Parliamentary Committee. Charges of political collusion came to a head in June 1993 when Mehta alleged before the Joint Parliamentary Committee that he had delivered Rs.1 crore to Prime Minister Rao himself. The prime minister, already under a cloud of suspicion because of his son's financial dealings, stoutly defended himself and eventually disproved the allegation. But the mere fact of the allegation and the willingness of many to believe it revealed the extent to which the crime-politics connection had gripped the public imagination.[23]

For many years political observers decried the "corruption" of politics in India; nowadays they add "and criminalization" to draw attention to the increasing use of violence and intimidation and the intensifying links among professional criminals on the one hand and politicians, administrators, and the police on the other. Bihar was always the state most notorious for its crime-politics nexus, dramatized in recent elections when several known criminals with police records ran successfully for assembly seats. Alas, Bihar is no longer a special case: the criminalization of politics seems nearly ubiquitous in urban India. The Bombay bombings and the stock exchange scam have forced a new awareness of the extremes to which the problem can go. India is no longer witnessing simply "crime from below," which is small-scale and localized (if increasingly violent), but also "crime from above," in which much larger stakes, organized professionals, and international transactions are involved.

---

22. "Securities Scandal: Spreading Shock Waves," *India Today* (North America), June 30, 1992, pp. 40–48; see also S.K. Barua and J.R. Varma, *The Great Indian Scam* (New Delhi: Vision Books, 1993).

23. "The Harshad Disclosure: Republic Heading for Disaster," *Times of India* (Ahmedabad), June 18, 1993.

Gujarat may not lead the country in criminalized politics, but it does not lag either. One factor, since the defeat of the Soviets in Afghanistan, has been the phenomenal spread of drug- and weapons-trafficking, which follows overland routes through Pakistan and sea routes from the Persian Gulf into India. Gujarat's long border with Pakistan and its Arabian Sea coast provide easy access for smugglers. There are payoffs for all who participate, including officials whose cooperation can be purchased. Throughout 1993, the *Times of India* (Ahmedabad) carried numerous stories of drug seizures, as well as discoveries of arms and ammunition dumps, bomb-making units, and plots to flood the economy with counterfeit money. Ominously, there was one report in August of the discovery in Surat of an immense cache of explosives and a bomb plot for that city equivalent to the ones that rocked Bombay and Calcutta.[24] More recently, investigators have turned up evidence that the explosives used in Bombay were sent from Dubai to Bombay via Porbandar and Surat.

This "crime from above" connects with relative ease to the "crime from below" that has flourished in urban Gujarat for decades. In Ahmedabad, crime bosses *(dadas)* operating extortion, bootlegging, gambling, prostitution, and illegal land development rackets have allegedly traded financial support for police and political protection. Drugs, weapons, and strong-arm thugs are now part of their stock-in-trade. The immediate reason for political involvement, besides personal greed, is the continually escalating cost of elections. The longer-range reason is the steady decay of political institutions and authority brought about by the willingness of officials and elected representatives to resort to "anything goes" tactics in their desperate drive to win—or, at least, to prevent others from doing so.

Related to this decay is the difficulty of seeing justice done because of the delay and slippage involved in bringing criminals to book in India. The investigation of the Bombay Stock Exchange scam—like the Bofors scandal or the Bhopal restitution case before it—dragged on from May 1992 to December 1993 and produced an equivocal result. The Joint Parliamentary Committee's report on the scandal indicted several ministers and officials of the Reserve Bank of India but left many questions unanswered regarding the precise culpability of vari-

24. "They Had Planned Many Blasts in Surat," *Times of India* (Ahmedabad), August 18, 1993.

ous officials and even what happened to the stolen money.[25] Dr. Manmohan Singh was criticized for various "acts of omission," but Prime Minister Rao rejected his offer to resign as finance minister. Meanwhile, the allegation that Harshad Mehta had paid Rs.1 crore to the prime minister was largely ignored by the Joint Parliamentary Committee, although it suggested that the Lok Sabha speaker "consider" initiating contempt proceedings against Mehta for "persistently misleading" the committee. As of March 1995, the Central Bureau of Investigation was still conducting its inquiry and promising that Mehta and others would soon be prosecuted and tried.[26]

Backward and Forward in Caste Politics

One issue that has remained relatively quiet in the mid-1990s, but because of past contentiousness is nevertheless significant, is the Rao government's handling of the reservations for "backward" castes and the Mandal Commission reforms. The commission's report, delivered to Prime Minister Indira Gandhi in 1980, recommended an increase of 27 percent in reservations of government jobs and higher education positions for Backward Castes (BCs), over and above the 22 percent reserved for the Scheduled Castes and Tribes. Neither Indira nor Rajiv Gandhi would touch this politically explosive issue. Eventually, it was Prime Minister V.P. Singh who announced the decision to implement the Mandal reforms in August 1990. The announcement sparked violent protests across northern India (including self-immolations by 75 young people) and led to Singh's parliamentary defeat in November 1990.

In October 1991, the Rao government took its stand on the BC reservation issue by adopting the Mandal reform recommendations with two amendments: first, within the 27 percent BC reservations, preference would go to candidates from the poorest sections, and second, an additional 10 percent of positions would be reserved for the poorest sections of the "forward," that is upper, castes. The whole policy was then reviewed in a Supreme Court judgment presented on November 16, 1992. The court endorsed the constitutionality of the Mandal Commission's basic proposals, including that caste, not class, should be the criterion for identifying "backwardness." But it added several important qualifications. First, neither the advanced sections,

25. "Uneven Indictment," *Times of India* (Ahmedabad), December 23, 1993.
26. "The Return of Harshad's Ghost," *India Today* (North America), March 31, 1995.

the so-called creamy layer among the BCs, nor the poor among the "forward" castes should receive reserved benefits. Second, the BC list should be divided into "Backward" and "More Backward" categories, to ensure that members of each received benefits, and "Backward" castes already well represented in government service should be excluded. Third, in order to uphold the merit principle, "backwardness" should be considered only in appointments, not promotions. Moreover, recruitment to certain technological posts in research, medicine, engineering, aviation, and the military should be by merit only.[27]

During 1993, the Rao government had the sensitive task of identifying the "creamy layer"; it eventually specified the children of top constitutional office holders, top civil servants, top military officers, big-property owners, and professionals earning over Rs.100,000. Separating the "more backward" from the "backward" castes posed opportunities as well as problems; in states where coalitions of certain BCs had come to power, designating other castes as "more backward" could be seen as a central government ploy to entice these to the Congress Party. In August 1993, the government set up the National Commission for the Backward Classes to deal with the question of inclusion and other details of policy implementation.[28]

When the Mandal issue became politically volatile at the all-India level in 1990, Gujaratis greeted it with feelings of both apprehension and déjà vu. Gujarat was not the first state to have extended reservations to the BCs, but it was the first where the reservation issue had become violently contentious on a large scale. As far back as 1981, protests by medical students in Ahmedabad against various administrative aspects of the reservation system had led to riots in which more than 50 people, mostly from Scheduled Castes, were killed. However, the riots of 1985 caused the greatest upheaval and damage: 275 people were killed in anti-reservation violence that did not let up until the Congress government of Madhavsinh Solanki resigned.

Narasimha Rao's government seems to have heeded the lessons of Gujarat's bitter experience with reservation policy where V.P. Singh's did not. The first lesson is that "playing politics with caste" is extremely dangerous. The BCs are too mobilized to be ignored, but

27. "Reservation Not Advisable in Technical Posts," *Times of India* (Ahmedabad), November 19, 1992.

28. "A Tightrope Walk: The Centre Starts Implementing Mandal," *India Today* (North America), September 30, 1993.

promising benefits to them in an obvious attempt to woo votes inevitably provokes a backlash by upper castes. The latter, who feel their children's futures are threatened by reservations, can retaliate with great force. Second, legislating an extension of reservations in a rapid, uncompromising way is counterproductive. Solanki and his coalition of "backward" castes, ex-untouchables, tribals, and Muslims may have won power in a legitimately democratic way. Suddenly legislating reservation benefits for their supporters, however, invited an angry reaction.

In virtually all of the larger Indian states the political self-assertion of the "backward" castes and *dalits* (the oppressed, including ex-untouchables and tribals) can no longer be disregarded. Their ability to capture power was proved in the political success of Yadavs (an agricultural caste, traditionally cowherds) in Bihar, manifested in the government of Janata Dal leader Laloo Prasad Yadav, and confirmed in the dramatic November 1993 election victory of the Samajwadi Party coalition in Uttar Pradesh. This coalition of "backward" castes led by Mulayam Singh Yadav, combined with ex-untouchables of the Bahujan Samaj Party led by Kanshi Ram and Muslims alienated from Congress by the Babri mosque debacle, cut deeply into vote banks hitherto controlled by the Congress.

During 1994, the reservation system was widely seen to be politically abused. Despite a Supreme Court limit of 50 percent on reservations, the Rao government amended the constitution so that Tamil Nadu and Karnataka could have 69 and 73 percent reservations respectively; other state governments, usually under electoral pressure, talked of following suit. In Bihar and Uttar Pradesh, many saw the Yadav-dominated governments as using the reservation system to promote the interests of Yadavs, for example in police recruitment.[29] The result was a great deal of animosity, including among the Yadavs' coalition partners. But in Bihar's March–April 1995 state election, Laloo Prasad Yadav campaigned as a champion of the disadvantaged and won an impressive majority.

The Gujarat experience suggests caution. Solanki's similar government of the disadvantaged lost its cohesion after the furor of the anti-reservation riots in 1985, and Amarsinh Chaudhury, his successor as chief minister, was forced to include higher-caste members in his cabinet. The overall trend seems to be that lower caste and *dalit* politicians are increasingly recruited by all parties in places where caste arithmetic

29. "Racketeering in Quotas," *India Today* (North America), November 15, 1994.

indicates they can win elections. Careful implementation of the Mandal reforms—which means avoiding a Gujarat-style backlash—should add to the trend and increase the political assertiveness of the "backward."

Narmada: Development, Environment, Human Rights

A new pass was also reached by the mid-1990s in yet another critical issue: the degradation of the environment and of the rights of people adversely affected by development projects in India. For more than a decade, local battles over deforestation, the pollution of air, water, and land, and the victimization of "development refugees" had broken out periodically between developers and protectionists.[30] Following the 1992 Earth Summit at Rio de Janeiro, where India was one of the most prominent representatives of the South, environmental and human rights groups proliferated widely in India and forced governments at all levels to take their demands more seriously.

Recent visitors to India cannot have helped noticing some of the adverse effects of its economic development and rapid population growth. In the cities, overcrowding, increasing strain on civic amenities and services, power and water shortages, and particularly air pollution are reaching alarming proportions. In the rural areas too, the pressure on land, the deterioration of forests and soil, the endangerment of wildlife, and the loss of biodiversity are making life and work increasingly difficult. Luckily, Indian tradition includes reverence for the natural world. Although "development" has been a priority since independence and is becoming even more aggressive thanks to economic liberalization, there is growing pressure in India to stop or at least to regulate its adverse effects.

The conflict that has arisen over the damming of the Narmada, India's largest west-flowing river, is the most important case in point.[31] It has placed Gujarat in the glare of national and international

---

30. See *The State of India's Environment: The First (Second, Third) Citizen's Report* (New Delhi: Centre for Science and Environment, 1982, 1985, 1990).

31. For critiques, see Claude Alvares and Ramesh Billorey, *Damming the Narmada: India's Greatest Planned Environmental Disaster* (Dehra Dun: Natraj Publishers, 1988), and Vijay Paranjpye, *High Dams on the Narmada: A Holistic Analysis of the River Valley Projects* (New Delhi: INTACH, 1990). The government position is set out in *Planning for Posterity: Sardar Sarovar Development Plan* (Gandhinagar: Sardar Sarovar Narmada Nigam, 1989) and Mahesh Pathak, ed., *Sardar Sarovar Project: A Promise for Plenty* (Gandhinagar: Narmada Planning Group, SSNNL, 1991).

publicity because of the human and environmental costs of the project. Construction of the mammoth Sardar Sarovar dam in Gujarat near the borders of Madhya Pradesh and Maharashtra began in 1987 after several decades of disputes among the three states over allocation of water and hydroelectric benefits. A tribunal award reached in 1978 set the height of the Sardar Sarovar dam, allocated costs and benefits to the participating states, and specified resettlement terms for the nearly 67,000 people in 248 villages who would be displaced by the dam's reservoir.[32]

The Gujarat government has clung to the award's terms and proceeded with construction of Sardar Sarovar at breakneck speed because of the political and economic pressures created by the state's perennial water shortage. The extension of Narmada water by canal through central and northern Gujarat into Rajasthan is expected to increase agricultural production in the area by more than six times and make drinking water available to some 3,800 villages and 147 towns. But the effectiveness of the water delivery system will depend on the construction upstream in Madhya Pradesh of a series of large and small dams that will store water for gradual release to Sardar Sarovar. Moreover, a whole new agricultural system based on careful water management techniques will have to be developed in order to avoid waterlogging and salinization in the command area.

No one anticipated any outcry from environmental or human rights protectionists at the time of the tribunal award. But a new rights consciousness had been building in India during the 1970s and 1980s, focusing on the injustices suffered by human victims of development projects and on the ecological damage inflicted.[33] In the case of the Narmada, the Narmada Bachao Andolan (Save the Narmada Movement, NBA), which has sought to stop the project through mobilization of valley residents and protest demonstrations, has attracted the most attention. Actually, more concessions favoring the environment and the "oustees" (people displaced by construction) have been wrung from the Gujarat government by the more pragmatic Gujarati voluntary associations. They know that stopping the dam, already half-built,

32. Government of India, Narmada Water Disputes Tribunal, *Report,* Vols. 1–5 (Delhi: Ministry of Water Resources, 1978).

33. See Smitu Kothari, "Social Movements and the Redefinition of Democracy," in *India Briefing, 1993,* pp. 131–62.

is politically impossible for any Gujarat government and have concentrated instead on getting the optimal package of resettlement benefits—land, money, draft animals, implements, insurance, and so forth—for each oustee family. They can do little, however, to reach the majority of project-affected people in Madhya Pradesh and Maharashtra, where the NBA has a larger following.

Since the World Bank had provided a start-up loan of $450 million for Sardar Sarovar and was negotiating other loans for canal construction and environmental protection projects, it too became a target of criticism by the NBA and allied international protest groups. Eventually, the bank responded by appointing an independent review of the project. Its report, published in 1992, was severely critical of both governmental and World Bank failure to live up to the terms of the award and other funding agreements regarding both the oustees and the environment.[34] It also pointed out that nothing had been done to protect the interests of the people living downstream from Sardar Sarovar or in the path of canal construction.

Eventually, the review created enough international opposition to the dam that the bank's executive directors split over whether to stop funding the project.[35] A compromise giving India six months to achieve certain targets in oustee rehabilitation and environmental protection finally led, on March 30, 1993, to India's announcement that it would forego the remainder of the loan. At the same time Prime Minister Rao gave assurances that the central government would continue to support the project. Doubts were raised, however, about the prospects of finding the finances needed to continue construction, and there were indications that Madhya Pradesh might renege on its commitment to the terms of the tribunal award. Union Water Resources Minister V.C. Shukla succeeded in assembling a meeting of government officials, the NBA, and a number of "independent observers." Gujarat Chief Minister Chimanbhai Patel steadfastly refused to attend the meeting or to allow any alteration of the tribunal award's terms. He was well within his rights, for according to the award (which cannot be challenged in any court), without unanimous agreement among the participating states the terms cannot be changed until 2025.

---

34. *Sardar Sarovar: Report of the Independent Review* (chairman: Bradford Morse) (Ottawa: Resource Futures International, 1992).

35. See John R. Wood, "India's Narmada Dams: Sardar Sarovar Under Siege," *Asian Survey*, Vol. 33, no. 10 (October 1993), pp. 979–84.

With the closing of the dam's sluice gates and the arrival of monsoon rain, the water in the Sardar Sarovar reservoir began to inundate the nearest villages. NBA protesters swore to commit *jalsamarpan* (suicide by drowning), and the police made scores of arrests. By totally blocking access to the dam and arresting NBA leaders, the Gujarat government temporarily wore down resistance to the dam's construction. But it was clear that until the project's completion in 1997, similar protests would be launched with every village's submergence.

The Gujarat Election: Harbinger for 1996?

The Gujarat state election results announced on March 12, 1995, brought more bad news for the Narasimha Rao government. The Congress Party was routed by the BJP, which won a solid majority of 121 seats in the 182 seat assembly, compared to 45 for Congress and 16 for independents and others. Eighteen out of 35 Congress ministers were defeated, and Congress representation was virtually wiped out in 11 of 18 districts. As he congratulated Keshubhai Patel, the new BJP chief minister, all-India BJP President L.K. Advani recalled that Gujarat had been the first state where the Janata Party had won en route to defeating Indira Gandhi's Congress Party in the 1970s. "Gujarat," he said, "is the shortest cut to Delhi."[36]

Rhetorically perhaps, Advani was referring to Gujarat's leading role in Indian political change, this time with an eye to the Indian general election expected in 1996. Gujarat gave the BJP its biggest victory in 1995, but it was not alone in rejecting the Congress, which lost elections in four other major states in 1994–95: Andhra Pradesh, Karnataka, Maharashtra, and Bihar. Currently, Congress governs only 12 out of 27 states and territories, most of them small, and if the present trend continues, its all-India defeat in 1996 seems likely. The BJP now governs three states—Gujarat, Maharashtra (in coalition with the Shiv Sena), and Rajasthan—and also the territory of Delhi. With a solid footing in only a few more (mostly northern) states, it seems improbable that the BJP's victory in Gujarat could be replicated nationally. However, it is intriguing to examine the explanations given for the BJP success in Gujarat, for these are linked to the all-India issues discussed above.

36. "Cashing In on Corruption," *India Today* (North America), March 31, 1995.

First, the explanation cited most often is voter impatience with corruption and criminality, long associated in many Gujarati minds with the ruling party. Even after the death of Chimanbhai Patel, his successor, Chhabildas Mehta, could not shake images of Congress underworld connections and *goonda raj* (rule of thugs). Second, the communal issue, although initially played down by BJP moderates, was revived when Narasimha Rao imposed a ban on the militantly Hindu Vishwa Hindu Parishad in January 1995. During the campaign this provoked defiance and prompted Hindutva issues to resurface. Secular appeals by Congress carried little conviction; there was widespread dissatisfaction with the government's handling of post-Ayodhya events, including among Muslims, who withdrew their traditional support for the Congress.

Third, a major factor in the Congress defeat was the divisiveness in party ranks during the run-up to the campaign. One measure of the factional infighting was the presence of 104 rebel candidates—those denied the Congress nomination—contesting over 80 seats. According to one report, the faction most thwarted in the Congress seat distribution was that of Madhavsinh Solanki, the acknowledged leader of the "backward" castes.[37] The Solanki rebels reportedly siphoned off Congress votes in many contests. It may be difficult for the party to recover from such disunity in time to fight effectively in the 1996 election.

What may be most significant is that whereas elsewhere in India the Congress has lost much of its support among the "disadvantaged" to new "backward" caste and *dalit* coalitions, in Gujarat it lost it to the BJP. The BJP has generally been seen as a party dominated by high and middle castes. In the Gujarat election, however, the BJP won 15 of 26 Scheduled Tribe seats and 10 of 13 Scheduled Caste (ex-untouchable) reserved seats.[38] We can only speculate whether the swing is simply explained by the general anti-incumbency mood, and whether the BJP will become a more pluralistic party capable of managing its new diversified composition.

Conclusion

Looking at contemporary events in India from the perspective of Gujarat raises many questions about the diffusion of political change

37. "The Spreading Lotus," *India Today* (North America), February, 28, 1995.
38. "Cashing In on Corruption."

across a terrain of great complexity and diversity. The issues discussed here provide a useful starting point for analysis, but there are many other momentous happenings and concerns—the separatist struggles in Kashmir, Punjab, and northeastern India, the controversies over the structural adjustment of India's economy, and the attempts to reform the electoral system, to name only a few examples with multilevel political causes and effects.

What is of interest is the interaction between the all-India level and the state level. In several cases, a phenomenon occurring at the all-India level, such as the Congress-BJP competition that led to the communal confrontation at Ayodhya, triggered events in Gujarat. But Gujarat already had its own equation between the Congress and the BJP and its own history of communal trouble. The Ayodhya confrontation sparked reaction in Gujarat, but much of this reaction was shaped by Gujarat's unique circumstances and problems. Significantly, it acted out its own version of the crisis as the holocausts in Ahmedabad and Surat took on lives of their own.

To take another example, the Bombay bombings highlighted an issue of all-India importance: criminal terrorism. In this case, the crisis was visited upon India from outside, by criminals headquartered in the Persian Gulf. In the weeks following the blasts it was revealed that Gujarat too was in the vortex of criminal terrorist activity as a main supply route for smuggled arms and explosives. In effect, the crime-politics nexus in Gujarat was contributing to and being stimulated by the all-India phenomenon.

Then there are the cases in which Gujarat seemed to play the "harbinger" role more directly, when a local crisis foreshadowed its all-India manifestation—for example, the struggle over the increase in reservations of governmental jobs and educational opportunities for "backward" castes. The conflicts that erupted over this issue in Gujarat in 1981 and 1985 were replayed at the all-India level in the Mandal crisis that brought down the V.P. Singh government in 1990.

Again in the struggle over the Narmada River dam a local crisis eventually developed all-India proportions. Because Gujarat was the site of the Sardar Sarovar dam, it became the battleground where environmental and human rights activists fought developers. But the initial conflict occurred between local protectionists and the Gujarat government. The Narmada Bachao Andolan, consisting mostly of non-Gujaratis, entered the struggle after the main concessions on resettlement and rehabilitation had been made. No doubt the conflict will continue and extend far beyond Gujarat, since the Narmada's development involves other states and some central government financing.

In all of the evidence reviewed here, it is striking that, again and again, Gujarat is "on the periphery" but also "in the thick of it." This raises the question of whether Gujarat's peripherality is itself a factor in the patterns of change discussed here. Ordinarily, core areas take the lead because of a superabundance of resources, talent, and energy. In India, the Hindi-speaking core contains some of the largest and most populous states; they send a correspondingly large proportion of India's parliamentarians to New Delhi. However, while people from the peripheral states may refer often to "northern dominance" or "Hindi-belt imperialism," the Hindi-speaking states (Haryana is an exception) are not among India's more economically successful ones. Bihar, in fact, is on most development indicators the farthest behind.

Alternatively, it may be argued that change originates at the periphery. However, many of India's geographically peripheral states do not present consistent patterns of either leading or following vis-à-vis the core. Thus, Gujarat's active role may have less to do with "peripherality" and more with its particular location in western India in the pathway of historical change, and also with its orientation to the all-India political economy. Gujarat's distinctive experiences of colonialism and nationalism and its entrepreneurial spirit and modern economic dynamism may each be somehow associated with peripherality, but peripherality alone explains little. Clearly, most of the explanation for why Gujarat is often "in the thick of" India's major political events lies in the historical and contemporary evidence of its social, economic, and political modernizing proclivities.

"Modernizing proclivities" do not, alas, mean a cleaner or more peaceful politics. Recently, power struggles among Gujaratis have acquired a sinister element, and it would be naïve to expect that with the advent of a new party in power the corruption and criminalization so prevalent in the 1990s will disappear. The new availability of guns and explosives, in fact, predicts increasing violence in an increasingly competitive society. This includes, unfortunately, state violence, which rarely resolves problems. In 1994–95, Gujarat became notorious as the state with the most detainees under the Terrorist and Disruptive Activities (Prevention) Act (TADA), India's most draconian and most abused preventive detention law. Fortunately, in May 1995, probably with an eye to the general election, the Rao government announced it would allow TADA to lapse.

Finally, looking to the the issue of whether development, the protection of human rights, and the preservation of the environment are compatible goals, again Gujarat provides a valuable laboratory in which to observe change. In the case of the struggle over the development of the Narmada River, the Gujaratis' penchant for developmental entrepreneurship has collided with a new philosophy that questions the wisdom of development based merely on measures of productivity and material gain. Virtually all Gujaratis feel that it is imperative to tap the Narmada's water. The new BJP government, no less than that of the Congress Party, will stand firm against any attempt to stop the project. Generally, government officials have learned a great deal from the activists, and from being "in the thick of" not only a national but an international controversy. If present trends continue, tensions may escalate, but it seems likely that Gujarati pragmatism will find a way out of the current impasse.

Suggested Readings

Datta, Prabhat. *Regionalization of Indian Politics* (New Delhi: Sterling Publishers, 1993).

Manor, James, ed. *Nehru to the Nineties: The Changing Office of Prime Minister in India* (Vancouver: University of British Columbia Press, 1994).

Omvedt, Gail. *Reinventing Revolution: New Social Movements and the Socialist Tradition in India* (Armonk, N.Y.: M.E. Sharpe, 1993).

Venkataraman, R. *My Presidential Years* (New Delhi: Indus, 1994).

Verghese, B.G. *Winning the Future: From Bhakra to Narmada, Tehri, Rajasthan Canal* (New Delhi: Konark Publishers, 1994).

India's Chief Ministers and the Problem of Governability

James Manor

It has never been easy to govern India. The country is huge, its society is the most diverse on earth, and it is beset by poverty, scarce resources, and marked inequalities. Over the past two decades, India's voters have become progressively sophisticated and impatient. People in every section of society—including the poor and least educated—have become more aware of their collective strength and self-interest, more insistent in demanding responses from politicians, and more willing on election days to punish those who fail to respond. This has made India a more genuine democracy than it was in the first phase after independence in 1947, when prosperous groups dominated politics and poorer people settled for tokenism. But it has also made it an even more difficult country to govern.

Politicians have found it harder to meet these rising demands because political institutions—the instruments through which they govern—have undergone decay. Political parties have been plagued by mounting corruption, indiscipline, and factional squabbling. The autonomy, flexibility, and resources of formal institutions—especially legislatures, the bureaucracy, and the police—have all deteriorated. This decay gathered momentum in the Indira Gandhi years, especially from 1971 to 1975; then the Emergency (1975–77) featured an orgy of deinstitutionalization. After two and a half years of confused and fragmented Janata Party rule, the process of decay resumed in Mrs. Gandhi's last premiership (1980–84).

Things have become still more difficult since India embarked on

This chapter is the first report on a major research project on chief ministers, funded by the British Economic and Social Research Council. A book-length study will emerge in due course.

economic liberalization in 1991. That has entailed cuts in government spending, leaving politicians with fewer resources to distribute among increasingly impatient voters. It has also begun to force those in power to base their popularity less on their ability to deliver goods and services controlled by the state, and more on their ability to attract private investment by offering incentives to market forces. This fundamental shift in the very purpose and thrust of government is exceedingly difficult to make.

It is hardly surprising, then, that many commentators have begun to ask whether India is becoming ungovernable by democratic means. Their concerns take various forms. Some focus mainly on the potent social forces that have emerged as the result of socioeconomic change and the openness of the political process. They question the capacity of the democracy to contain and respond creatively to conflicts among classes, castes, and religious and ethnic groups, and between those groups and the state. Others fix mainly on the decay of political institutions, especially political parties. Still others worry that those in authority depend so heavily on the use of coercion against discontented groups that the democratic process may be subverted or abandoned. While their emphases differ, they agree that something close to a crisis is at hand.[1]

How anxious should we be about all of this? To assess the capacity of democratic politics to provide stability and adequate governance, this chapter examines a crucially important group of politicians—the chief ministers who preside over state-level governments in India's federal system. Their role is similar to that of the prime minister at the national level. But since state governments loom large in the implementation of most of the national government's policies, and since the states have immense powers in their own right, chief ministers are

1. See, for example, Paul R. Brass, *The Politics of India Since Independence. The New Cambridge History of India,* 2d ed., Part 4, Vol. 1 (New York: Cambridge University Press, 1994); James Manor, "The Electoral Process amid Awakening and Decay," in *Transfer and Transformation: Political Institutions in the New Commonwealth,* ed. Peter Lyon and James Manor (Leicester: Leicester University Press, 1983), pp. 87–116; "Party Decay and Political Crisis in India," *Washington Quarterly,* Vol. 4, no. 3 (Summer 1981), pp. 25–40; Francine Frankel, "Introduction," in *Dominance and State Power in Modern India: Decline of a Social Order,* Vol. 1, ed. Francine Frankel and M.S.A. Rao (Delhi: Oxford University Press, 1989), pp. 1–20; and Atul Kohli, *Democracy and Discontent: India's Growing Crisis of Governability* (New York: Cambridge University Press, 1990).

much more intimately involved in the day-to-day dilemmas of governance than anyone in New Delhi.[2]

They have to wrestle incessantly with concrete manifestations of institutional decay. The struggle to maintain political legitimacy in the face of demands from the electorate is a pressing concern for them. They, far more than India's national leaders, grapple with both the painful adjustments and the opportunities that follow from economic liberalization. Since the composition and character of society vary greatly from state to state, they are far more thoroughly enmeshed in the complexities of state-society relations than any prime minister can be. So it is mainly their decisions that determine how, and indeed whether, the institutions of state are integrated with society. They make the key judgments about the distribution of government resources among various interest groups, about the pursuit of political accommodation or the use of coercive force. Most of the actual governing in India takes place at the state level and below, and at those levels, chief ministers are critically important.

Like India's prime minister, they achieve office by leading a party or coalition that can muster a legislative majority. They form state-level cabinets of ministers to oversee a broad array of government departments. They remain in power for a five-year term, provided that they defeat any attempts within their parties to oust them and avoid majority no-confidence votes in the legislature. If they lose such a vote, their government falls, and either another leader is given the chance to rule or a state election occurs to choose a new legislature.

The Indian Constitution arms state governments with formidable powers. It gives them exclusive control over a long list of subjects including public order, local government institutions, public health and sanitation, agriculture, land, animal husbandry, and fisheries. State governments also share responsibility with the central government for much else, including the administration of justice, forestry, industrial disputes, social security, family planning, education, and the provision of electricity.

State influence has been eroded by the authorities in New Delhi

---

2. This is apparent from several of the studies in *Nehru to the Nineties: The Changing Office of Prime Minister in India,* ed. James Manor (Vancouver: University of British Columbia Press, 1994).

over the last 20 years or so. The central government has encroached into areas supposedly reserved for the states and has taken a larger role in areas of shared responsibility. It has also denied state governments essential funds.

But despite this, state governments and the chief ministers who head them have actually become more important in recent years. The opening of India's economy to market forces since mid-1991 has in many respects increased their autonomy. Intrusions from on high have declined since the national election of 1989 ended the Indira/Rajiv Gandhi dynasty's time in office. The hung parliaments (in which no party had an overall majority) that emerged in 1989 and 1991 made prime ministers somewhat less inclined to intervene at the state level.[3] The decay of political institutions means that more rides on the decisions of individual leaders.

To understand the role of chief ministers, we need to begin where they do. Their overriding preoccupations are to ensure their political survival and extend their influence. This is not a criticism but a statement of fact. India rightly takes pride in having produced this century's greatest political moralist—Mahatma Gandhi—but his saintly legacy is often used as an unfair basis for judging (and condemning) the behavior of chief ministers and others. We need to consider objectively what these politicians have done to tackle the daunting array of problems that they face.

Chief ministers loom large in this chapter and in the politics of their states because nearly all of them lack strong party organizations that would enable them to interact systematically with other forces in their states. This leaves them badly exposed and compels them to wheel and deal frantically in order to survive politically. Their performance becomes disproportionately important to the fate of their states.

This is a relatively recent development. During the first two decades after Indian independence, chief ministers from the Congress Party ran nearly every state, and the Congress organization in those days had both sinew and reach. It operated in the various Indian states like the political machines that used to dominate politics in many American

---

3. The Congress government of Prime Minister P.V. Narasimha Rao took office in June 1991 with slightly less than half the seats in the Lok Sabha (the dominant lower house in India's parliament). By late 1993 it had enticed enough members from other parties to join it that it had achieved a small majority.

cities. A disciplined network of skilled political managers coordinated the distribution of government-controlled goods and services to a large number of key interest groups. It extended from the state capitals down to district, subdistrict, and local levels. Chief ministers thus had instruments of governance that were usually more than adequate to their task.

But the Congress organization was systematically crippled by Indira Gandhi, who saw it more as a threat to her personal dominance than as a tool to help her govern well. In most states, the parties that have arisen to challenge Congress have also failed to develop strong organizations linking the state capitals to the grass roots. This makes it difficult for chief ministers from those parties to govern effectively—though they are partly to blame for inadequate party building. This chapter describes how chief ministers cope in these unhappy circumstances.

"The Job Makes You Crazy Sometimes"

In the last few weeks of 1990, Hyderabad, the capital city of Andhra Pradesh, witnessed fierce rioting between Hindus and Muslims. The security forces had great difficulty imposing order, partly because dissidents within the ruling Congress Party were fomenting violence to undermine the position of their own chief minister, Dr. M. Chenna Reddy. At the height of the crisis, an exhausted and traumatized Dr. Reddy held a press conference to try to reassure the public. When a reporter asked him to comment on the use of automatic weapons by both sides, he astonished his audience by saying, "This only shows that the people of Andhra do not lag behind in this respect."[4]

This bizarre remark was all the more remarkable for being uncharacteristic. Chenna Reddy was one of the more intelligent state-level leaders in India. After taking command of the Congress Party in his state when it was in opposition and disarray, he had mounted a series of protests that galvanized the party organization and carried it to victory at the next state election.

Several months later, when Dr. Reddy was in temporary retirement, a visitor asked him how he came to make that remark. He paused for a moment, then said quietly, "The job makes you crazy sometimes." He explained how much more difficult the job of chief minister was in the early 1990s than in the late 1970s, when he had previously held this post. In that earlier period, conflict had been more manageable, voters

4. *Indian Express,* November 29, 1990.

had been more patient, resources had been more plentiful, and the party organization had been more formidable.[5]

By the 1990s, many more interest groups had become politically active than before. They tended to come into conflict with one another earlier and more aggressively, so that managing conflict was no longer easy. They had also grown more strident in their demands on the government, and it took more resources to satisfy them. Poor, low-status groups that once settled for tokenism and a few crumbs now insisted on substantial benefits. The electorate had become sophisticated enough to have thrown out the Congress Party, which had once been unassailable in this state, from 1983 to 1989 when the Telugu Desam was in power. As a result, here and in every other state Congress now faced a powerful opposition with experience of government. In short, Reddy was describing the cumulative effects of a political awakening that had been proceeding among ordinary people for decades.

He went on to say that the resources available to his and other state governments had shrunk as a result of mounting corruption among politicians and bureaucrats. The Congress Party's organization was wracked by feverish factionalism that would have been unthinkable 20 years earlier. To placate various factions, and to prevent individual legislators from becoming dissidents, Reddy had to commit huge amounts of resources and time to flattering them and buying them off. This left him exhausted, undermined his health, and denied him the time to deal with matters of high policy. He implied that his government, like many others across India, had therefore become rudderless. The effectiveness not only of the Congress Party, but of many formal political institutions had declined, so that it was difficult to meet soaring demands and to prevent social conflicts from spinning out of control.

In other words, Reddy was painfully aware of the dangers posed by the combination of political awakening and institutional decay. It so undermined his position that he was eventually forced by dissension within his own party to resign. Even while he had held office, his life had been so unpleasant, even desperate, that the job hardly seemed worth having—although at the same time, he clearly mourned his loss of power.

Chenna Reddy's experience is reasonably typical, particularly but not only of chief ministers from the Congress Party, where activists'

5. Interview, Hyderabad, February 11, 1991.

unbridled, unsavory, and often illegal doings have long been a serious problem. Conditions vary from state to state. In some, both the Congress (which remains an important force in all but a few states) and rival parties have suffered less decay than in Reddy's Andhra Pradesh. In others, decay has gone farther. But nearly all chief ministers to some degree face the problems Reddy encountered.

This is worrying, especially since few chief ministers are as intelligent as Reddy. Yet some have coped more impressively than he did. Consider two recent examples. Their methods will tell us more about chief ministers' troubles as well as their powers and opportunities.

Bhairon Singh Shekhawat of Rajasthan

In November 1993, voters in the state of Rajasthan elected a legislature in which the Hindu nationalist Bharatiya Janata Party (BJP) held the largest number of seats, but fell just short of a majority. It duly formed a government. A few days later, a woman legislator from the Congress Party (the main opposition party) was surprised to be contacted by the chief minister, Bhairon Singh Shekhawat. He invited her to explain the needs of her constituency. She rattled off a list of development projects and other benefits, and Shekhawat astonished her by saying that he would see to it that most of them were delivered by the end of his five years in office. The legislator left feeling elated, since she had feared that, as a member of the opposition, she would be cut off from government goods and services.[6]

There were good reasons for the chief minister to feel satisfied too. He could now depend upon this woman (and numerous others in opposition with whom he had had similar chats) to refrain from attacking the government, lest she jeopardize her access to resources. He would allot a small number of benefits to her constituency in the first few months, to give the impression that his promises would be kept. He could decide later about whether to deliver further concessions, in the light of the political situation at the time.

By mid-1994, it was apparent that Shekhawat would not need to maintain the flow of spoils to all of the opposition legislators whom he

6. The section of this chapter on Shekhawat is mainly derived from daily newspapers and research in Jaipur during February 1994, when I interviewed numerous politicians, journalists, civil servants, academics, and others. I am especially grateful to Sanjeev Srivastava, G.K. Bhanot, and Robert S. Jenkins.

had met. He had engineered the defection of enough opposition members to the ruling party to give himself a majority. He had promised them sizable benefits, but once they had joined his party, he handed over only a few of these—knowing that these new recruits were locked in. The explanation for this lies in India's anti-defection law, which requires that a group of defectors constitute at least one-third of the legislators in the party they wish to leave. It was easy for Shekhawat to entice one-third of a tiny opposition party to join his, but once they were members of the huge BJP delegation, they could not defect out again without taking dozens of others with them—an impossibility.

This chief minister is clearly a devious (or if you prefer, ingenious) master of realpolitik, but he is more complex than that. For example, he is by turns tough and generous. On the one hand, he often seeks to get things done by threatening to reveal compromising information about politicians or bureaucrats. On the other hand, when confronted with pressure for benefits, he tends to promise more than he can deliver to spare himself the embarrassment of saying no, even though his failure to live up to commitments causes more resentment than would an initial refusal. One sympathetic observer, referring to this habit, described him as "often a liar in little things."

At times, however, Shekhawat remains generous when he need not be. Even after securing majority support in the current legislature, he continues to provide patronage to numerous opposition legislators. He does so partly because it mutes criticism of his government and may prove useful if his position deteriorates, but also because patronage is part of the amiable political culture that has always existed in Rajasthan (though not in most other states). Those in power cultivate members of the opposition, and when chief ministers and leaders of the opposition spar in the legislature, they visibly restrain themselves from going for the jugular.

Shekhawat learned this kind of politics during a long spell in opposition, observing a great Congress chief minister, Mohanlal Sukhadia, who offered him and his colleagues the same enticements that Shekhawat now provides to his opponents. A former senior aide insists that he does this not just because it makes political sense, but because he is "essentially a kindhearted person." On many occasions, he has gone out of his way to assist adversaries who are in personal difficulty or distress. These actions have won him a good deal of grudging affection.

His observance of old fashioned Congress-style courtesies (which include a tendency not to seek excessively partisan behavior from bureaucrats) and his pragmatic approach to politics have often set Shekhawat at odds with some members of his Hindu nationalist party. This is particularly true of his relations with the zealots from the Rashtriya Swayamsevak Sangh (RSS), an extremist association that looms large in the BJP organization everywhere.

Two things help him to maintain the upper hand. The first is the widespread and accurate belief that Shekhawat is indispensable—that no one else in the party in Rajasthan can match his deft skills and experience (he has been chief minister twice before). The second is the small size of his legislative majority. This enables him to persuade his legislators that the party's grip on power is tenuous, and that they must discipline themselves lest wayward behavior upset the delicate balance. A large majority would, of course, provide him with certain advantages, but it would allow legislators to relax and it would make dissidence in the party much harder to contain. This is why he and many other chief ministers prefer small majorities or even minority governments.

The RSS faction is strong enough to give ministers who belong to it considerable autonomy from the chief minister, and freedom to pursue policies dear to the Hindu right. Shekhawat, who is (or some say, poses as) a liberal, handles this in two ways. He places some of these people in posts where their rightist views will make little difference: as one wag put it, "What is the Hindu theory of road repair?" He also signals his differences with them by leaning leftward on certain issues, to compensate for their biases. This was vividly apparent during his first term in office, when he created a program to target the five poorest families in each village for special benefits.

This was an example of Shekhawat's uncanny ability to come up with programs that are inexpensive, but touch a sympathetic chord at the grass roots. Another such initiative is his "your village, your work" scheme, which enables local communities to complete small projects that meet their most urgent needs. Recent research suggests that such programs, which respond to a ferocious popular appetite for long-neglected microlevel development projects, hold greater promise of popularity at less cost and risk than any other option open to chief ministers.[7] They assisted Shekhawat in being the only BJP chief minis-

7. This emerges in R. Crook and James Manor, "Enhancing Participation and Institutional Performance: Democratic Decentralisation in South Asia and West Africa," *Report to the Overseas Development Administration* (London 1994).

ter, out of the four whose governments were toppled after the destruction of the Babri mosque at Ayodhya, to be returned to power at state elections in November 1993.

Shekhawat is intensely preoccupied with gathering information. He is acutely aware that one serious consequence of the organizational weakness of his and other parties is that they cannot deliver reliable intelligence to leaders. Many chief ministers content themselves with what they learn from party colleagues, who often tell them what they think they want to hear, and from the police and a cursory perusal of the press. Shekhawat goes beyond this, actively seeking out well-informed people beyond his party. Over the years, he has built up an impressive network of sources who have knowledge of all of the state's regions, and he milks them effectively. Reporters say that he fritters away far too much time chatting with informants, but they acknowledge that he is immensely knowledgeable—the best journalist in Rajasthan.

For many years, he has meticulously maintained an extensive private set of files on policy issues and people—politicians, bureaucrats, journalists, and others. The files contain his own notes, official documents, and clippings from the daily press. In the legislature, these enable him to wear down opponents by citing details and statistics they lack. The files are also widely presumed to contain compromising information on all manner of people. It is exceedingly unusual for Shekhawat to make public use of this material—insofar as it actually exists—but it is not necessary for him to do so. Sometimes, the mere presumption that the chief minister possesses such information is enough to deter people from causing him problems.

Shekhawat, like most chief ministers, has maintained exclusive control over the posting of civil servants. He understands that legislators are inordinately concerned with securing appointments for their constituents, and that some collect sizable sums from bureaucrats who seek agreeable transfers. He also knows that he has to tread carefully here. He cannot ignore legislators' wishes entirely, but if he gives too much ground, he can dilute his authority and demoralize the bureaucracy—which he is loath to do. He has therefore invested much time and effort in finding a balance, and most observers regard him as unusually adroit at this fiendishly difficult game. He has been especially successful at placing talented senior civil servants in high posts within departments run by less dependable ministers—to monitor their actions and correct their mistakes.

Partly as a result of his unwillingness to give legislators a free hand, his control over events has not slipped away as Chenna Reddy's did. His indispensability to the BJP and his impressive political skills are important here, but he has also been helped by two other things. First, neither corruption in general nor a market in transfers has developed in Rajasthan to the extent that they have in most other states—thanks in part to the resistance nearly all of its chief ministers have offered to these tendencies. Second, he and his party are cleaner than the Congress and other centrist parties and leaders. In a country where many chief ministers own fleets of Mercedes, the only extravagance people mention about Shekhawat is that he has "a very nice jeep."

Praise for Shekhawat needs to be qualified, however. Knowledgeable sources who are repelled by Congress Party corruption nevertheless stress that Shekhawat and the BJP have often been less effective than more corrupt Congress governments in Rajasthan at the politics of resource distribution, at forging transactional ties to important social groups, and at responding to pressure from those groups. The Congress Party's profiteering has been sufficiently restrained in Rajasthan to sustain some of its effectiveness as an instrument of patronage distribution.

Shekhawat's ability to maintain considerable autonomy from the pressures of legislators and interest groups, and his preeminence within his cabinet of ministers, make it possible for him to dominate his government. Although this has many advantages, close observers say that he tries to manage too many things. Delays and mistakes sometimes follow. He is prepared to delegate authority to a few ministers and bureaucrats whose competence he trusts, but he does less of this than is good for overall performance.

On the other hand, Shekhawat has ensured that his governments have been reasonably effective, imaginative, corruption-free, and stable. Perhaps most crucial of all, he has created an environment in which the very large number of skilled political activists, who exist at all levels of this and nearly all other Indian states' political systems, are able to operate creatively. This is essential if goods and services are to be delivered efficiently to organized interests of all kinds, if government programs are to work reasonably well, and if the politics of bargaining is to adapt to change. Such an environment is especially important at a time when economic liberalization is accelerating the pace of change. These skilled people are a huge political and developmental asset that India possesses in far larger measure than other less-developed countries, because of its sustained experience of democratic politics.

Sharad Pawar of Maharashtra

It may seem odd to use Sharad Pawar—until recently, the chief minister of Maharashtra—as an example of an accomplished operator, since in March 1995 he was forced to relinquish office after losing a state election. But that happened in spite of Pawar's deft leadership, and the main blame for it falls on others. There are many similarities between Shekhawat and Pawar. The latter is also highly intelligent and experienced—he too has held the post on three occasions (1978–80, 1988–91, and 1993–95). He understands the advantages that small legislative majorities or even minority governments offer for maintaining control over party colleagues, and he has coped adroitly with the problems that arise in such circumstances. He has been an activist chief minister with a good network of informants helping him to check constantly on administrative details.[8]

This means that he, like Shekhawat, took on so many tasks that delays and errors sometimes occurred, but his skills as an operator minimized these. It also means that he sometimes interfered too much with bureaucrats and prevented them from getting on with things they were well equipped to manage. But like Shekhawat, he was open to persuasion from frustrated civil servants—especially when their arguments were couched in terms of his self-interest. Pawar was reluctant to say no when influential people asked the impossible, which led to disappointments later. He was highly adept at building bridges to opposition parties and at well-timed actions to split and undermine them.

There are, however, important contrasts between Shekhawat and Pawar. Pawar's Maharashtra is much larger (a population of 79 million in 1991) than Shekhawat's Rajasthan (44 million), so it is much harder for one leader to remain informed and in control there. Maharashtra is far more developed, industrially and agriculturally, than Rajasthan, so its chief minister has to cope with more lavishly moneyed interests. Maharashtrian interest groups—whether prosperous or impoverished—

8. This discussion of Pawar is mainly based on daily newspapers and interviews with informants in Bombay and Pune during two visits, in January–February 1992 and February 1994. I am especially grateful to Govind Talwalkar, Rajdeep Sardesai, and Robert S. Jenkins.

are more organized, assertive, impatient, and prone to conflict than their counterparts in Rajasthan. Furthermore, the instruments of governance available to Pawar were less formidable than those under Shekhawat's control, because his Congress Party is more decayed and undisciplined than Shekhawat's BJP.

Despite this, Pawar performed impressively in office—thanks to his skills at political maneuvering and his ability to adapt to his own use the approach of a distinguished predecessor, Y.B. Chavan, a Congress chief minister between 1956 and 1962. Like Pawar, Chavan was from the Maratha caste that dominates village life across most of the state, thanks to its numerical strength (it is a sizable minority) and control of land. This group provided the main foundation of Congress power in Maharashtra, but Chavan was quick to forge ties to other centers of wealth and influence.

He was also sufficiently canny (and statesmanlike) to see that it was in his and the Marathas' interests to make significant concessions to less powerful groups, when or even before they fully emerged as potent political forces. As a result, governments in Maharashtra have tended to be more broad-based and inclusive than their counterparts in many other states—although Marathas have received a disproportionate share of the spoils. Chavan also minimized discontent in the Congress organization by sharing spoils equitably among most factions, and he kept opposition groups off balance by coopting or incorporating them.

Pawar has operated in this tradition, on all of these fronts, with a shrewd Machiavellian sense and impeccable timing. For example, during the latter part of 1993 he quietly cultivated cordial ties with the leader of the Shiv Sena, one of two parties of the Hindu right in Maharashtra, in order to detach it from the second, the BJP. For a considerable time, he had some success at this—one senior official said that the Sena leader "became his dancing bear." But reports of the courtship threatened to alienate *dalit* (ex-untouchable) voters, who are suspicious of the Shiv Sena. This was dangerous for Pawar, especially after the Bahujan Samaj Party, based mainly on *dalit* votes, did well in a November 1993 election in the northern state of Uttar Pradesh and helped to form a government there. Leaders of that party planned to come to Maharashtra to try to pry *dalit* voters loose from their long-standing ties to Congress.

Pawar therefore moved quickly to grant a demand for which *dalits* had waged a prolonged and bitter campaign. He agreed to rename the

Marathwada University for Dr. B.R. Ambedkar, an eminent former leader of *dalits*. (To ease resentments among higher castes, he kept the word "Marathwada" in the university's name.) Pawar's decision reinforced ties between many *dalit* voters and the Congress Party, while signaling that his hobnobbing with the Shiv Sena amounted to little more than a ploy to divide the Hindu right.

Pawar, like his mentor, Y.B. Chavan, understood that economic development can pay political dividends, and he created and maintained structures to foster it. In particular, he encouraged links at the district (that is, county) level among rich agricultural interests, business people, industrialists, and Congress politicians. This nexus, which is stronger in this state than in nearly any other, was useful in promoting economic growth. It was also a source of constant pressure on bureaucrats and politicians to assist the private sector to develop the state economy. This alliance of interests created an environment in which people felt inclined and indeed compelled to deploy their political skills to adjust creatively to economic liberalization. Pawar deserves much of the credit for this.[9]

Nonetheless, Pawar has many detractors, who argue that he has no scruples and cannot be trusted. This derives in part from what one former aide calls the "sudden and secret sneak attack" that he launched to make himself chief minister for the first time in 1978. Despite being a minister in a Congress Party regime, he took a group of followers out of that party and formed a government with support from other parties (only to return to the Congress Party years later). The lack of trust in him engendered by these maneuvers has deepened in recent years as a result of his alleged involvement with corrupt, unsavory forces.

In Maharashtra, unlike Rajasthan, moneyed interests loom so large that it is dangerous to ignore or frustrate them. To make matters worse, Indira Gandhi imposed one utterly unscrupulous chief minister there, who lowered standards of public conduct and institutionalized the position of dubious groups in state politics. In such an atmosphere, it would be difficult for any chief minister to take a strong stand against corruption, but what worried many voters was Pawar's alleged cultivation of these interests. There was also resentment among some Congress Party legislators and activists that he had arranged matters in

9. I am grateful to Subrata Mitra and Robert S. Jenkins for help on this point.

ways that prevented them from obtaining as much largesse from these groups as they would have liked.

Pawar minimized such discontent by not centralizing so radically that politicians were denied opportunities to enrich themselves. But despite the fact that his system was only partially centralized, he managed to make himself the most effective state-level fund-raiser in India's recent history—thanks partly to the size and wealth of Maharashtra. Donors are said to have included the heads of powerful sugar mills (crucial figures in his initial political base), the state's many private industrialists, producers of both legal and illicit liquor, and the beneficiaries from hugely lucrative urban land deals in and near the state capital, Bombay.

These last two groups consisted in part of members of the criminal underworld—which looms larger in Bombay than in any other Indian city. Allegations that Pawar involved himself with them indiscriminately are serious overstatements, but there is evidence to suggest some connections. For example, two underworld figures who dominate pockets of the Bombay slums—where, in the words of a well-informed witness, "the rule of law does not prevail"—were Congress Party candidates for the state legislature at the 1990 election. They used their local influence to win their seats and were then allowed to select pliable bureaucrats and police officers to serve in their constituencies. These two men and other underworld figures allegedly connected to Pawar may have been involved in the January 1993 bombings in Bombay, which touched off a horrific spate of Hindu-Muslim rioting. But the most knowledgeable sources on that episode stress the obvious—that Pawar was not stupid enough to be mixed up in that. Indeed, the two dubious legislators were detained after the bombings and remained in custody for a long time, and that outbreak of violence resulted in Pawar's return to the chief minister's office in Bombay from a cabinet post in New Delhi—a move that was very unwelcome to him.

In early 1995, Pawar's Congress Party lost a state election to a Hindu revivalist alliance of the BJP and the Shiv Sena. Many commentators blamed this defeat on disenchantment among Maratha caste voters with Pawar's renaming of Marathwada University, and on more general displeasure over his alleged association with corrupt and criminal elements. There is some substance in these claims, but they overlook the decisive reason for the defeat.

As the election approached, Prime Minister Narasimha Rao decided to award a huge proportion of Congress candidacies for the state legislature to followers of Pawar's factional rivals in Maharashtra. He did this partly to prevent Pawar from emerging as a potent rival for the prime minister's post, and partly because he is temperamentally inclined to try to please all factions in the party. This decision was disastrous for Pawar, for the Congress, and ultimately for Rao himself.

Pawar knew that many of the candidates from rival factions were so weak that they stood little chance, and that those who might win would make it impossible for him to govern effectively should his party emerge victorious. He therefore had Congress Party candidates loyal to him stand as independent rivals to many official Congress candidates. He had to do this on such a vast scale that his organizational and financial resources were badly overstretched. Rival factions responded in kind, so that Congress Party candidates fought one another not just in a few pockets like in the last state election in 1990, but in fully 200 of the 288 constituencies.[10] Pawar still managed, remarkably, to get 45 of his rebel candidates elected. They, together with the 81 official Congress victors, brought him surprisingly close to a majority. But Congress infighting enabled the Shiv Sena to win 73 seats and the BJP to win 65, and they joined to form a government.

Had the prime minister done the sensible thing and backed his most effective chief minister when candidacies were awarded in Maharashtra, Congress could have won there. Pawar had governed well enough to be reelected at a time when an unusually strong anti-incumbent mood gripped the Indian electorate.

The Complexity of the Chief Minister's Task

The sketches of Shekhawat and Pawar suggest the intimidating range of problems faced by chief ministers. But their job is even more complicated than these surveys indicate. This complexity requires careful negotiation. Many chief ministers would like to centralize power in their own hands, but only a very few (mainly consisting of movie stars), whose vote-getting ability exceeds that of their parties, can manage this. Others who attempt it soon provoke rebellions from potent factions that can destroy them. If they are sensible, they adopt a dual strategy of playing factions off against each other and decentralizing some

10. For an excellent, detailed analysis of this see Lakshmi Iyer, "Pawar Masterminds Rebels' Strategy," *Hindustan Times* (New Delhi), January 24, 1995, p. 1.

power and resources in order to forge ties to powerful subordinates.

Those who decentralize in this way often grasp a crucial subtlety—that leaders at the apex of complex regional political systems in India make their influence penetrate downward more effectively by means of compromise than by seeking to dictate. Too much centralization can, paradoxically, weaken chief ministers by cutting them off from potential clients and backers. Many decentralizers still find, however, that their underlings are so undisciplined and desperate to grab whatever they can that factional strife rips apart carefully constructed transactional networks. They then spend much of their time and political capital patching up deals with contending groups.

One of India's leading political scientists, G. Ram Reddy, has seen so many ruling parties at the state level overtaken by infighting that he now suspects that destructive factionalism is a dangerous "national trait."[11] This sort of comment would have been pooh-poohed in academic circles a few years ago, but not today.

Chief ministers also need to decide how to handle corruption. Some centralizers seek to deprive subordinates of moneymaking opportunities—either to minimize corruption or to monopolize it in order to fill their own pockets, their party's coffers, or both. This inspires immense resentment from underlings, many of whom are in politics mainly to profiteer.

Others decentralize such opportunities, on the assumption that legislators who are busy enriching themselves will seldom rebel. This strategy often backfires, however, since legislators' appetites tend to exceed what a chief minister can offer, and there are always dissident leaders who promise them greater gain if they topple the man on top.

Many chief ministers resort to actions, postures, or promises intended to have mass appeal, especially among the poor. Some of these are downright reckless. The movie star/politician N.T. Rama Rao won an election and became chief minister of Andhra Pradesh in late 1994 by promising two things: total prohibition of alcohol and heavy subsidies on rice. Either of these measures would nearly cripple the state financially—the first because almost half of its revenues come from taxes on drink, the second because the proposed subsidies would cover more than 80 percent of the cost of rice. Rama Rao must either break his pledges or bankrupt his government—not a happy choice.

11. Interview, New Delhi, December 11, 1994.

Some populist gestures, however, are carefully designed not to imply specific promises, and they often work well. When Laloo Prasad Yadav of Bihar had himself photographed milking a cow, he reminded members of his cowherd caste that he delights in his and their humble origins. When Biju Patnaik, septuagenarian chief minister of Orissa, rode a bicycle to the office to dramatize the need to conserve fuel, he got a useful point across and reminded citizens of how extraordinary he is.

Still other gestures go at least partly wrong. The same Patnaik invited citizens to "beat up" errant officials (providing he gave prior approval), in order to deflect resentment about ineffective government onto bureaucrats. It worked for a while, but then he was embarrassed by requests for permission to thrash him for failing to fulfill commitments, and eventually angry civil servants assaulted him as he left the office.

Some chief ministers try to insulate bureaucrats from lobbying by legislators and others. This is a favorite device of centralizers, but it makes them seem dangerously unresponsive and undemocratic, and it often provokes anger and rebellion among their subordinates and leaders of powerful interests.

Others go to the opposite extreme by allowing legislators and political allies to browbeat bureaucrats into permitting illegalities. This wins support from those who gain wealth and influence as a result. But it demoralizes the bureaucracy, and chief ministers who try this often lose credibility and control over events amid runaway corruption. Cannier leaders seek a balance between these extremes, but that is an exceedingly tricky task that calls for constant shifts of emphasis that overburdened politicians are often unable to make.

All chief ministers try to channel patronage (funds, goods, and services) to social groups from whom they hope to receive votes at future elections. But this time-honored practice has recently undergone important changes. During the first two decades after independence, the Congress Party maintained its dominance in nearly every state by distributing resources, in a largely successful effort to keep every conceivable interest group happy. Prosperous groups got the lion's share, but there was at least a token for everyone.

Since the late 1960s, other parties have often gained power by targeting not 100 percent, but 60 to 70 percent of the population—whether the Hindu majority, clusters of disadvantaged castes, or other groups. Rising political awareness, even among the poor, has made it more difficult to paper over divisions between high castes and low, industry and labor, urban and rural dwellers. Congress too has often given way to this trend. But using patronage distribution to forge majority coalitions has become increasingly difficult for all parties, for several reasons.

Slow economic growth has meant that the resources available for distribution have not kept pace with the rising demands from interest groups. Mounting corruption among politicians means that money that might have been allotted as patronage has been skimmed off by individuals. Growing indiscipline within ruling parties has made them less capable of distributing resources effectively. And since mid-1991, economic liberalization has reduced the funds available to state governments. So while most chief ministers try to make the most of patronage politics, it yields fewer advantages than it used to.

Some chief ministers make extensive use of their coercive powers. This can entail threats of unwanted transfers or disciplinary action against civil servants to dragoon them into cooperating. Or it can mean the use of the bureaucracy, the police, or even gangs of toughs to intimidate or brutalize interest groups, nongovernmental organizations, opposition parties, and even opponents within one's own party.

Other chief ministers use both sticks and carrots in subtle combinations. While this often enhances their power, it is difficult to avoid contradictions between these two approaches. Those who depend mainly on tough tactics usually pay a heavy price at election time.

In recent years, chief ministers have had to face difficult new choices in their pursuit of economic development. Economic liberalization has forced them to devote more attention to attracting private sector investment and less to patronage distribution. But even more important has been the need to choose between huge development projects like dams, irrigation systems, or major hospitals and small-scale schemes at the village level—wells for drinking water, the building or repair of schools, medical dispensaries, rural roads, and the like. After years of emphasizing the former, they have seen governments in a few states become enormously popular by stressing long-neglected smaller projects that bring direct, highly visible benefits to villagers.[12]

12. This was vividly apparent both from the 1985 reelection of the Janata government in Karnataka after it had stressed such projects (most notably, 60,000 village tube wells) and from evidence gathered in a study of decentralization in that state. See Crook and Manor, "Enhancing Participation."

The issues discussed above include only a few of the tactical choices that confront chief ministers. They also need to decide whether to try to mobilize comparatively dormant social groups to broaden their base, or to divide, intimidate, or otherwise demobilize certain groups—or both at once. They must find a balance between fomenting social conflict and mitigating it; between dramatizing politics and lowering the political temperature and popular aspirations (as Prime Minister Rao has systematically done); between generous responses that assuage grievances and a hard line in the face of pressure from interests; between making themselves easily available and remaining aloof; between leftist and rightist policies—and much more.

With so many things to consider, their task is excruciatingly difficult. Little wonder then that one eminent political scientist has said that if a chief minister is not suffering from heart trouble, hypertension, or a nervous disease after just one year in office, he is not doing his job properly.[13]

Most chief ministers tend toward moderation in most of the tactical choices listed above. There is, of course, no correct set of postures to adopt in all situations. The appropriate choice will depend on the personality of the chief minister, the condition of his party and of the opposition, the socioeconomic milieu, and many other things. But most of those who have been at least partially successful share a few traits.

First, they have frequently adjusted their postures on these various issues to respond to changing circumstances. They have been compelled to do so by the volatility of Indian politics. This means that relations—within parties, between different parties, between parties and interest groups, and among various interest groups—tend to change quickly, often, and unexpectedly.

Second, relatively successful chief ministers have made these adjustments in a measured manner. It is usually unwise to make drastic changes, since this can give the impression of panic and earn a leader a reputation for wild inconsistency. Continuous fine-tuning is essential.

Finally, such chief ministers understand that if they shift their position on one issue, they may need to make adjustments on others—either to maintain consistency or, by contrast, to balance interests.

To succeed even partially at all of this is obviously difficult. To say that a chief minister is involved in a game of chess is to understate the

13. Interview with G. Ram Reddy, New Delhi, December 11, 1994.

complexity of his task. It is more accurate to see him as a frantic performer in a circus act, rushing back and forth along a long table, keeping 15 or 20 dinner plates spinning—and doing all this from the saddle of a unicycle.

As if this were not enough, in recent times chief ministers have found the ground shifting beneath them. The process of opening the economy to market forces is changing the fundamental logic of Indian politics.[14] In the past, governments at the national and state levels have succeeded or failed at winning reelection on the basis of their effectiveness at distributing the resources they control. In the future, they are likely to stand or fall mainly on the basis of their effectiveness at enabling market forces to generate growth. This change requires politicians to make huge adjustments in their thinking and tactics, and compounds their problems still further.

Chief Ministers' Overall Performance

In judging the overall performance of chief ministers, we need to recognize that the serious factional squabbles that most of them face within their parties have produced starkly different outcomes for the Congress Party chief ministers and those from other parties. Since 1980, many Congress chief ministers have been unseated between elections because Indira and Rajiv Gandhi were suspicious of strong state-level leaders and had the power to oust them when factional fighting (which the Gandhis often fomented) became too intense. (By contrast, the other parties were either purely regional or their state-level units had greater leverage than their national leaders, so ousters scarcely occurred.) Congress has held power in 12 of India's 14 major states in this period, and in 9 of these chief ministers have been toppled in this way.[15] Only two non-Congress chief ministers have left office in midterm, and one of them—Ramakrishna Hegde

14. James Manor, "The Political Sustainability of Economic Liberalization in India," in *India: The Future of Economic Reform,* ed. Robert H. Cassen and Vijay Joshi (Delhi: Oxford University Press, 1994).

15. A "major" state is one that sends more than ten members to the lower house of parliament. Congress has not held power in Tamil Nadu or West Bengal since 1980. Congress Party chief ministers have been toppled in Andhra Pradesh, Bihar, Gujarat, Karnataka, Madhya Pradesh, Maharashtra, Orissa, Rajasthan, and Uttar Pradesh. This has failed to occur only in Assam, Punjab (where Congress has held power only since 1992), and Kerala.

of Karnataka—went because he preferred to, not because he was forced out.

This does not mean that non-Congress chief ministers have overcome factionalism. It has plagued them and undermined their governments' effectiveness, often severely. But factionalism is usually less unbridled than in the Congress Party, and it is much less threatening for non-Congress chief ministers than for their Congress counterparts. Congress chief ministers whom national leaders have imposed after toppling others, continue to suffer extreme infighting, because their enemies within the party cling to the hope that if they can create enough havoc, yet another ouster may occur.

And yet, despite these and other difficulties and the extreme complexity of their task, a significant number of chief ministers have performed well enough to get reelected. Major Indian states witnessed 51 state elections between 1980 and March 1995, and 19 of these were won by incumbent governments. The defeat of the other 32 reminds us of the inadequacy of many chief ministers. But when we consider the immensity of their problems and the volatility of Indian politics, those 19 victories (37 percent of the total) are reasonably impressive.

How did this happen? This important question brings us to the heart of the debate over India's governability. The explanation is complicated. In part, it has to do with the quality of the people who have served as chief ministers. Few can match Shekhawat or Pawar for adroit leadership, but—crucially—few have been such wretched leaders that they were bound to fail. Such hopeless cases are not unknown among recent chief ministers, however.

Fortunately, incompetent chief ministers have done limited damage to institutions, for two reasons. First, Indian voters are perceptive enough to have thrown such leaders out on every occasion when they presented themselves for reelection, and replaced them with less destructive figures and parties. Second, the electorate has been able to do this because India's multiparty system, despite much decay, is creative enough always to have produced at least one alternative who—while he or she may not always have been particularly impressive—was at least a significant improvement on the incumbent regime.

What else explains the ability of a large minority of chief ministers to get themselves reelected? Most neither sink to the level of incompetence mentioned above nor rise to the ingenious heights represented by Shekhawat and Pawar. The majority of them have muddled and struggled along in the job, often in confusion and distress. So their own political skills clearly do not explain the electoral success of so many. If, however, we look beyond these leaders—or rather below them, to the people whom they lead—we will find enough vitally important skills to provide much of the explanation.

Compelling evidence has recently emerged from two sources to indicate that India's long experience with open, competitive politics has played a key role by enabling a huge number of activists at the local level to develop these skills. The first source is a study of the political implications of economic liberalization since mid-1991. It found that political operatives in state-level ruling parties have been remarkably successful at adapting political skills acquired before liberalization to the new circumstances. They have shown themselves able to forge political bargains, to share out both benefits and pain among key groups, to negotiate with varied interests, and to build coalitions; all of these skills have important uses in preventing liberalization from damaging the interests both of their parties and of most key interest groups. They have therefore been more adept than politicians in many other countries at coping with the political strains that liberalization brings.[16]

Even the factionalism that bedevils most parties in India has—to a limited extent—been creative. Factions sometimes play positive roles, like those parties used to play. They serve as instruments for the distribution of resources in ways that cultivate support from important interest groups and integrate state and society. They represent the desires and grievances of interests within the political process, and they mobilize voters at election time. They sometimes promote stability by restraining chief ministers and other leaders who might otherwise move too fast or too far. When circumstances change rapidly and unexpectedly, factions often adjust swiftly to them and thus contribute to the flexibility of the political system. These positive contributions are far outweighed by their damaging doings, but they are realities nonetheless.

The second source of evidence is a comparative study of attempts at democratic decentralization in India, Bangladesh, Ghana, and the Ivory Coast. The experiment in India has been far more successful than in

16. This study has been done by Robert S. Jenkins. His work will soon emerge in the form of articles, a report to the British aid ministry, and a doctoral dissertation at the Institute of Development Studies, University of Sussex.

the other three countries, where democracy has enjoyed an intermittent existence at best. A crucial factor in India's achievement was the ability of political activists there to accomplish things that most people in the other countries found impossible.

When elected councils were created near the grass roots, a sizable army of political operatives in India knew how to develop creative relationships between elected councillors and low-level civil servants—because they had seen how it was done at higher levels over several decades. They knew how to maintain contact with constituents, how to articulate constituents' views to elected councils, and how to ensure that councils and bureaucrats would respond to those views. They knew how to make adversarial relations between rival political parties within councils work in ways that were civilized but nevertheless ensured that a lively opposition acted as a check on the excesses of the majority party. They knew how to communicate with representatives of India's free press, to keep citizens informed on council affairs, and to reveal and thus restrain excesses by those in power. They also found it easier to make democracy work at lower levels because both politicians and citizens shared a belief that elected representatives had heavy obligations to voters—an idea that was largely absent in the other three countries.[17]

The evidence from these two sources provides a further explanation for the ability of such a large minority of chief ministers to gain reelection. These political skills are found in abundance at all levels of the political system in India, and in nearly all states and parties. They tend to enable organized interests (which India has in abundance) to exert pressure on state institutions and to extract concessions. They facilitate frequent adjustments and renegotiation in state-society relations to respond to change. They permit many (though not all) conflicts between caste, class, religious, and other groups to be fought out in semicivilized ways. They tend to enhance the authority of those in power and the legitimacy of open politics.

Chief ministers who can maintain a minimal amount of rationality and order in the political process—as a sizable minority have done—create conditions in which activists can deploy these skills to deliver reasonably adequate governance. There are numerous ways in which chief ministers can help to achieve this. It is usually possible for them

17. Crook and Manor, "Enhancing Participation."

to prevent corruption from soaring out of control and to avoid committing huge proportions of the government's resources to giveaway programs such as subsidies on foodstuffs.

Those who achieve these things should have enough funds available to help skilled activists at lower levels to arrange a politically advantageous distribution of goods and services to key social groups. It is usually possible for chief ministers to structure their daily routines in ways that leave time for consultations with ministers and bureaucrats on matters of policy and political strategy. If they do that, there is every chance that their governments and the activists at lower levels who assist them will remain focused on a manageable number of programs that address citizens' needs. Chief ministers with theatrical skills (and that includes most) can use oratory, slogans, symbolic acts, and the like to dramatize and clarify their aspirations and achievements. This is a way of cultivating popular support, but it also gives political activists a clear understanding of the government's main aims and of the social groups that government is targeting for benefits in its effort to develop a solid social base.

Among the many other things that chief ministers can do to facilitate the work of lower-level activists, one is often crucial. By containing and managing factional conflict within the ruling party, they can limit its potential damage and enable activists working within various factions to play constructive roles.

Factions inside a ruling party often can assist the party to make government responsive to important social groups. Activists within factions collect information on felt needs and discontents among citizens and transmit it to politicians. They help to engineer responses by those politicians and to explain politicians' views and problems to citizens. Factions recruit skilled activists who can perform these tasks, and they mobilize support for faction leaders (which often means support for the larger party) at and between elections. They criticize excesses by leaders and members of other factions, and this sometimes helps to check such behavior. If a chief minister can prevent factional conflict from getting out of control, he or she can maximize these benefits.

By doing this and some of the other things mentioned above, many less-than-ingenious chief ministers have gone a long way toward creating conditions for skilled activists to work constructively. Some of them have been sufficiently skilled to ensure the reelection of their governments and to suggest that India is governable through its existing democratic institutions. When chief ministers fall short, another democratic institution—the electoral process—rids the system of the failed regime and produces an alternative government that may be more successful.

There is no denying that corruption, brutalization, and institutional decay are serious problems in India. But that is not the whole story. The accommodative skills of political activists are capable of repairing some of the damage that institutions have suffered, and of restoring minimally civilized social relations after periods of severe conflict. Under even mediocre chief ministers, decay can be checked and this kind of rebuilding can occur.[18]

So commentators who have voiced alarm at the disintegration of party organizations in India have overstated the problem.[19] To have exceedingly good government, strong party organizations are essential. But such organizations are lacking in nearly all Indian states and are very difficult to reestablish. And yet, reasonably adequate governance is often possible in their absence if chief ministers create congenial conditions for the skills of lower-level activists to operate constructively. Those skills are a major national resource that India has in far greater abundance than most other Asian and African countries.

The picture of India's politics that emerges here is ambiguous. This is not a full-throated anthem to chief ministers or the system in which they work. But while the sense of crisis in many writings on India is not to be dismissed lightly, the country is less ungovernable than many have suggested. Enough has been achieved there to warrant appreciation for the practical utility of Indian democracy, and to discourage despair about its prospects.

Suggested Readings

Brass, Paul R. *The Politics of India Since Independence. The New Cambridge History of India.* 2d ed. Part 4, Vol. 1 (Cambridge: Cambridge University Press, 1994).

---

18. See in this connection, James Manor, "Political Regeneration in India," in *The Multiverse of Politics,* ed. A. Nandy (forthcoming), and the forthcoming work of Robert S. Jenkins.

19. See the references in note 1, especially the work of Atul Kohli and this writer.

Cassen, Robert H., and Vijay Joshi, eds. *India: The Future of Economic Reform* (Delhi: Oxford University Press, 1994).

Frankel, Francine, and M.S.A. Rao, eds. *Dominance and State Power in India: Decline of a Social Order.* 2 vols. (Delhi: Oxford University Press, 1990).

Jeffrey, Robin. *What's Happening in India? Punjab, Ethnic Conflict, and the Test for Federalism.* 2d ed. (London: Macmillan, 1994).

Kohli, Atul. *Democracy and Discontent: India's Growing Crisis of Governability* (New York: Cambridge University Press, 1990).

Manor, James, ed. *Nehru to the Nineties: The Changing Office of Prime Minister in India* (Vancouver: University of British Columbia Press, 1994).

Vanaik, Achin. *The Painful Transition: Bourgeois Democracy in India* (London: Verso, 1990).

Economic Reform: Stalled by Politics?

Meghnad Desai

The Indian economic reform program was launched in mid-1991, following the general election in which the Congress emerged as the largest single party, though not with an absolute majority. Following the death of Rajiv Gandhi in May 1991, in the midst of the election campaign, P.V. Narasimha Rao was elected leader of the Congress Party, and he duly became prime minister in June 1991. He chose as his finance minister Dr. Manmohan Singh, who had previously been deputy chairman of the Planning Commission and governor of the Reserve Bank of India.

The need for reform was urgent. In January 1991, when foreign exchange reserves fell to a very low level and India's credit rating was downgraded, the country had been surprised and somewhat humiliated by the sudden prospect of defaulting on its international debt.[1] India at that time had foreign exchange reserves covering only two weeks' worth of imports, so a loan had to be raised in a hurry against the gold reserves of the Reserve Bank of India. The minority government of Chandra Shekhar, which had come into power only a few months previously, failed to do much to address this emergency. It was even unable to present the budget for 1991–92 at its usual time in February, because the Congress Party, which supported the minority government but was facing a particularly difficult election in the state of Tamil Nadu, did not wish to take responsibility for the higher taxes that had to be imposed. The presentation of the budget was therefore postponed, and in its place, a simple revenue statement was issued. Thus even at a time of severe economic crisis, short-term and partisan political considerations had obstructed economic reform.

1. See Deena Khatkhate, "India on an Economic Reform Trajectory," in *India Briefing, 1992,* ed. Leonard A. Gordon and Philip Oldenburg (Boulder, Colo.: Westview, 1992), pp. 49–52.

The economic reforms subsequently launched by the Congress government surprised the world by their boldness. It seemed that the government was willing at last to jettison all the policies of the Nehru era. It took steps to abandon the dogma about self-sufficiency and fear of foreign capital; to cut tariffs and expose the economy to foreign competition; to end the special privileges enjoyed by big business by way of interest subsidies and favorable licenses to import and to expand capacity; to unleash the energy of small and medium-sized firms; and to contemplate the shutting down of loss-making public sector enterprises. All in all, this was a radical turnaround.

The surprise was that unlike the reforms in Eastern Europe, this radical change was not being initiated by a new party or even by new personnel. The same cadre that had been the guardian of the old order emerged as the champion of the new; the same ministers and officials who had defended the policies of protection and state guidance were now advocating and implementing liberalization programs. Was this a genuine conversion or electoral window dressing? Will politics, unreformed and unrepentant of its role in causing the economic crisis, win again and stall the reforms before they have drastically changed the Indian economy?

Reforms: A Brief History

Reform was forced on India as much by the country's external debt position as by the liquidity squeeze caused by the Persian Gulf war, which increased the oil bill and reduced the remittance payments of nonresident Indians, since large numbers of Indians were working in Iraq and had to flee from Kuwait. Moreover, as significant as the external debt, there was also a mounting internal debt. Although domestic savings had risen substantially between 1961 and 1990, from 12 percent of GDP to 24 percent, the government had begun to eat into this source of funds since the mid-1970s when it began to be a net borrower on both the revenue (consumption) and capital (investment) accounts. The deficit on the revenue account mounted steadily through the years. Interest payments on the internal debt now amounted to one-fifth of the central budget. Something had to be done to tackle both external and internal debt.

During the first two years of reform there was progress on both fronts. Since then, foreign capital has flowed back, both in terms of portfolio capital and as direct investment. The budget deficit has come down. The foreign-exchange reserve position has dramatically improved since January 1991, to the point where $20 billion sits in the Reserve Bank's coffers and threatens to push up the rupee vis-à-vis hard currencies. Structural changes have been undertaken, in radical rejection of the Nehru-Mahalanobis strategy of developing India as a by and large closed capitalist economy with a leading public sector.[2] Tariffs are being cut; quotas are being converted into tariffs; restrictions on the expansion of private sector industries are being relaxed. Foreign capital is now being welcomed into a longer and longer list of activities—power, telecommunications, and oil exploration. Foreign collaboration with Indian private capital is also proceeding apace.

The 1992–93 budget (the Indian fiscal year runs from the first of April to the end of March) had been bold in freeing the rupee from restrictions on the trade account, and the budget deficit was being cut along the lines laid down in the memorandum of understanding with the International Monetary Fund (IMF), reducing it from just over 8 percent of GDP in 1990–91 to a projected 4.7 percent of GDP in the budget of 1993–94. This radical budget, which liberalized the economy further, was an antidote to the fears raised by the Ayodhya events—the riots and turmoil in the wake of the destruction of the Babri mosque by militant Hindu nationalists in December 1992—that the Indian political system might not stand the strain of communal violence.[3] The liberalization of the rupee gave the signal that the reforms would not only continue but could accelerate.

Growth was, however, sluggish, and did not attain even the 5.5 percent per annum rate reached in the 1980s. Another problem came from the considerable fear among the employees of public sector enterprises that they would lose their jobs as soon as an exit policy was in place, removing the restrictions that had made it all but impossible for management to fire workers in response to changed business conditions. During 1993 their fears were echoed by some of the leaders of the Bombay Club, an informal group from some of the largest Indian business houses, who met privately to coordinate their complaints

2. For the Nehru-Mahalanobis strategy see Meghnad Desai, "Is There Life After Mahalanobis? The Political Economy of India's New Economic Policy," *Indian Economic Review, Special Issue in Memory of Sukhamoy Chakravarty,* Vol. 27 (1992), pp.155–64.

3. See Ashutosh Varshney, "Battling the Past, Forging a Future? Ayodhya and Beyond," in *India Briefing, 1993,* ed. Philip Oldenburg (Boulder, Colo.: Westview, 1993).

about the liberalization process.[4] They articulated complaints about foreign capital being favored and voiced the need for a level playing field to protect Indian capital.

Prime Minister Rao has never been a bold man. While he backed his finance minister to the hilt, he failed to generate any enthusiasm for reform. There was no platform in the party or in the country for drumming up popular support for the reforms. At the Davos Conference in February 1994, Rao articulated a cautious philosophy. He said that the collapse of communism did not necessarily mean the total acceptance of a market economy, and that India had been saved from "political submission and economic dependence" because it had followed a "middle path" between the two.[5]

Much of the rest of 1993 was quiescent on the reform front. The reason for this was obvious. The government was facing midterm elections in some of the larger states in North India—Uttar Pradesh, Madhya Pradesh, and Rajasthan—and in Delhi and Himachal Pradesh. Electoral considerations can never be ignored in a democracy, and in the Indian federal polity elections come often. Since 1972 elections to state assemblies have tended not to coincide with the national general elections, particularly since the 1980s. Each set of elections compels caution at the national level as well as at state levels, as the party in power hopes to improve its fortunes. The Ayodhya events had put Congress on the defensive vis-à-vis the Bharatiya Janata Party (BJP), which had captured power in Uttar Pradesh and Madhya Pradesh in the previous round of state elections. So the Congress decided that pushing reform too far, too fast might cost it valuable seats in the 1993 elections.

As it happened, the BJP's onward march was checked during those elections: although it won handsomely in Delhi and retained power in Rajasthan, it lost power (but not vote share) in Uttar Pradesh and Madhya Pradesh. Although the economic reform was not an issue in those elections, the pace of reform did not resume during 1994. The 1994–95 budget was a cautious one: the finance minister did not even attempt to cut the deficit and gave a signal thereby that the political resistance to cutting subsidies to farmers and to public enterprises was gaining ground.

---

4. The formal existence of the Bombay Club, which is also referred to as the Bombay Group, is difficult to confirm.

5. See the report in the *Times of India* (Bombay), February 2, 1994.

Not only was the budget deficit not cut, it was stabilized at a relatively high level of 6 percent, despite the fact that the deficit for 1993–94 had actually turned out to be 7.3 percent as against the projected 4.7 percent. There were rumors that the rupee might be liberalized further, allowing for convertibility on the capital account—restricted convertibility on the current account had already been introduced—but nothing was done in the budget about it.

Since early 1994 the reforms have been confined to areas outside the scrutiny of parliament. Thus the government gave a formal assurance to the Reserve Bank that it would be restrained in its short-term borrowing and not finance its deficit by selling short-term Treasury bills (which banks could then use to expand their loans). In effect this meant printing money, an indication that in order to finance its expenditure, the government was not willing either to increase taxation or to borrow with interest from the public. There was also a deregulation of the money markets and interest rates. Both these moves were accomplished by bilateral negotiations between the Ministry of Finance and the Reserve Bank, requiring no parliamentary discussions.

But apart from these technical moves, reforms were put on hold. In November 1994 there was yet another round of state elections, this time largely in South India—Andhra Pradesh (the prime minister's home state), Karnataka, and Goa, along with Sikkim in the north. Congress lost power in Andhra Pradesh, and decisively so, coming in third behind Telugu Desam and the Communists. In Karnataka too, the Congress lost, and the Janata came to power again, with the BJP pushing Congress into third place. It was not at all clear whether the reforms were at fault, but many commentators claimed that the poor felt they had been neglected in recent years and that the reforms were benefiting only the middle classes. Whatever the truth of the matter, with the Congress having lost in three of the four major states that went to the polls in February and March 1995, the prime minister is unlikely to push reforms farther at the present juncture.

As has often happened before—in the 1950s, 1960s, and 1980s—questions arise as to whether India can politically sustain radical economic policy, or whether politics will mold economics in its own conservative shape. Has reform had its day until the next crisis?

In its 44 years of planned economic development, India has repeatedly experienced short bursts of radical action on the economic front, which were then checked or reversed by political considerations. The first such episode was the launching in 1955 of the bold framework for the Second Five-Year Plan by P.C. Mahalanobis, then an unofficial but very powerful adviser to the prime minister. The Mahalanobis framework was not only a plan for eventual self-sufficient development of the Indian economy, but it was also a decisive move away from a laissez-faire strategy for Indian industrialization, as well as from the Gandhian strategy of decentralized, village-level, agriculture-oriented development. It asked for a big resource commitment by way of voluntary savings as well as taxation. Taxes on income, expenditure, and wealth were proposed; imports were to be curtailed, especially for consumer goods. This was the boldest move yet toward a "socialist pattern of society," a goal that had been approved by the Congress Party at Nehru's behest at the Awadi All-India Congress Committee meeting in 1954.

By 1958 there was a foreign-exchange crisis, and the plan had to be pruned. It turned out that imports had been inadequately controlled, perhaps willfully so, by the then–finance minister, T.T. Krishnamachari, no friend of Nehruvian socialism. Taxation could not be increased because of resistance within the Congress as well as from the rich and the middle classes, so the government had to borrow abroad or get foreign aid. In addition, food shortage was imminent, dictating a resource transfer to agriculture, hitherto a low priority item in the Mahalanobis plan. And so the plan was pruned (the Planning Commission lowered the targets, protecting projects in iron and steel, power, railways, and the like, but cutting allocations to social services, among other things)[6]; U.S. aid was welcomed; and the need to keep food prices low was recognized.

The next such episode, though in the reverse direction from the leftward thrust of the 1950s, was in the mid-1960s. The Third Five-Year Plan had continued the Nehru-Mahalanobis strategy of industrialization, but the outcome of the first two years was disappointing. The China-India war in 1962 further undermined Nehru's reputation and brought on the added burden of increased defense expenditure. After Nehru's death in 1964, there was an attempt by the new prime minister, Lal Bahadur Shastri, to change the emphasis and direct the plans more toward agriculture. There followed two bad harvests, reinforcing

---

6. See Francine Frankel, *India's Political Economy, 1947–1977: The Gradual Revolution* (Princeton, N.J.: Princeton University Press, 1978), pp. 147–49.

the need for agricultural development. The Fourth Five-Year Plan, scheduled to start in 1965–66, was postponed; indeed, a four-year "plan holiday" was declared. At the same time, the first "miracle seeds" that made the Green Revolution possible were introduced. This turnaround from industry to agriculture, from rapid growth of capital goods to slow but consolidated growth in food output, constituted an alternative path of development for India, much more Gandhian and conservative, much less dirigiste and socialist. Even after the sudden death of Shastri in January 1966, his successor, Indira Gandhi, continued on this path. Her government devalued the rupee, as a gesture toward market-friendly policies, though not without extreme pressure from the United States.

This market-friendly, agriculture-oriented policy was reversed within three years. By 1969, Mrs. Gandhi had decided to break with this pattern and go for another bout of nationalization, this time of commercial banks, and she reverted to the autarchic Mahalanobis strategy. Apart from a much more comfortable position in food grain supply, what had caused the reversal from the "rightist" to the "leftist" policy was the exigencies of domestic politics. Mrs. Gandhi had been elevated to power by the right-wing Congress "syndicate," a group of powerful regional bosses who thought they could manipulate her. Her bid for independence was couched in political terms as a change in policy and, with support from the two Communist parties (Communist Party of India [CPI] and Communist Party of India–Marxist [CPM]), she was able to carry it through. With the nationalization of the 14 largest banks and Indira Gandhi's backing of the rival presidential candidate against the syndicate's nominee, the Congress Party was split and India began the period of personalized politics.

This radical lurch lasted until 1974. Not only banks but insurance companies were nationalized. There was even an attempt at nationalizing wholesale trade in food grains, which backfired and had to be abandoned. The limits to this policy were again political, though this time the pressures were due to widespread unrest caused by inflationary pressures. Consumer agitation, an impending strike by railworkers, and a threat to Mrs. Gandhi's position and power, triggered by a court decision that would have barred her from elective office, brought about the Emergency, in which, among other things, opposition leaders were jailed, press censorship imposed, and a series of constitutional amendments passed that curbed the power of the judiciary vis-à-vis parliament. During the Emergency, despite the rhetoric, policy became less left-oriented.

With the Janata Party's defeat of Mrs. Gandhi in the General Election of 1977, there was again a reversal in policy, though more in words than in implementation. The protectionist regime continued, as did the suspicion of foreign capital, symbolized by the steps that forced the departure of IBM and Coca-Cola. But as in the mid-1960s the emphasis was on rural development, on Gandhian principles, and on reserving a significant amount of manufacturing for the small-scale sector. Again, something akin to a plan holiday occurred, with reduced activity on the part of the government as a way to boost private investment. The Janata experiment fell apart in battles over policies and position between groups and parties as diverse as the Hindu nationalist Jan Sangh, former Socialist Party leaders, and peasant farmer leaders. General elections in the beginning of 1980 brought Mrs. Gandhi back, with her slogan "a government that works."

The next episode of radical policymaking came under Rajiv Gandhi, who succeeded his mother after her assassination in October 1984. Mrs. Gandhi had already moved toward borrowing from the IMF to relieve resource constraints due to the impact of the second "oil shock"—itself a major departure for a Nehruvian. To be sure, the last installment of that record-sized approved loan was not taken, mainly because of left-wing political opposition, both within the Congress and without, to U.S.-influenced international financial institutions. But Rajiv Gandhi accelerated both the borrowing and the opening up of the economy, instituting a policy of import liberalization and industry deregulation. The exchange rate was actively manipulated to depreciate the rupee and thereby encourage exports. Incentives were given to exporters: half of export profits were deductible for income tax purposes: for example, the interest rate on export trade was reduced from 12 percent to 9 percent, and duty-free input of capital goods was allowed in selected export industries. This policy did not touch the public sector, nor was the public sector given priority for new industrial products and processes. Rajiv's was a policy of accelerating growth by borrowing, but without any drastic restructuring of the economy.

Again by 1988, the policy had run aground. Political problems caused by unrest in Punjab, as well as allegations that bribes given by the Swedish defense manufacturer Bofors had been accepted at the highest level, led to a loss of confidence in the government, which produced the election result of late 1989. Rajiv Gandhi lost, inaugurating the period of minority party governments.

Continuity and Change

Thus, one way of characterizing the Indian economic scene is as a series of experiments in changing policy, with each experiment halted on account of political exigencies. Usually the pressures are democratic—consumer agitation, as in 1974, or electoral considerations, as in 1977, 1980, and 1989. This view of the Indian polity as subject to frequently reversed lurches of policy is not the usual one.[7] Bardhan, Chakravarty, and others have argued that the Indian economy has been stalemated by a delicate balance of class forces. They have put this explanation forward to model the 30 years of low but persistent growth: at about 3.5 percent per annum from 1950 to 1980, this was the so-called Hindu rate of growth ("so-called" only because the technical term for such a long-term growth rate is the "secular" rate of growth and the contrast between "secular" and "Hindu" has a unique Indian flavor, suggesting a long-term increase, but at a rate barely above stagnation). The argument is that the prosperous farmers, the big industrialists, and the urban unionized workers, along with the urban middle classes, each constitute a powerful force, but none so powerful as to dominate the others. In order to maintain the social balance, each has to accommodate the demands of the other. The farmers want subsidized inputs and high output prices; big business wants tariff protection, interest subsidies, and low income taxes; and the urban middle classes want job security and inflation-proof salaries. Together this leads to a wastage of resources and a low rate of accumulation and growth. If any one class could dominate, then a clear and bold accumulation policy, albeit in the interests of that class, would emerge.[8]

This explanation is partial in many respects. It was first advanced to explain the low growth of the Indian economy between 1950 and 1980

---

7. In a recently published book, Little and Joshi similarly periodize 1964–91. See I.M. D. Little and Vijay Joshi, *India: Macroeconomics and Political Economy, 1964–1991* (Washington, D.C.: World Bank, 1994).

8. Pranab Bardhan, *The Political Economy of Development in India* (Oxford: Basil Blackwell, 1984) and Sukhamoy Chakravarty, *Development Planning: The Indian Experience* (Oxford: Clarendon Press, 1987); see also a different approach in Jagdish Bhagwati, *India in Transition* (Oxford: Clarendon Press, 1993) and Deepak Lal, *The Hindu Equilibrium* (Oxford: Clarendon Press, 1988).

when, as mentioned above, GDP grew at an average rate of 3.5 percent (1.25 percent per capita). The 1980s witnessed an acceleration in this average to around 5.5 percent (3.5 percent in per capita terms). Thus both the stagnation and the acceleration need explaining. But even in the earlier period the growth rate was characterized by volatile fluctuations around a steady trend. Take, for example, the 20 years between 1961 and 1980, when the GDP growth rate per annum averaged 3.5 percent, but ranged from 3.7 percent in 1965–66 to 9.0 percent in 1975–76. Since 1980 the average has been higher, at 5.5 percent, but the range has been from 10.4 percent in 1988–89 to nearly zero in 1991–92.

Thus a pattern of short-run dash and reversal is a better way of characterizing the growth rate than "slow and steady." While Latin American economies have been notorious for their hyperinflation and East European economies in transition have experienced the same disease,[9] India has had a remarkable record in never having experienced sustained inflation at double-digit levels, measured annually. Only in three, widely separated periods (1967–68, 1973–75, and 1980–81) has it reached that level for any length of time, and only in nine years out of the last thirty-five. However, inflation was a crucial issue in 1974—when measures to control it may have contributed to the challenge to Indira Gandhi—and in the 1980 election, where the price rise in onions was used as a symbol of inflation.

The political economy of India has to be rethought to explain both the low but volatile income growth, with occasional spurts due to radical policy change, and the absence of runaway inflation. It can be argued that a class analysis, though not wrong, is only a partial answer. What strikes the observer of the democratic political sphere—the arena of parliamentary elections and government formation and rule—is not a stable stalemate of class formations but a kaleidoscopic shift of alliances and groupings based on caste (*jati*), region, language, and religion. As we have seen, the 1970s witnessed a breakdown of the monolithic Congress Party, which split into personalized factions. The merger of disparate parties to form the Janata in 1977 was quickly followed by their dissolution.

Since 1967, again with the exception of the Emergency, there has

9. Michael Bruno, *Crisis, Stabilisation and Economic Reform* (Oxford: Oxford University Press, 1993).

also been a shifting pattern of one- or multiparty rule at the state level. Purely regional parties dominate today in Tamil Nadu (Dravida Munnetra Kazhagam or All-India Anna Dravida Munnetra Kazhagam), Andhra Pradesh (Telugu Desam), Punjab (Akali Dal), and West Bengal (the CPM is, despite all, a Bengal party). Often, the party at the center (usually the Congress) is not in power in a majority of the states, a situation rarely encountered before 1967. Except for the Indira/Rajiv Gandhi government of 1980–89, national governments have not been able to rely on one party for support. Mrs. Gandhi relied heavily on Communist support in the 1967–77 period, and every other government has been forced to act similarly.

There is, however, a high level of competence in the country's civil service and technical personnel. Thus any government that fears inflation, and the consequent unpopularity, has at its disposal an effective set of officials who know how to reverse inflation; indeed, every government minority, coalition or otherwise, that has had to deal with this problem has, by and large, done so successfully. In addition to fiscal tightening, this has usually required importing food grains or other essential commodities, or releasing food grains from available stocks. There has been occasional delay, as in the sugar scam of 1994 when, whether because of bureaucratic and political incompetence and infighting, or something even less savory, the central government overestimated domestic sugar production and consequently was forced to enter the international market when prices had increased substantially. This led finally to the resignation of Food and Civil Supplies Minister Kalpanath Rai. But overall, especially when a short period of double-digit inflation has led to unrest, the system has responded quickly.

It has been much more difficult to pursue growth-enhancing policies consistently, because in an inflationary situation, those who gain are a small minority: traders, hoarders, and speculators, for example. Growth requires resource mobilization, continued sacrifice of consumption in order to increase investment, and differential rewards. Growth raises distributional issues that divide the polity in different ways depending on the policy pursued. Thus while the Green Revolution helped all farmers, those who grew wheat benefited more than those who grew other crops, and larger farmers benefited more than small farmers, especially when they had access to cheap water and power. Policies of retrenching the public sector to let the private sector expand, or deregulating interest rates so as to level the playing field between large and small business, benefit some factions and hurt others. A reduced public sector hurts trade unions linked to political parties, for example.[10] Interest rates that are allowed to fall to market levels make loans to many small businesses less attractive.

It is difficult therefore to build up a sustained coalition for reform. For a time the gainers support and the losers oppose, and a large proportion of the population stands in the middle waiting for the fruits of reform. But if the process falters or is seen to benefit particular groups persistently, then democratic opposition mounts. The coalitions that form the fragile majority are broken up. This process may start at the state level or at the national level, and change at one level feeds into the other. Thus the Congress Party's electoral defeats of late 1994 and early 1995 at the state level will have an impact on the government at the center, even though its own majority is formally not at risk. And there is already a factional split developing in the ruling party, with the expulsion of Arjun Singh and the fall of the Kerala government headed by Prime Minister Rao's ally Karunakaran in March 1995.

The fragility of the ruling coalition at the state and at the national level is heightened by the first-past-the-post electoral system, in which the winner takes all even when he or she does not command an absolute majority of the votes cast. This leads to small swings in the overall share of the votes translating into large swings in the number of seats won or lost. The system puts a premium on broad, all-encompassing coalitions representing every shade of opinion or every known vote bank. But by the same token, since their components have nothing but the desire to win office as a cement, these coalitions fall apart at the first whiff of likely defeat.

This is of course not an iron law. In the 1950s and 1960s, the Congress was a single broad-based party that represented such a coalition, but a well-disciplined one. The Congress leadership—the so-called High Command—gave orders to those levels below, who in turn fed back grassroots reactions to policy changes. The presence of a nationally recognized, charismatic leader, Jawaharlal Nehru, also helped. Since 1969, when Indira Gandhi split the Congress Party, not only has the discipline gone but so has the feedback mechanism. All that remains is the high-handedness of the High Command, which

10. See E.A. Ramaswamy, "Organized Labor and Economic Reform," in this volume.

often dismisses provincial Congress chief ministers and party leaders only to settle personal scores.

Indian democracy can thus be seen as a continuous process of coalition formation, whatever the formal party labels of the people in power. This coalition formation is the result not only of the fragmentation of the once hegemonic Congress Party, but also of the articulation of interest groups that are able to manipulate the electoral system by shifting large quantities of votes from one party to another in return for favors. Log-rolling and pork-barreling, well-known phenomena in American politics, are constantly at play in India. Loan *melas* (literally, "fairs"), where generous and not-to-be-repaid loans are given out by the touring minister, are one example of pork-barreling. Large budget deficits run by individual states eager to spend money but not to tax their citizens, and a similar indulgence at the central level only writ large, are elements in the same shifting equilibrium.

The Problem Today

Brief periods of implementing necessary but politically distasteful economic measures and exercising fiscal restraint have been quickly reversed; the recent course of reform is no exception. The initial budgets under the reform regime did succeed in cutting the deficit, from 8.25 percent of GDP for 1989–90 and 1990–91 to 5.8 percent in 1991–92, and just 5 percent for 1992–93. For 1993–94, a lower budget deficit of around 4.7 percent was envisaged, but, as had often been seen in the prereform days, as a consequence of the failure to reduce certain subsidies, among other things, it actually increased to 7.3 percent. The remarkable feature of the 1994–95 budget is that even the attempt to bring the deficit down was abandoned. By forecasting a deficit of 6.5 percent the finance minister signaled that there was no longer a sense of urgency in the government of India about economic reform.

True, to a limited extent the higher deficit of 1993–94 and the high deficit that came to pass in 1994–95 are due to the sluggishness of the economy. With import duties having been cut, and with the necessary upsurge in imports having failed to materialize, the revenue outcome was disappointing. But the prime culprit was the overrun in expenditure. Despite the higher-than-planned 1993–94 deficit, the finance minister still increased planned expenditure above previous projections. In 1993–94, expenditure was Rs.12,549 crores higher (about 9 percent) than the projected Rs.131,323 crores, while revenue was Rs.8,117 crores (or about 9.5 percent) less than the projected Rs.84,867 crores. The expenditure overrun consisted of items like Rs.900 crores extra for fertilizer subsidies as well as Rs.632 crores toward assistance to states for providing concessions to farmers on decontrolled fertilizers. Rs.856 crores were given to states to cover their open deficits, and Rs.2,320 crores extra were given for defense. All these items, though individually minor, are signs of business as usual having resumed in the Indian polity.

It was no surprise also that for 1994–95 the nonplan expenditure was to be raised from Rs.97,846 crores to Rs.105,117 crores, while the plan expenditure was to be Rs.70,141 crores. (The category "nonplan expenditure" corresponds to current consumption, and plan expenditure is capital/developmental expenditure, i.e., planned investment in particular projects—a new railway line, for example—or in a sector of the economy.) The pattern of nonplan expenditure exceeding plan expenditure, outturn exceeding estimates, and rising interest payments has come back as before.

It is not because of its inflationary impact that the size of the deficit is important. It was quite correct for the finance minister to say that the stocks of food grains, at 32 million tons by mid-1994, are an adequate guard against inflation. But what he did not say is that in such a case there was no call to offer the farmers higher procurement prices. It is not sound economics to subsidize food production when adequate buffer stocks exist. It is, however, a symptom of the ambivalence of Indian political circles about the reforms. Apart from the prime minister and the finance minister, no one else in the cabinet has come out enthusiastically for the reform. No popular political platform in support of reform has been established. This has allowed opposition parties to build up an anti-reform coalition. The BJP has joined this coalition, despite its earlier image as a pro-business party. The BJP rhetoric is now economic nationalist, and repeats many of the things the Left used to say and still does: that foreign companies should not be allowed free rein to produce goods Indian companies make; that economic decision making has shifted to Washington (they made a great fuss over the alleged transmission of the budget to the IMF before it was presented to parliament); and so on.

The BJP and the Left claim, not without some justification, that the reforms have only helped the rich. But it is more accurate to say that the reform has cleared a space in which business can grow and the middle classes will benefit, and that the reforms have not gone sufficiently deep in removing older vested interests—of the subsidized farmers, the loss-making public enterprises, and the interest-subsidized industries—in order to create room for redistribution to the poor.

The enemies of the reforms are those who did well out of the old subsidy/protection/license/permit Raj. Politicians and bureaucrats were able to extend their patronage (by ensuring that industries hired far more workers than needed, for example) and often extracted large bribes from business executives, either to fight elections or to line their own pockets. While their rhetoric is pro-poor, in actual practice the politicians and bureaucrats delivered slow growth in income and slower alleviation of poverty than in, for example, Indonesia, Malaysia, or even Pakistan.

The defeat of the Congress Party in the recent state elections can be traced in part to sophisticated voting behavior by the Muslims and the lower castes, who no longer gravitate naturally to the Congress. Rao's compromises and delays on the Ayodhya temple problem and his reluctance to challenge the BJP on secularism may be as potent reasons as the reforms for Congress losses. But it is easier for the opposition to try to convince voters that India's sovereignty is under threat because the reforms are imposed from the outside. It will be very tempting for the Congress to soft-pedal reform.

The Anti-Reform Platform

The reforms have been attacked on several fronts: first, exit policy, changed laws that permit the closure of factories and other company units, including those in the public sector, at the complete discretion of the owners; second, "entry policy," the conditions under which foreign capital, including nonresident Indian capital, can buy into Indian firms; and third, the GATT treaty and liberalization of the trade regime. On each of these issues the government seems to have preferred to play down reform and introduce it almost by stealth, certainly without fanfare, and the popular stake in the success of the reforms has not been canvased.

Exit Policy

The main resistance to an exit policy comes, of course, from trade unions supported by Left parties. The celebration for the third anniversary of Narasimha Rao's accession to power was spoiled by a nationwide strike on July 14, 1994, in which all trade union federations except the Congress-affiliated one joined. Although the 2.3 million workers who honored the strike represent a small minority of workers, or even of industrial workers, the political impact was considerable.

The government has failed to make clear to the public that losses in the public sector create high deficits, which in turn require high taxes and high interest rates.[11] It has not exposed the contribution to this problem that comes from the relatively privileged position of public sector workers, whose earnings have risen faster than per capita GDP over the last 25 years. In 1992–93, 104 of 237 state-owned units recorded losses amounting to Rs.40 billion. Of the remaining 133 units, many have low returns, while few have been highly successful.

The cautious approach to privatization has been to issue equity in the successful public sector units first. Thus on the eve of the 1994–95 budget, it was announced that seven major state-owned enterprises would sell part of their equity. These were the Steel Authority of India Ltd., Hindustan Petroleum, Bharat Heavy Electricals Ltd., Hindustan Machine Tools Ltd., Bharat Petroleum, Hindustan Zinc Ltd., and Bharat Earth Movers Ltd. This partial equity sell-off, mainly to domestic buyers, was expected to raise Rs.35 billion (Rs.49.5 billion had been raised up to March 1995). There has also been a move to allow Videsh Sanchar Nigam Ltd. to raise capital abroad, and although the initial bid to raise $1 billion of global depository receipts, via Euroissue, had to be withdrawn, this will be accomplished sooner rather than later.[12]

But it is not enough to divest shares of profitable companies. The exit policy has been sluggish in shedding failed enterprises. Ironically, many of the loss-making industries in the public sector, such as the textile mills, do not fulfill any of the criteria of the original industrial policy strategy laid down in 1956. They are consumer-goods-producing, nonbasic industries that were taken into the public sector as a way of nationalizing private sector losses, and they have continued to make losses. The National Renewal Fund, which was set up to cushion job

11. Meghnad Desai, "Capitalism, Socialism and the Indian Economy," Exim Bank Lecture, Bombay, January 1993.

12. Global depository receipts allow foreign investors to buy equity in India by proxy: an agent of a bank buys equity in India and puts the certificates in a safe deposit box in India. The receipt of deposit is traded in European and American markets.

losses, had spent Rs.78.62 billion by October 1993 on 60,000 workers.[13] Only 59 companies have been referred to the Board for Industrial and Financial Reconstruction to evaluate their solvency. Given the size of the workforce that could be let go without harming production, and the number of companies in deep financial trouble, these are very small steps.

The government's dilemma is clear. While it can partially or wholly privatize the profitable companies, loss-making companies cannot be privatized, since no one will buy equity in a negative net worth company. They have to be either shut down or kept open just to provide jobs. The latter "solution" is epitomized, in the extreme, by the Hindustan Fertilizer plant at Haldia, which employs 1,550 workers but has no production whatsoever! Indeed, the plant has produced nothing since 1986 when it was commissioned. As the *Financial Times* reported, "There is a canteen, a personnel department, and an accounts department. There are promotions, job changes, pay rises, audits, and in-house trade unions. Engineers, electricians, plumbers and painters maintain the equipment with a care that is almost surreal."[14]

It is doubtful that there will be any rapid move on exit policy. Since the National Renewal Fund is spending roughly Rs.1.3 million per redundant worker, the budgetary burden itself will be heavy. The recent election results will make exit policy even more problematical. Like China, India may live with an inefficient public sector for a long time.

Entry Policy

There has been much greater progress in throwing the economy open to foreign investment, though even here there are considerable doubts about loss of sovereignty, unfair competition from abroad, and the like. Thus the state telephone monopoly has been ended and private foreign capital has been invited to compete. Foreign companies have been allowed to enter the field of oil and gas exploration. The Industry Ministry announced on June 6, 1994, that it had cleared 73 new foreign investment proposals worth Rs.10 billion ($322.5 million). These ranged from food processing to textiles and agro products, software,

13. Ministry of Finance, Government of India, *Economic Survey, 1994–1995.*
14. Stefan Wagstyl, *Financial Times* (London), June 6, 1994.

banking, information processing, medical instrumentation, and more. Foreign equity participation even up to 51 percent will be allowed in high-priority sectors, and 100 percent foreign-owned units will be allowed elsewhere.

This move toward opening out the economy did not meet with total enthusiasm on the part of the large industrialists, the organized private sector. Having lived for so many years behind the shelter of tariffs, subsidized interest rates, and valuable licenses, Indian big business finds the prospect of competition unnerving. The complaint was that these foreigners, including nonresident Indians, have special advantages inasmuch as they can borrow abroad at cheaper rates and have better deals regarding capacity expansion than the local business people. Yet, as 1994 progressed and direct foreign investment flowed in, many of the same business leaders were able to enter into collaborative arrangements with foreign companies. Business was, by the end of 1994, much happier with the reforms.

The opposition parties continued to be ambivalent, however. The BJP moved during the year to a much more accommodating position on foreign capital, criticizing only the kinds of product lines in which foreigners were entering. The Rashtriya Swayamsevak Sangh, the core "cultural" organization of the Hindu nationalist "family," is much more uncompromising about allowing in foreign capital. The election reverses of the Congress Party, and the BJP's gains in Karnataka, Gujarat, and especially Maharashtra, may yet revive the nationalist fervor.

The indicators of business performance, despite misgivings on the part of business, look bullish. The Centre for Monitoring the Indian Economy reported in July 1994 that for a sample of 1,200 companies, net profits for 1993–94 were 83 percent higher than in the previous fiscal year. This is partly a result of changes in company law interpretations that permitted a lower provision for depreciation than previously, but is also due to lower interest rates. Tax incidence fell from 33 percent in 1991–92 and 27 percent in 1992–93 to 16 percent in 1993–94. Sales growth in real terms also doubled between 1992–93 and 1993–94. But despite a fall in the interest rates, the ratio of interest to sales has grown over the last three years. The organized private sector is one interest group that stands to gain from accelerated reforms via lower interest rates as well as lower taxes.

GATT

Nowhere did economic nationalism show up more virulently and somewhat absurdly than in the Indian agitation against the Dunkel draft of the General Agreement on Tariffs and Trade. All sorts of unfounded fears were raised in the public mind about the likely effect of the GATT treaty on India. For example, the provision for patenting biotechnology innovations was alleged to mean that if they refused to pay royalties, Indians would be barred from planting *neem* trees, which scientists have shown to have important medicinal qualities (as Indian villagers have long believed). The campaign was a well-financed one based on the fears of industries such as pharmaceuticals that the new law on intellectual property would restrict their present evasion of the spirit of patent law (Indian law now protects processes but not ultimate product; one can thus legally "reverse engineer" an imported product and develop a different method of making it). The government for a long time did little to counter some of the more absurd fears. Its attempt to forge a unified line for the G77 ("Group of 77" countries—now many more—that represent the South, or industrializing countries, in international debates and organizations) during the Uruguay Round negotiations had borne no fruit. This was because the initial impetus behind the Uruguay Round came from the industrializing countries themselves, as is clear from the Uruguayan origin of the conference. There is as much fear in the industrialized countries of competition from the cheap labor of the South as there is fear in India of the old adage that "free trade equals neoimperialism."

It is some indication of the isolation of Indian politicians of all parties that there was a serious demand to "cancel the pact," or a fond hope that at the last minute the world would stop and modify the GATT treaty to suit India's demands. No one had pointed out that not signing the GATT treaty would lose India its Most Favored Nation status around the world and damage exports severely. While China is impatient to join GATT, India thought it could choose to leave it.[15] No one in the government was honest enough or bold enough to counter some of the wild propaganda. As in other areas of economic policy,

15. For some popular fears, see Hardev S. Sanotra, "Anti-GATT Movement Spreading Waves of Confusion," *India Today,* May 15, 1994. Even this excellent periodical did not deal with the GATT until the date of signing the treaty.

reform is seen as a technical matter, to be defended only by the finance minister and his civil servants. All the other ministers and leading politicians are waiting to see if the reforms will succeed or falter, and keeping their powder dry for either eventuality. Now, with the defeat of Congress governments and some major leaders such as Sharad Pawar in state elections, some politicians may openly jump onto the anti-reform bandwagon.

The Prospect

In the short run, the Congress cannot disown the economic reforms. It has few other achievements to its credit. But, as was indicated by the prime minister in his first major speech on economic reform since the election reverses in late 1994 and early 1995, there will be a slowdown in opening the economy. The entry policy will be tightened and the exit policy will be put on hold. The budget for 1995–96 presented in mid-March 1995 confirmed this. The outcome for the budget deficit for 1994–95 was above the projected 6.5 percent, but only slightly. For the coming year, there will be no attempt to bring it down much below 6 percent, and the outcome may yet end up at 6.5 percent. A gesture was made to increase rural employment, but no attempt was made to cut fertilizer subsidies or accelerate the exit of loss-making public sector units. While the budget did not go so far as giving a subsidy for rice for the poor, the message is that populism will be pursued.

There are systemic reasons for this, as I have argued above. A sustained reform package would require a government at the center with a substantial majority. This government would have to have its party in power in a large number of states. It would help if it were led by a nationally recognizable prime minister rather than one who has a fragile regional base. Such a leader might be able to build a pro-reform coalition from all the fractions that stand to gain from the reforms: small and big business; employees in the unorganized sector; rural and urban poor, who would benefit if the burden of taxation and the benefits of subsidies were more equitably distributed; and consumers, who will enjoy lower prices as the tariffs come down; among others. Rajiv Gandhi created such a coalition briefly in the mid-1980s, as did Indira Gandhi for a different sort of platform in the early 1970s. But both these leaders also discovered that it is not enough to have the rhetoric for reform: there has to be effective delivery of change while, at the same time, careful watch is kept on any adverse turn in the economy that might exacerbate the negative effects. This means controlling inflation above all, securing steady food supplies, and taking swift action against unanticipated shocks like the recent outbreak of plague.

Such a powerful governing coalition seems highly unlikely, even in the long run. It is improbable that the number of parties will decrease, or that the parties will become more disciplined or ideological. The best prospect would be for a revived Congress Party that could fold back into itself some of the smaller fractions that have wandered off into the many Janata parties existing today. Such a Congress might even be able to reform the electoral rules to ensure proportional representation and greater stability in the political system. Economic policy requires a medium-term perspective to be effective. As of now, the political system cannot guarantee such a perspective. It is too dominated by electoral pressures and, given its current fragile state, elections occur far too often and cause far too many reversals of policy. An unreformed political system is an obstacle to fundamental and irreversible economic reform.

Suggested Readings

Bardhan, Pranab. *The Political Economy of Development in India* (Oxford: Basil Blackwell, 1984).

Bhagwati, Jagdish. *India in Transition* (Oxford: Clarendon Press, 1993).

Chakravarty, Sukhamoy. *Development Planning: The Indian Experience* (Oxford: Clarendon Press, 1987).

Desai, Meghnad. "Is There Life After Mahalanobis? The Political Economy of India's New Economic Policy," *Indian Economic Review, Special Issue in Memory of Sukhamoy Chakravarty,* Vol. 27 (1992), pp. 155–64.

Lal, Deepak. *The Hindu Equilibrium* (Oxford: Clarendon Press, 1988).

Little, I.M.D., and Vijay Joshi. *India: Macroeconomics and Political Economy, 1964–1991* (Washington, D.C.: World Bank, 1994).

Organized Labor and Economic Reform

E. A. Ramaswamy

The contemporary history of the Indian labor movement is intimately linked with the protectionist economic policies that the government of India followed for 40 years. Organized labor has been among the major beneficiaries of an economic arrangement that insulated the private sector from competition and the public sector from crippling losses. Segments of the industrial economy that did not have to battle for survival in a competitive market could be persuaded, with only a show of resistance, to share their good fortune with labor, and trade unions made the most of the opportunity. While this participation in the benefits of a protected economy is in itself unexceptionable, the downstream consequence of the windfall has been to warp, perhaps even pervert, labor's own perceptions.

As the spoils of protectionism began to trickle down, trade unions came to focus rather closely on sections of the workforce for whom the most benefits could be obtained with the least risk. This was perhaps inevitable, given the history and structure of the Indian labor movement. With unions fragmented along lines of ideology and personality and engaged in a competitive bid for support, the one sure way to stay ahead of rivals was to demand an even larger slice of the pie, which was more easily achieved within the charmed circle of protected industry. In a process that gained momentum, especially with the lifting of the Emergency toward the end of the 1970s, trade unionists began to churn familiar ground, organizing the already organized. Raiding each other's territory and luring new members with ever bigger promises became the accepted norm, and basic organizing ground to a halt.

Industrial workers have notched up impressive gains as a result of these developments, but the labor movement itself is caught up in a gathering storm. The consequence of a narrow focus on the protected segments of the economy is alienation from the unorganized sector, where most Indian working people are. Trade unions are undoubtedly powerful in large enterprises that they can cripple with the snap of a finger, but their constituency is steadily shrinking because of capital's policy of shifting work to the unorganized sector. What trade unions have accomplished as a result is to obtain more and more money for fewer and fewer people, which cannot go unnoticed in a poor country like India with its struggling millions. Thus, while unions can paralyze vital sectors of the economy, they scarcely have friends in the wider society.

Moreover, the labor movement is hopelessly fragmented, lost in obsolete strategies, and saddled with a gerontocratic leadership. One hundred years after its birth in the textile mills of Bombay, the labor movement is in its greatest crisis ever. Economic liberalization comes at this particularly inopportune time. For the beleaguered labor movement, the move to abandon protectionist policies in favor of free market economics could be the proverbial last straw. Protectionism and organized industry are the *summum bonum* of its existence, and the new policies are specifically targeted at both.

The Organized and Unorganized Sectors

The Indian labor movement is built on a narrow base and is more than a little cloistered. Employment can be viewed in two ways. One is to look at the numbers employed in the three major sectors of the economy: agriculture, industry, and services. The National Sample Survey, which is generally considered to be a more reliable source of statistics than the census, indicates that agriculture, with 67 percent of the working population, is by far the biggest employer. Employment in industry has stagnated at 12 percent since 1960, but the service sector has grown from 15 percent to 21 percent in three decades. It is not particularly helpful to know how many are employed in producing goods or providing services, however, as this tells us nothing about conditions of employment. The more useful method is to consider the "organized" and "unorganized" sectors of the economy.[1]

1. "Organized" and "unorganized" are the most common usages, but some prefer "formal" and "informal."

The unorganized sector, comprising agriculture, small enterprises employing fewer than ten persons (at least on paper, since actual employment can be several times higher), and self-employed people accounts for 92 percent of the country's working population. This is the abode of the unprotected worker in whom trade unions, which have concentrated on the 8 percent employed in the organized sector, have no interest.

The unorganized sector, absorbing about 292 million of India's working population of some 317 million, is a vast and diversified universe about which few generalizations can be made except that conditions of employment are in general quite exploitative and in sharp contrast to those in the organized sector. There is no such thing as employment security here, nor even the payment of statutory minimum wages unless enforced through collective effort, which is uncommon. The unprotected worker in the unorganized sector is so far removed from the raging debate on economic liberalization and its consequences for employment security that this debate could well be taking place on another planet.

Women, children, migrant workers, and bonded laborers are among the segments of the unorganized sector's workforce whose conditions of employment are especially deplorable. There are an estimated one-quarter million bonded laborers in the country—primarily in agriculture and drawn essentially from tribal and semitribal groups—who are tied to lifelong servitude to settle debts incurred by the family. Despite the existence of laws abolishing bonded labor and the efforts of voluntary groups organizing raids to free bonded laborers, the practice has not been eradicated. In addition, there are migrant laborers, especially in agriculture, who travel vast distances in search of work.

The number of working children below 15 years of age is variously placed at 13.6 million (by the 1981 census), 17.3 million (by the Planning Commission), and 44 million (by the Operations Research Group, a prominent research and consultancy outfit), with all three estimates considered understatements.[2] Although agriculture is the chief employer of child laborers, some industries are also heavily dependent on them, the more important ones being safety matches and firecrackers, *bidi* (cigarette) rolling, catering, construction, and carpet weaving.

The unorganized sector is the prime source of employment for

2. Parveen Nangia, "The Situation of Working Children in India," in *Protecting Working Children,* ed. William E. Myers (London: Zed Books, 1991), p. 46.

women. The 1991 census places the number of employed women at 90.6 million, of whom no more than 4.2 percent are absorbed by the organized sector. The organized sector has been steadily pushing out women workers, and is now left with just one woman to every six men.

The unorganized sector also accounts for close to 90 percent of all employed men. Their conditions of employment are bad by any reasonable yardstick, although better than those of women and children.[3]

Broad comparative data indicating differentials in pay among men, women, children, and migrant laborers of all ages are not easy to find, but case studies offer a clear pointer. A recent study of the hosiery industry in Ludhiana (in Punjab, among the most developed parts of the country) shows, for example, that migrants are paid less than local workers, and women less than men. Only local adult men earn statutory minimum wages; migrant men come next with a drop of some 20 percent, and women's wages are lower by up to 50 percent depending on the job.[4] Such evidence of women being paid considerably less than men, besides being relegated to low-end jobs involving little skill or interface with machines, can be easily replicated.[5]

But this is not all. Every large enterprise operates a segmented labor market, with a core of permanent workers and a growing periphery of apprentices, temporary workers, casual laborers, and nonemployees who are not even on its payroll. The trend everywhere is to downsize the permanent force in favor of these segments. The law is actually in labor's favor, forbidding the deployment of contract workers to perform core jobs and requiring the employer to confer permanent status on temporary hands who have worked for a length of time, but trade unions, which have little interest in these forms of labor, are by and large content to let management do as it wishes. A recent paper by Ajit Ghose for the International Labor Organization (ILO) in New Delhi notes:

> The most striking fact is that the 1980s has been the best decade in terms of economic growth but the worst in terms of employment gener-

3. For a detailed account of the unorganized sector, and in particular of women's work, see *Shramshakti: Report of the National Commission on Self-Employed Women and Women in the Informal Sector* (New Delhi: Government of India, 1989).

4. Manjit Singh, *The Political Economy of Unorganized Industry* (Delhi: Sage, 1990), pp. 163–72.

5. For such evidence pertaining to a wider range of industries and parts of the country, see *Indian Women in a Changing Industrial Scenario*, ed. Nirmala Banerjee (New Delhi: Sage, 1991).

> ation. During 1978–83, GDP grew at an annual rate of 3.1 percent while employment generation grew at 2.8 percent. In 1983–88, the rate of growth of GDP accelerated to 4.3 percent per annum while that of employment decelerated to 1.3 percent per annum.

This pattern is also present in the organized sector, where, as Ghose points out, employment growth has been decelerating since the 1970s.

> The deceleration in the '80s, moreover, was due solely to the sharp decline in employment elasticities. This decline was fairly general; but it was much sharper in manufacturing than in other sectors. The employment elasticity was actually negative in private organized manufacturing. . . . The consequence of all this was a decline in the share of the organized sector in total employment, which was small to start with.[6]

Although Ghose says that "the underlying reasons for these tendencies are not known," he also notes that in the 1980s there was a "growing informalisation of employment." Indeed, the organized sector has not grown because work is being siphoned off to the unorganized sector to circumvent restrictive laws and take advantage of cheap labor. The single dominant objective of the management of the organized sector, public and private, during the last decade has been to shift work from workers to nonworkers and nonemployees. It has farmed out production to small enterprises; transferred work to laborers hired by contractors, although working within its premises; enlarged, especially in high-technology industry, the employment of supervisory and managerial staff, if necessary by promoting workers to these positions; invested in capital-intensive technology that reduces or eliminates the requirement for labor; and even done away with "workers" altogether. The textile industry has shifted weaving operations to power looms, and the drugs and pharmaceutical business has taken advantage of "loan-licensing" to produce its branded goods through the informal sector. Every firm in high-technology areas engages contract workers for labor-intensive tasks, though this is sometimes done not to reduce the cost of labor but to use it more effectively.

At the upper echelons of technology, some elite firms have dispensed with "workers." Modi-Xerox, an affiliate of the American Rank Xerox, not only does not have anyone who carries the designa-

6. Ajit K. Ghose, "Economic Restructuring, Employment and Safety Nets: A Note," in ILO-ARTEP, *Social Dimensions of Structural Adjustment in India* (New Delhi: ILO, 1992), pp. 94–101.

tion "worker," but encourages employees to aspire to upward mobility rather than this lowly status. A high-technology thermal power plant has managed to avoid employing workers by entrusting production (consisting essentially of monitoring automated processes) to supervisors and managers and maintenance (which is more labor intensive) to contractors. The success of some of these managerial strategies was visibly demonstrated recently when Hindustan Lever (an associate of the Anglo-Dutch multinational) posted its highest profits and distributed the largest dividend even though its biggest manufacturing facility was under a yearlong lockout. With the market well supplied by small-scale producers, running the plant was no longer of strategic importance to capital. The locked-out workers resorted to all kinds of strategies, including hawking on the streets of Bombay a rival brand of detergent named "Lockout," produced by the same subcontracting firms Hindustan Lever used; but they had to back down because their employer could hold out indefinitely.

Workers from these two different worlds—the organized and the unorganized sectors—can be found not only within the same factory but sometimes within the same shop, doing the same job on adjacent machines with vastly differing treatment and compensation. To the casual and contract workers in industry, not to speak of women breaking stones on a construction site, children weaving carpets, agricultural laborers, and numerous others at the bottom of the pile, permanent workers in the organized sector are the ultimate object of envy. With secure jobs, wages that go upward with every settlement, a cost-of-living allowance that compensates for inflation, health care, retirement benefits, job descriptions that cannot be altered against their will and interests, and employers who will not push them around for fear of annoying their union, they appear to be wallowing in luxury.

The Labor Movement

The Indian labor movement is essentially an outcrop of politics.[7] The socially and economically deprived industrial workers of the late 19th

7. For a discussion of the history of the Indian labor movement, see V.V. Giri, *Labor Problems in Indian Industry* (Bombay: Asia Publishing House, 1959); Sukomal Sen, *Working Class of India: History of Emergence and Movement—1830–1970* (Calcutta: K. P. Bagchi, 1977); Rakhahari Chatterji, *Unions, Politics and the State: A Study of Labor Politics* (New Delhi: South Asia Publishers, 1980).

and early 20th centuries could scarcely have hoped to match the power of capital, especially British capital, were it not for the politicians and middle-class intelligentsia who took the first steps to organize them and provide leadership. Along with politics, however, came issues workers barely understood, let alone empathized with. Nationalists and communists, who made up the leadership of the All-India Trade Union Congress (AITUC), formed in 1920, were constantly at war over distant ideological issues—such as, for example, affiliation with international organizations like the League Against Imperialism and the Pan-Pacific Secretariat—which hardly mattered to a workforce struggling at the margins of existence. While some of the early differences within the labor movement could be papered over, the first irrevocable split was brought on by World War II.

The nationalists under Gandhi decided not to cooperate with the British war effort, whereas the communists, who swore undying opposition to imperialism, lined up behind the British the moment the Soviet Union joined hands with the allies. When Gandhi launched his famous "Quit India" movement at the peak of the war, the British presented the communists with the opportunity of a lifetime: they threw nationalist politicians and trade unionists into jail, leaving the communists to annex the AITUC. Nationalist trade unionists, who had no labor organization to return to when released from jail, responded by forming the Indian National Trade Union Congress (INTUC), the second labor federation and chief rival to the AITUC, in 1948. Two more federations were formed around this time, both on ideological lines—the Hind Mazdoor Sabha by socialists, who had always been a distinct group within the AITUC, and the United Trade Union Congress by a radical group from West Bengal.

Reflecting on these events some 50 years afterward, the communists admitted that it had been a mistake to oppose "Quit India"; this action had well and truly damaged the labor movement. Regional political parties, which mushroomed in subsequent years, have formed their own front organizations, adding further to the rift in the labor movement along political lines.

Structure

The dominant organizational form of the Indian labor movement is the industrial union, although craft unions are by no means absent. Industrial unions can either organize an entire industry in a large city or region, with branches in individual enterprises, or limit themselves to a single firm or factory. The former pattern is typical of older industries, the textile workers of Bombay and Coimbatore being, for example, organized by unions spanning each city. The trend in newer industries, of which there is a growing profusion, is to form unions limited to a single firm or factory. These industrial (and craft) unions are the building blocks of the labor movement, with a membership and an identity under the trade union law of the country. Since this law permits any seven workers to form a union, employers may have to deal with several unions organizing the same body of workers: a public sector steel plant has no fewer than 100 of them, although a handful is more typical.

A further complication is that, in the absence of an agreed verification procedure, unions claim vastly exaggerated membership, making it difficult for employers to weed out pretenders. The check-off system, wherein workers authorize employers to collect union membership dues, addresses some of these problems, but only partially. Not all employers offer the facility, nor do all unions accept it: the communists in particular have serious reservations about the check-off system.

Additionally, it is not uncommon for workers who treat membership as a form of cheap insurance to sign up with more than one union. This bewildering confusion is further confounded by the absence of a law requiring capital to recognize a union or to bargain with it. Employers have their own ways of dealing with such complexity, but that is another story altogether.

The next layer of the labor movement is made up of an indeterminate number of federations seeking to affiliate individual unions. The larger and better known of these apex bodies are explicitly political: political parties control them to varying degrees (although some federations deny any link with a party at all) and supply the top crust of their leadership. These leaders—called outsiders because they have not risen from the ranks of workers—may preside over dozens of affiliated unions in far-flung locations while simultaneously holding positions in the party and even the government: Jyoti Basu, the longtime chief minister of Marxist-ruled West Bengal, for example, presides over some Calcutta unions. In addition, numerous nonpolitical federations—built around an industry, city, region, or even a leader—offer affiliation, with the result that individual unions can literally shop around for a federation. They may also decide against any kind of affiliation, as is increasingly the case.

The politically aligned federations and their affiliates at industry and enterprise levels are the most visible facet of the labor movement and the most common referent when people speak of organized labor—but this is beginning to change. Workers have grown tired of being divided along political lines, dictated to by political parties, and dominated by external leaders. The result is a new breed of unions—commonly referred to as "internal" or "independent" unions—anchored in the enterprise, led from within, and deliberately distanced from any kind of ideology or wider linkage. This arrangement offers two immediate advantages: greater unity and higher membership density. Unlike political unions, which are divisive, internal unions not only have kept workers within an enterprise united—no mean achievement in a country where seven workers can form a breakaway group—but also have an impressive record of enrolling everyone.

Political unionism, on the other hand, is invariably associated with low density. There may be a dozen or more competing unions in a single factory, but all of them together would account for no more than one-half to two-thirds of the labor force. When faced with a surfeit of unions, workers tend not to sign up with any, knowing that one or the other can always be approached in case of need. Membership is one of the everlasting mysteries in factories where multiple unions operate: no one quite knows who belongs to which union, and how many workers are nonunion. With an internal union, this is never a problem because there is hardly any nonmember. The disadvantage of this form of unionism is that it is devoid of wider linkages. The typical internal union is a free floater, limited to a single enterprise, or even to a single manufacturing unit or office and its permanent workers, shutting every window to the wider world and oblivious even to another such union in the factory across the road. Internal unions can be claustrophobically isolationist, but it is isolationism born on the rebound, resulting from workers' disgust with political unions for whom the wider world is almost everything and the enterprise a relatively minor player. Bombay, the premier industrial city and the home of literally hundreds of independent unions, has no network to bind them together. As a result, unions find it difficult to mobilize fraternal support or gain access to the bureaucracy or the political executive of the state during a crisis.

Some unions have attempted to overcome this limitation by forming firm-specific federations: large firms such as Pfizer, Blue Star, Hoechst, Hindustan Lever, and Philips have federations knitting together far-flung factories and offices, although hostile employers have dismantled some of these formations. Yet others have turned to outside leadership, despite their distrust of it. Although the preference is to induct an outsider, especially a lawyer, as adviser, high-powered leaders have sometimes been elected to an office in order to counter a militant employer or deal with a politically charged environment. Hindustan Lever is an interesting example: although well educated and organized, its workers have always sought outside leadership to meet their management on level ground. But no outsider is entirely above suspicion: workers pack the executive committee, hold every other office, and are vigilant for any trace of skulduggery.

The stock of outsiders has been declining in all kinds of unions, whether independent or not, reflecting the general disenchantment with messianic leadership. The most recent in the line of messiahs, which includes such names as the communist S.A. Dange and socialist George Fernandes, along with Gandhi and Nehru who too had occasional brushes with trade unionism, was Datta Samant, who stood industry on its head with unconventional methods, such as the destruction of company balance sheets.[8] His aggressive strategy worked well in profitable firms, but not in the Bombay textile industry, which was already in its death throes by the time he stepped in to make his characteristically inflated wage demands. Under his leadership, one-quarter of a million mill workers went out on a strike in 1982 that lasted over a year and has never been officially called off.

This inconclusive strike destroyed the textile industry, and along with it Samant's image as an invincible gladiator. Moreover, it demonstrated the essential isolation of internal unions. The striking mill workers enjoyed little fraternal support even from Samant's own unions, despite the fact that he was then at the peak of his power. The historic strike was a turning point for the labor movement: with the collapse of Samant in the mid-1980s, workers began to hold their leaders accountable through democratic checks and balances.

Internal unions are a growing force, with a strong appeal to young,

8. For an elaboration of this phase of trade unionism, and in particular the strategies that catapulted Samant to the zenith of the Bombay labor movement, see E.A. Ramaswamy, *Worker Consciousness and Trade Union Response* (Delhi: Oxford University Press, 1988).

educated workers in the newer industries and enterprises. They are individually powerful and well organized, but it is doubtful if they add up to a labor movement, or even a segment of it, because of their isolationist ways. Moreover, only unions with political links have any influence over public policy.

Political Links

Parties expect support from unions and unions from parties, although their relationship is neither straightforward nor without variation from one federation and party to another. In spite of these complexities, organized labor has been the battering ram of party campaigns. When parties organize *bandhs* (a kind of forced paralysis of a city, state, or even country), they count on trade unions to shut down factories and offices and ensure that trains and buses do not run. Equally, when they want to make a political point by defeating an opponent's *bandh*, they turn to labor to keep up an appearance of normality. Organized labor is also a useful ally at election time, if only in a few urban constituencies where workers preponderate.

The quid pro quo for labor comes in the form of favors that a party in power can dispense to unions in a state-mediated system of industrial relations. Labor ministers and chief ministers have a long history of using their power over the bureaucracy and clout with capital to benefit favored unions. Indeed, they can often tilt the balance merely by choosing to unfurl the union flag in front of a factory gate: the civil administration, the police, and the employer (who is dependent on politicians for licenses in a regulated economy) would have to attend such a ceremony, sending powerful signals to workers about which union to support.

In addition, the vast public sector is susceptible to political pressure over a range of issues, from recruitment, promotion, and transfer to wages and benefits. State government enterprises (which vastly outnumber those under the central government) in particular give the impression that patronage distribution is the very purpose of their existence. Politicians appointed to chair their boards have turned them into fiefdoms, limiting appointments and promotions to the party faithful and encouraging unions headed by political lieutenants.[9]

9. See ibid. for a discussion of how Marxists have used employment to promote their unions in West Bengal. Every political party has done this, although perhaps not so blatantly.

Labor's mainstay in the early years of independence was the Indian Labor Conference, a tripartite body modeled after the ILO representing labor, capital, and the government. Although the conference now meets less frequently and is taken much less seriously by the government, considerable prestige attaches to membership, since it is the only forum giving labor a say over major policy issues. Labor's representation is limited to political federations, however, leaving other segments with no influence in spite of their growing membership. Every political party, it seems, attempts to keep out the nonpolitical segments of the labor movement, giving the impression that membership in the conference is yet another benefit in the system of spoils.

Labor also relies on political parties to stall unwanted changes in legislation by raising a stink in parliament. It is this strategy used in tandem with industrial action that has enabled labor to fight off attempts at amending trade union and industrial relations laws so repeatedly and successfully. With the advent of economic liberalization, this strategy is in evidence yet again.

Support Base

It is impossible to tell how many workers are actually enrolled in trade unions, since there is nothing to go by except the vastly exaggerated claims of the unions themselves. Of the 45,904 registered trade unions in 1986, the last year for which published figures are available, only 7,667 had actually filed the mandatory returns giving details of membership. Their claimed membership during this year was 6.4 million, but few take this figure seriously.[10] The area of relative certainty is the following of the ten federations recognized by the government as having a national presence, whose membership is verified by the chief labor commissioner through a system of random checks and penalties for false claims. The 6,543 unions affiliated to them (roughly 20 percent of all registered unions) had a verified membership of 6.1 million (against a claimed 12.4 million) in 1980, the last year for which con-

10. Membership is compiled on the basis of returns that unions are required to file annually: only about 20 percent actually do. State governments, which compile the statistics, do not often transmit them to the Labor Bureau for publication, with the result that the same membership figures could be repeated year after year: the fine print states that the figures for the past two decades are provisional. The Labor Bureau, for its part, takes about a decade to publish the data, and what comes out at the end are exaggerated claims that would have us believe there are more trade unionists than there are workers.

firmed data are available. The Indian National Trade Union Congress, aligned with the Congress Party, topped the list with 2.2 million members; the Bharatiya Mazdoor Sangh (BMS), linked to the Bharatiya Janata Party, with about half that number, was the only other federation to have more than a million members. Another verification round was held in 1990, but only provisional results are available. Some observers believe that INTUC was pushed to second place by the BMS, with 3.1 million members. Perturbed by the ascendance of the allegedly communal BMS, every other federation has challenged the finding.

Manufacturing and mining contribute 40 percent of the membership of the ten federations, transport 23 percent, services 12 percent, and plantations (tea, coffee, and rubber) 9 percent. Agricultural workers make up another 9 percent, with 82 percent of them coming from three federations whose activities are confined to West Bengal. INTUC has only 26,000 members (1 percent of its following) in agriculture. Even in manufacturing and the services, trade union presence is limited to large and medium-scale enterprises. Their absence in the unorganized sector is difficult to establish statistically, however, since the industrial classification goes by the nature of the activity and not its scale. A very rough approximation is nevertheless possible: activities typically located in the unorganized sector (tobacco, tanneries and leather goods, glass and pottery, coir, brick kilns, wood and wood products, quarrying, and building and public works) account for no more than 5 percent of union membership.

Neither the old (political) nor new (independent) unions have much interest in the unorganized sector. Their constituency is small, but there is a clear pattern to the way they have divided the pie. The political federations have greater sway in the older, smokestack industries like textiles, coal mining, ports and dockyards, transport, and plantations. Independent unions have a firm grip over such sunrise industries as fertilizer, pharmaceuticals, chemicals, petroleum refining, power generation, and electronics. Thus, independent unions are likely to become more and more significant.

The change in the social profile of younger workers, compared to older generations, reflects this change in industrial mix. Industrial workers in India come increasingly from a background of formal education and middle-class parentage. A census of 10,000 workers in a large public sector electronics plant showed, for example, that less than a quarter had not completed school education, whereas more than 50 percent had gone beyond ten years of schooling to obtain diplomas in engineering, industrial training certificates, and even degrees in the sciences, humanities, and engineering.[11] This is a 40-year-old factory, with 60 percent of its workforce in the age group 40–49, which stopped recruiting long ago. Newer plants employing younger workers would be even more likely to require specialist qualifications like an engineering diploma or at least technical training, and would certainly not consider employing anyone with less than ten years of schooling. With such a background, workers expect to move with experience and seniority to skilled white collar and supervisory jobs. This changing workforce will be less and less likely to obey distant leaders, either heads of party-linked federations or messianic individuals like Datta Samant.

The Public Sector

The public sector is a category apart, distinguished from sunrise and sunset industries in the private sector by a centralizing tendency, reflecting the bureaucracy's desire to control this vast empire. Among its centralizing features is a system of wage bargaining whose objective (although never fully achieved) is wage parity—a common wage pattern across a range of industries and enterprises that are inherently noncomparable. When public enterprises head for a round of wage bargaining, they look to the Department of Public Enterprise in New Delhi, which issues guidelines to enterprise management, scrutinizes settlements, and decides whether they merit its stamp of approval. Knowing where power lies, many public enterprises have located their corporate offices in New Delhi although their manufacturing facilities may be nowhere near, and the top brass of those that have not done so spend their time shuttling to the capital. Trade unions need a presence in New Delhi and a structure that spans the country to deal effectively with public enterprise management, but only the larger political federations have this. Independent unions led from within and lacking wider linkages are severely handicapped in this regard. A union confined to a particular steel plant, for example, cannot deal effectively with management that is constrained to bargain according to policies set not just for the public sector steel industry as a whole (which would be bad enough) but for all similar kinds of industries in the public sector.

11. Based on unpublished data collected by the author for a consulting assignment.

Public sector workers are the government's gift to the federations, but with liberalization this source of membership is in danger of evaporating. With many enterprises in the midst of wage negotiations, the government has recently dismantled the regime of centralized directives and bureaucratic approvals to let enterprise management reach whatever settlement it deems fitting. Labor is alarmed at the prospect that the principle of wage parity might fall by the wayside.

In the new environment in which public enterprises are left to fend for themselves, the demand that all enterprises pay the same wage does not make sense. Unionists are willing to make concessions to the changed context, but not to abandon the concept altogether. For them parity is more than money; it is also the basis of solidarity, the cementing force that keeps the labor movement together. Trade unionists prefer therefore to discuss parity within disparity—or disparity within parity—but not to let every firm go its way. They have even more difficulty in accepting the dilution of the public sector. Just as parity is more than money, the public sector is more than employment. It is also the fountainhead of the labor movement, the bastion of trade unionism.[12]

Strikes

Trade unions of all descriptions are decidedly adversarial in their attitude to management, private or public—the one-line article of faith for the average union is that the employer must necessarily be wrong. Squabbling unions can quickly come together against the employer: even unions that cut secret deals with capital ("yellow" unions) fall in line when a strike is called. This deep-seated sense of adversity (to which capital has handsomely contributed) has made impossible the evolution of more participatory forms of industrial relations. In an atmosphere where cooperation with capital is indistinguishable from collaboration, even well-meaning trade unionists hesitate to publicly admit that the employer may on occasion be right. When it is not about politics, therefore, the history of Indian trade unionism tends to be about conflict. Strikes can drag on for weeks and months in the face of extreme adversity: some have continued even after an express ban by the government and imprisonment of striking workers. Few unions

12. *The Public Sector: A Dialogue*, ed. E.A. Ramaswamy (Bangalore: Industrywatch, 1994), pp. 23–24.

have the money for a strike fund, although every worker has a kinship network to fall back on.

No strike is beyond political meddling, and long, drawn-out ones are especially apt to run into a political quagmire. Three strikes are memorable: the railway strike in the mid-1970s, the public sector strike in the early 1980s, and the Bombay textile strike already described. The railway strike (to demand, among other things, a 48-hour work week), which the government crushed by deploying the army, was the harbinger of the Emergency that Indira Gandhi imposed on the country in 1975. When public sector manufacturing industries were crippled by a major strike in 1981 to demand wage parity with a better-paying firm, the government-as-employer allowed workers to go on strike, but retaliated when their spirits began to flag. Switching over from the role of employer to that of government, it then ruled that the workers could not go before a tribunal because their dispute did not merit adjudication. This was an astonishing decision, considering that petty disputes are routinely found to have merit. In yet another political twist, the dispute was promptly dispatched to a tribunal when the government changed, but more than a decade after the event an award is still awaited. The government also had a major hand in the Bombay textile strike, which was the longest and largest (in terms of workers involved) in the annals of Indian labor. It stood behind the mill owners on the flimsy ground that Samant's union had no *locus standi* in the dispute (since INTUC, aligned to the ruling Congress Party, was labor's official spokesman). The strike was an indictment as much of INTUC as of conditions in the textile industry, but the government was more interested in the fate of its favored union. In the event, the mill owners were content to sit back and let the government beat Samant down.

The incidence of strikes has declined in the decade since the collapse of the Bombay textile strike, although conflict persists. Reflecting the changing power equation, the offensive lockout (as distinct from a defensive one responding to a strike) has emerged as capital's strategic weapon, especially in the private sector. In the Marxist-ruled state of West Bengal, lockouts have been accounting for between 80 and 90 percent of the worker-days lost to industrial conflict. The Marxist chief minister, Jyoti Basu, who considers strikes to be un-Marxist, has reined in the militant union wing of his party, but capital has become more bellicose. West Bengal, with its declining industries steeped in the culture of adversity, is hardly typical of India; the more troubling circumstance is the use of extended lockouts by multinationals such as Bata and Hindustan Lever to bring labor to heel.

The failure of labor and capital to graduate to a more mature and sensible relationship has been the subject of much comment, although not of very much action. The National Labor Commission recommended 25 years ago the gradual withdrawal of the government to allow more efforts at bilateral agreement, but this suggestion was squelched by labor leaders and politicians who had developed an interest in tripartism. In subsequent years, there has been much halfhearted talk by governments and government-appointed committees of industrial-relations reform and the promotion of participatory forms of management. The inertia of the government and the indifference of capital have suited the labor movement, which is in any case opposed to every form of change.

Voluntary Organizations

While mainstream trade unionism remains in this state of infancy, the unorganized sector has witnessed a fresh mobilizing effort. The new push comes from voluntary organizations that, though they have the legal status of trade unions and resemble them, avoid calling themselves unions and certainly do not work with them. Since they operate in a vastly different environment, these voluntary groups tend to adopt different methods to organize and service their constituency. Their organizing effort is directed to the community in which workers live. Being anchored in the community, they must address such issues as housing, water supply, sanitation, and health and not be limited to economic issues in the manner of conventional unions. Moreover, their members' problems may not be with employers—because an employer is either nonexistent as in the case of the self-employed, or elusive and constantly changing as with much of the unorganized sector—but with the police, the municipality, and the government. Collective bargaining and strikes may not be the most appropriate methods when it comes to defending vegetable vendors' right to the pavement and fishers' right to the waters before the police and the administration. All in all, the voluntary groups employ the kind of mass mobilization strategies that trade unions have long since forgotten. And they are a lot less adversarial and much more constructive than the average union. As the secretary of a voluntary organization observed in a recent paper:

> Trade unions have a "hard" image. The strategy and tactics of a trade union lead to confrontation as [its] task is to articulate conflict and contradiction. The relationship of a trade union with other parts of society is therefore often non-harmonious. With this type of image, the union often loses potential allies such as the press, the middle class or any other part of society with which it has no conflict. This loss of allies and support can reduce the strategic options of the trade union.[13]

Some of the most successful of these organizing efforts are by women. The best known is the Self-Employed Women's Association (SEWA) in Ahmedabad, which has organized some 30,000 poor women engaged in vending and hawking, portering (carrying goods on their heads), handcart pulling, rag picking, and other forms of self-employment. The association trains members in business and technical skills, helps them procure materials and market the product, provides legal assistance, and even has its own bank with 24,000 savings accounts to extend credit and encourage thrift. Interestingly, SEWA started off as the women's wing of one of the best-known trade unions in the country—the Textile Labor Association (TLA), organizing the mill workers of Ahmedabad, which had the benediction of Gandhi's leadership—only to be expelled because "the growing personal and political strength of the women . . . was disconcerting to the TLA leadership in a society where women are taught to defer to men."[14]

Construction workers in some parts of the country are also well organized, with local unions or associations and an apex body in the National Federation of Construction Workers.[15] Fishing folk in coastal areas have similarly organized themselves and affiliated to the National Fishworkers' Forum.

These voluntary initiatives make up a third strand of the labor movement, which is in many ways more vibrant than the politically

13. Renana Jhabvala, "Self-Employed Women's Association: Organizing Women by Struggle and Development," in *Dignity and Daily Bread: New Forms of Economic Organizing Among Poor Women in the Third World and the First*, ed. Sheila Rowbotham and Swasti Mitter (London: Routledge, 1994), p. 133.

14. Kalima Rose, *Where Women Are Leaders: The SEWA Movement in India* (London: Zed Books, 1992), p. 75.

15. See Geetha, "The Tamilnadu Construction Workers' Union," in *A Space Within the Struggle: Women's Participation in People's Movements*, ed. Ilina Sen (New Delhi: Kali for Women, 1990); Theo van der Loop, *Industrial Dynamics and Fragmented Labor Markets* (Utrecht/Amsterdam: Royal Dutch Geographical Society, 1992).

inspired national federations and the enterprise-level independent unions. They are as yet a diminutive force, an occasional bright patch in a vast sea of unorganized labor, but they will undoubtedly grow. They will also seek wider influence, including in the formulation of labor policy. SEWA has already demanded admission to the closed world of the Indian Labor Conference. More ominously for mainstream trade unionism, SEWA, construction workers, and fishers have come together recently to form a national confederation of labor in the unorganized sector.

Government, Labor, and Economic Reform

The battle lines are clearly drawn three years after the process of economic liberalization began, although no real change has so far taken place. There are major conflicts that must come to a head if the government intends to carry through the reform program. Labor has important strengths as it faces these challenges, but also fundamental weaknesses.

The Regulatory System

Labor's power flows in good measure from the legal system. There is hardly a facet of labor relations untouched by law, although the conversion of statutory promise into practical advantage is not automatic. However, this is a sphere where labor has done quite well for itself. Workers and their unions have not only taken advantage of the statute but produced a body of jurisprudence by stretching its limits in law courts. For labor, and for industrial relations generally, the case law resulting from years of litigation is at least as important as the rules on the statute book.

The basics of the legal system trace back to World War II when India was a British colony. Since the country was a supplier of materials to the Eastern theater, the British did not want industrial action that might impede the war effort. This was the basic reason behind the promulgation of the Defence of India Rules, which virtually banned strikes and lockouts, forcing the disputants to go before a conciliator and further seek a judicial decision in a court of law if conciliation failed. With independence, the Defence of India Rules became the Industrial Disputes Act, which continues essentially unchanged to this day. The justification for state regulation of industrial relations in post-colonial

India was provided on the one hand by the Gandhian ideology of nonviolent protest and on the other by the need for unhampered production to make a success of the five-year plans. Successive labor ministers raised in the Gandhian tradition held up state regulation as a superior Indian alternative—quite unlike the wasteful and uncivilized method of collective bargaining—which balanced the interests of labor and capital without recourse to conflict.

The Industrial Disputes Act, like its predecessor, gives sweeping powers to the bureaucracy to conciliate industrial disputes and refer them for adjudication when conciliation fails. Labor and management are not required in this system to reconcile on their own, nor even permitted to do so, strictly speaking. Among the forces inhibiting voluntary effort are the restrictions placed on industrial action. Labor must serve the bureaucracy with a notice of strike 14 days in advance, go through conciliation for an indefinite period until the bureaucracy gives up, and wait, once again for an unspecified period, for the government to decide to refer the dispute for adjudication.[16] No strike can be called before all this is accomplished nor is one likely to be called afterward, since no union can sustain the momentum indefinitely.

The realities of industrial relations, it must already be clear, do not quite match the formal blueprint. Conciliation, on which so much faith was placed, has been the main casualty: the National Labor Commission observed in 1969 that it had become a waiting room, an inevitable preliminary to adjudication. Collective bargaining has grown to fill the vacuum, although unsupported by statute. The de jure denial of the right to strike and to practice lockout might appear to hamper collective bargaining, but it is available de facto in the absence of enforceable sanctions. Despite the fact that the law makes strikes and lockouts an impossibility, India has plenty of both, neither side being deterred by questions of legality. Collective bargaining has of course to survive in the shadow of state regulation, since the government can always intervene in an industrial dispute if it so chooses. It is within the government's power to ban an illegal strike and jail striking workers, although such interference would in practice be extremely rare.

16. Such stringent conditions apply only to public utilities, but the government can bring any industry within this classification. In a recent case, the government of Maharashtra declared that bakeries were a public utility.

While collective bargaining has gained favor as a method of dealing with interests, the establishment of rights has become the realm of courts and tribunals. Although capital is far better endowed to fight law suits, labor in fact has fared better. Inspired by notions of social justice and inclined to view labor as the unequal partner in the industrial relationship, the judiciary has pronounced a series of landmark judgments that have bolstered labor's power.

Employment Security

Employment security is the most important of the individual and collective rights that labor has expanded through the courts. Jobs in industry are for life. While workers can be dismissed for serious misconduct (after an inquiry that can be challenged in court), the employer can do nothing about surplus labor. Reducing redundancies requires government permission, which has never been given. Government permission is also needed before losing enterprises can close down, and this has never been granted either.

While the law protects employment by forbidding retrenchment and closure without the government's consent, such a cast-iron guarantee is available only to "workers" in "industry." The judiciary has interpreted both of these terms in the broadest possible way so as to extend the protection of law to the greatest number. "Workers" have been defined as those who perform work of a manual, clerical, or technical nature regardless of how much they earn. Supervisory employees can also claim to be "workers," but only if their pay is below a fairly low ceiling. An important demand of many managers and supervisors above the ceiling, and therefore without protection, is to be recognized as "workers," on the ground that their work is more clerical or technical and not so supervisory. The demand is especially strident where managers are organized into their own separate trade unions, which is the case in much of the public sector. The judiciary has tended to rule that managers are not really managers (even if so called) if their work is more technical than supervisory, but such judgments have so far been confined to individual managers who have challenged a dismissal. The next step in the chain is for collectivities of managers to claim the status of workers, and such a case is already pending before the courts. It comes from the managers of a public sector consulting firm who have argued that consultants with no subordinates to manage cannot be said to be engaged in supervisory work. It is a case whose outcome is keenly awaited.

One has not only to be a "worker" but also to be employed by "industry" to be secure. In a landmark judgment given in 1978 in the case of a water supply and sewage disposal board, the Supreme Court ruled that the essential criterion for a place of work to be considered an "industry" is the employment relationship and not the pursuit of profit. With the exception of sovereign functions (such as the police and the armed forces) and tiny firms employing fewer than ten persons, any systematic activity that brings together an employer and his employees in a cooperative relationship to produce goods or render services that satisfy human wants is an industry in the eyes of the law. An entire range of organizations from universities and hospitals to temples, churches, and charitable institutions that offer an employment relationship, or "nexus of employment" as it is often termed, are now covered by the Industrial Disputes Act even though they may not aim to make a profit.

The prospect of closure has recently become less remote: the Board for Industrial and Financial Reconstruction (BIFR) can order closure if there are no suitors willing to resuscitate a losing firm, but the process can take years. For employers who want to pare the workforce or close down an unprofitable line, voluntary retirement offers the only viable option. A recent example is Hindustan Ciba-Geigy, an affiliate of the multinational Ciba, whose Bombay factory had to retire every one of its 650 workers before it could shut down. This is an expensive course: knowing that they cannot be retrenched, workers prefer to wait until the parting package is suitably hefty.[17] The less expensive, if also less wholesome, method is for an employer to vanish after stripping the firm of its assets. Whatever the law, every employer knows that no government can force him to run a business against his will. The firm could in effect be shut down through the simplest of expedients, such as, for example, nonpayment of electricity and water bills. Vast sums are owed to the banks by firms vandalized by their owners, but none of it can be recovered because they have not gone into liquidation. It is a

17. Employers do in fact adopt a variety of tactics to push out the unwanted. Chronic absentees and poor performers may be counseled, for example, to accept early retirement (and the package that goes with it) if they wish to escape disciplinary action (which of course carries no package). This course is risky in that if coercion can be established, voluntary retirement can be struck down by a court.

problem the country has in any case to face up to, but liberalization is forcing the pace.

Service Conditions

Employment security is not the only bone of contention, although it has cornered much of the limelight. The regulatory framework also confers on labor the right to be consulted before any changes are made in service conditions. The law requires employers to serve labor with a three-week notice of changes in conditions of service, which could in effect encompass almost every aspect of work organization. If workers do not consent, the dispute may end up before courts and tribunals that take years to move. A cussed trade union can virtually immobilize the employer by taking advantage of this restrictive provision to block all change. As a commentator observes:

> [A]ny management that wishes to modernise its factory or office will find that the Industrial Disputes Act has prescribed a game of hurdles. . . . The only permitted course of action under this Act is to take all the right decisions at the start of the business, and then grow with a fossilized organization and frozen technology. . . . The law gives workers quasi–property rights over their jobs which cannot be changed to their detriment.[18]

Obsolete Laws

There are other aspects of the legislative framework that require reexamination, although they may not be so central to the liberalization process as employment security and restrictive labor practices. The archaic Trade Unions Act is in desperate need of amendment. Enacted by the British in 1926 when workers were too fearful to stand up to their employers, the law aimed to encourage mobilization by allowing a handful of workers to combine under the leadership of nonemployees who could not be bullied. Whatever the early benefits, few today would deny that the law has played havoc by fragmenting the labor movement and handing over its leadership to outsiders. The Industrial Disputes Act, with its emphasis on state mediation and indifference to

18. C.K. Johri, "Industrialism and Industrial Relations in India: The Task Ahead," in *Industrial Relations in India: The Coming Decade,* ed. J.S. Sodhi and S.P.S. Ahluwalia (New Delhi: Shri Ram Centre for Industrial Relations and Human Resources, 1992), p. 32.

union recognition, is no less obsolete. Trade unions have done their best to block any change in these antiquated laws. They are not keen on increasing the membership requirement nor at all in agreement on a credible method of checking inflated membership claims, a prerequisite to formal recognition. They are also inclined to limit attempts by the government to reduce dependence on external leadership as an intrusion into their internal affairs.

Industrial Relations

Although the need for change is widely recognized, there has been little evidence so far of the government's will to act. Labor has such a long and successful record of resisting change that any government that ventures to clean up industrial relations must brace itself for a prolonged battle.

Attempted Legislation

There have been five distinct occasions in the past 15 years when the government of the day was forced by mounting labor protest to abandon a bill placed before parliament. The first was in 1978 when the Janata Party, the opposition alliance that came to power by defeating the Congress Party, brought before parliament a comprehensive Industrial Relations Bill. It raised a storm of protest from trade unions, even those that supported the constituent parties of the Janata government. The government itself collapsed not long after, taking the bill with it. Four years later, in 1982, Indira Gandhi's Congress Party asked an expert committee headed by a trade unionist to come up with recommendations on industrial relations reform. Based on its report, the Trade Unions and Industrial Disputes (Amendment) Bill was placed before the upper house of parliament, but never got beyond that stage. V.P. Singh's Janata Dal government brought another bill before parliament in 1990, this time to promote participatory management, a consensual method of decision making that gives labor representation —usually parity representation—with capital at various levels from the shop floor to the board. Labor opposed yet again, but its opposition was now more subtle: what the unions wanted was not worker participation in management but trade union participation. They said that worker participation already existed in the form of collective bargaining, but they did not object to participatory management if unions were given the sole right to nominate labor's representatives to participative forums. The employers were in any case bitterly opposed to the bill. This government too fell, and with it vanished any hopes that might have been entertained for participation.

In addition to these attempts at cleaning up industrial relations, two bills specifically addressing employment security have also been beaten back. The parliament passed a bill in 1982 exempting certain industries from the definition of "industry" (with obvious implications for employment security), but this never became law because the government refrained from announcing the date when it would take effect.[19] Another bill in 1987 seeking to exempt hospitals, educational institutions, and charitable trusts from the definition of "industry" was also abandoned. Attempts at reforming industrial relations have not ceased, although they rarely seem to progress. The government has before it the report of yet another committee, the difference this time being that it is not an expert body but one providing equal representation to labor and management and headed by the president of INTUC, still thought to be the largest trade union federation in the country. The members of the committee are apparently agreed on the need for change, but cannot decide on the direction. The disagreement is not merely between labor and capital; the many factions of the labor movement are themselves at odds over vital issues.

Issues

Four issues are likely to dominate the confrontation between organized labor and the government, when it does come: exit policy, the future of the public sector, the opening up of monopolies to greater competition, and the entry of multinational corporations.

Exit Policy. The government is under pressure from international agencies and foreign investors to come up with an exit policy that would enable firms to shed unwanted workers and unprofitable activities. Most people agree that direct foreign investment, especially in manufacturing,

---

19. A bill becomes an act when it goes through both houses of parliament, gets the assent of the president of the republic, and the date on which it is to take effect is announced in the government's gazette. The final step is a technicality, rarely considered a hurdle to legislation. That an attempt to dilute employment security could be stymied at this stage shows how unpopular it is to tamper with it.

will not pick up so long as jobs carry a cast-iron guarantee. On the other hand, employment security is what unions the world over are after. It is difficult to see how any labor movement can surrender such a precious possession and hope to survive. Not surprisingly, the very mention of an exit policy has become anathema to labor.

Future of the Public Sector. India has a vast and diversified public sector whose presence covers the entire spectrum of industrial and commercial activity, stretching from insurance and international trade to the baking of bread and hatching of eggs. By 1990 the central government alone had invested Rs.993 billion in 244 enterprises employing 2.3 million people.[20] About 100 of these enterprises are in the red, with quite a number having wiped out their capital base, and the return on capital for the sector as a whole is around 4 percent. Many of the profitable ventures have the benefit of administered prices and monopolistic markets, prime examples being insurance, oil and gas (exploration, refining, and distribution), and telecommunications.

The public sector is as much sinned against as sinning. While politicians have routinely bemoaned its inefficiency, they have also denied it the freedom to be businesslike. Entangled in a web of bureaucratic controls and political interference, public enterprises scarcely have the autonomy to take vital business decisions. Liberalization has placed this huge sector in the eye of the storm. What is to become of the numerous enterprises with their vast employment and enormous investment? The government appears to lack any strategy: all it has done so far is to divest a small portion of equity and announce its unwillingness to bail out losing firms. Neither reform nor privatization is on the agenda—reform is needed even to privatize, since there will be no takers for most firms unless they are first turned around.

Labor has raised the banner of revolt, making known its opposition to privatization even as the government is undecided about its next move. The case of the Indian Iron and Steel Company (IISCO), in the

20. This relates only to firms registered under the Companies Act. Economic activities directly under the control of various ministries, such as the railways, post, and telegraph and telecommunication, all of which are large employers, are excluded. Also excluded are an estimated 875 enterprises under the control of state governments with an investment of Rs.382 billion. There is hardly a state government that does not operate an electricity board and a road transport corporation, besides sundry other enterprises, most of which are awash in red ink.

politically turbulent state of West Bengal, offers what is possibly the best evidence of labor's resolve. Mukand, a leading private sector firm making steel from scrap, was willing to take over IISCO, which is deep in the red and in desperate need of capital to modernize its plant, but the government was forced by stiff opposition in parliament to withdraw a bill that would have put the sale through. The unions do not have many options, however. If they want to save IISCO from liquidation—which is what the BIFR might order if there are no takers—government or the public sector Steel Authority of India would have to be pressured into nursing the firm. Neither appears willing. Labor is undoubtedly concerned about IISCO's workforce of some 30,000 employees, which privatization is sure to trim, but this is not all. Privatization threatens the very survival of the labor movement, for reasons we shall consider. For now, the message from the trade unions is clear: they not only want jobs, but want them in the public sector.

Monopolies. Monopolies that have thrived for 40 years under the regime of planned economic development are suddenly faced with the prospect of competition. Banking and insurance represent the biggest and most powerful monopolies—the latter even more than the former—and they are both solidly in the public sector. Two committees appointed by the government have recommended that both industries be opened up to competition, but the unions are up in arms. As it happens, some of the most powerful trade unions in India are to be found in these two industries. Not only is the clerical and subordinate staff well organized but managers right up to fairly senior levels have their own unions (euphemistically termed "associations"). It is a powerful network that runs from the smallest branch in a remote village to the apex of the banking system in the big cities and cuts across almost the entire hierarchy, from messengers and errand boys to senior managers. With the exception of a small clutch of very senior managers, bank employees across the spectrum have made common cause in the past and will do so in the future. They have already organized a series of one-day strikes to protest privatization. For all this, the government has not gone beyond making an occasional noise, usually feeble, on the need to clean up banking. Moreover, it is competition rather than privatization that is on the anvil. What is raising labor's hackles is evidently the threat to the monopolistic advantage that public enterprises have so long enjoyed.

Multinationals. Trade unions have been able to address some of these issues from the moral high ground, even though their essential interests are sectional. The public sector has been at the cutting edge of the policy of import substitution and national self-sufficiency that has inspired Indian industrialization since independence. By contrast, most Indians have viewed the private sector as motivated by profit rather than national interest. In the past multinationals were barely tolerated.[21] Even now, most Indians believe that their role should be limited to using marketing savvy to peddle mass-consumption goods. All kinds of groups opposed to the reform process have been able to play on suspicion of multinationals, with deadly effect. A motley collection of Gandhians, former socialists, and environmentalists succeeded, for example, in beating back a recent proposal by Cargill, an American multinational, to manufacture common salt.[22] Cargill's offices have been repeatedly ransacked by farmers alleging that it was forcing them into dependence by patenting seeds. Allowing multinationals to buy into public sector enterprises, if and when this happens, could be fraught with difficulty. The government would find it hard to counter the allegation that enterprises built with the nation's wealth—even if they are seriously in the red—are being given away to foreigners.

This environment enables labor to argue that national interests are being forsaken under pressure from international lending agencies in the name of liberalizing the economy. Banking and insurance are especially relevant in this context, since the public sector has taken them to the farthest corners of the country. Public sector banks may not be terribly efficient or profitable, but they are everywhere. Labor's argument is that a vast network painstakingly built is being handed over to foreign interests. It is like selling the family silver, and selling it cheap. The communists have accused the Congress Party of sacrificing

21. The Foreign Exchange Regulation Act of 1973 requires foreign firms to dilute their equity to 40 percent unless they are engaged in high-technology industries or export at least 40 percent of their output. It was under this law that George Fernandes, the socialist trade unionist who was then industry minister, ordered IBM and Coca-Cola to wind up their operations in the country.

22. Salt, once a British monopoly, has been the symbol of India's defiance against imperialism ever since Gandhi organized his famous salt *satyagraha* at the peak of the Civil Disobedience movement in 1930. Being a shrewd tactician, Gandhi decided that Indians would defy British rule by marching in their millions to the vast coastline and evaporating sea water to make salt. This symbolic gesture had profound effect, and is considered a turning point in the independence movement. Ironically, Cargill sought to set up its salt works in Gujarat, the very state where Gandhi personally led the march.

Nehruvian socialism at the altar of multinational greed. The government has countered with the weak and unconvincing retort that liberalization is in fact a continuation of Nehru's vision.

It is difficult to see how the process of industrial liberalization can advance without addressing these issues: they can neither be ducked nor resolved through sleight of hand. The government is for the moment lying low, but a confrontation is inevitable if India is not to turn its back on industrial liberalization. For all its seeming strength and invincibility, organized labor will be forced to contend with the many chinks in its armor when that confrontation does come. It is true that law and jurisprudence have conferred on labor an enormous advantage, acting no doubt on the assumption that it is the weaker of the two partners to the industrial relationship and therefore in need of protection. But the benefits of this dispensation have been limited to a tiny minority, because mainstream trade unionism has failed to reach the vast multitude of working people. By turning a blind eye to exploitation outside their narrow circle, trade unions have rendered themselves vulnerable to criticism. Unionized workers, often called a "labor aristocracy" and worse, are among the favorite targets of the intelligentsia and the mass media, let alone the captains of industry.

What Lies Ahead?

Change is never easy, and in India it is especially difficult, occurring only when there is no alternative. Certainly, little has changed so far on the labor front, although the lightning and thunder witnessed in the past two years would have us believe that much has. The labor minister has promised before every session of parliament to bring up an Industrial Relations Bill, but nothing of the kind has happened. On the specific question of employment security, the government's ministers have in fact backtracked on their earlier stand and now deny that an exit policy is even under consideration. It would indeed be a social and political disaster to throw millions out of employment without a safety net. It was claimed in the early stages of economic reform that the newly created National Renewal Fund would be used to rehabilitate surplus labor by imparting useful skills, but the money has been used only to finance voluntary retirement in the public sector.

Apart from divesting some equity and financing some early retirement, the government has not done much with the public sector either. It has neither initiated steps to improve its performance nor carried out its threat to stop budgetary support to losing firms. Many firms cannot pay wages without the government's dole, and there has been no case of payments being stopped. The Board for Industrial and Financial Reconstruction is the only institution currently in place to deal with losing firms, public or private. Of the 1,895 firms referred to the board in the seven years of its existence, revival packages have been put together for 295 and another 225 have been ordered to close. The BIFR has its critics: not only is it ponderous, but revival packages recommending soft loans and other favors to dying firms, critics argue, amount to throwing good money after bad. Luckily for them, the board cannot issue a fiat to the banks; it can only identify firms where an infusion of capital might help recover old investments. In any case, it is not yet apparent whether the BIFR has an answer to the problems of the public sector. The decision to refer public enterprises to the board was taken only in 1992, and no case has so far been disposed of.

Organized labor has not made it easy for the government to resolve these complex problems. Its stand is by and large that nothing needs to change. This view has been most vociferously put forward by radical Marxists, who attribute every problem to international lending agencies. They are in particular opposed to tampering with employment security and state ownership of the public sector. The finance minister has offered to write off the accumulated losses of public enterprises if workers would take them over, but labor is hardly enthusiastic. The Marxist response is that worker ownership is itself a form of privatization that would detract from social ownership.[23] Their answer to the problems of the public sector is better management, to which they would, however, make no contribution either by helping to put together a reform package or by actively clamoring for one. In keeping with labor's tradition of the most extreme position winning out, the Marxist stand has in effect become organized labor's stand. In spite of the numerous squabbles between the federations and the political influences that pull them in different directions, middle of the road groups have thrown in their lot with the radicals, at least in public.

23. When the State Bank of India, the largest and most successful public sector bank, made a public offer of equity, the unions advised their members not to accept the preferential offer made to employees. The members, however, spurned this advice and picked up the blue chip.

Nor has capital done much to lighten the government's load. All it has asked for in the last two years is an exit policy and a share in the National Renewal Fund. Management not only wants the right to fire, but thinks that this is how the rest of the civilized world deals with labor. Captains of industry have spoken time and again of the (presumed) freedom offered by Western capitalism to issue pink slips in the evening, asking workers not to report to work the next morning. Furthermore, capital is not even certain that its interest is limited to getting rid of surplus labor. Industrialists have repeatedly claimed that industrial relations would be set right and productivity improved if only the government would allow them to get rid of 10 percent of the labor force. Serious doubts arise as to who this 10 percent would be: surplus workers, or trade union activists? Capital—especially private capital—gives the impression of waiting for an opportunity to settle scores with organized labor. Even the most ardent supporters of economic liberalization may not be with capital on this, being loath to see India treat organized labor the way Third World dictatorships do.

When the crunch comes, all the federations are likely to join in defending labor's edifice. While the entire public sector would be affected by labor action, the impact would be especially severe in banking and insurance. Banking is the one sector that can be struck with deadly effect on the rest of the economy, as the mid-1994 one-day strikes demonstrated.

It is however doubtful if the federations can convince the independent unions to join them in industrial action. While employment security is as dear to them, on some aspects of trade-union and industrial-relations reform the independent unions disagree more with the federations than with the government. There are also signs that enterprise-level affiliates of the national federations in the public sector might rethink their position: they are beginning to accept that public enterprises will not survive if they do not cut themselves loose from government aid and stand alone as economic enterprises. Moreover, what matters to unionists at this level is the future of their own enterprise and not of the sector as a whole. They would be quite willing to cut a deal with enterprise management on productivity, wages, and personnel policies regardless of what happens to other firms. Some of them are already frustrated to find the national-level leadership insisting on wage parity even when agreement with enterprise management is within reach. These tensions will increase and may even cause some unions, especially in the more profitable and better-managed firms that have a future, to disaffiliate. This is a major centrifugal force that has the potential to undermine the federations' base.

Moving farther afield, the voluntary movements that make up the third strand of the labor movement have even less reason to join this battle. The unorganized sector is far less affected by liberalization, although it has not exactly welcomed it. The fear is that workers squeezed out of the organized sector would flood the already overcrowded unorganized sector and make it more difficult for everybody to eke out a living. Beyond this, the voluntary organizations hardly have common cause with trade unions.

Whether and when the government will take the next steps depend on whether it believes there is no alternative. The scarcity of foreign exchange was one of the factors pushing the government to reform the economy, but with money pouring into the stock markets the pressure has eased considerably. The government, which did not obtain a Congress Party majority in parliament until well after it took power, has little reason to rock the boat immediately, whatever the feelings of international investors and lending agencies. The next move will probably await the parliamentary elections, due by June 1996.

Suggested Readings

ILO-ARTEP. *Social Dimensions of Structural Adjustment in India* (New Delhi: ILO, 1992).

Johri, C.K. *Industrialism and Employment Systems in India* (Delhi: Oxford University Press, 1992).

Ramaswamy, E.A. *Worker Consciousness and Trade Union Response* (Delhi: Oxford University Press, 1988).

Rose, Kalima. *Where Women Are Leaders: The SEWA Movement in India* (London: Zed Books, 1992).

Reading India

Ainslie T. Embree

"What is this India, apart from her physical and geographic aspects?" Jawaharlal Nehru asked from prison in 1944 in his notable literary statement *The Discovery of India.* The record of India's cultural achievements, he wrote, gave only a partial answer, for they seemed to have little to do with the present realities of "appalling poverty, superstition, and the crushing burden of British rule."[1] In the same vein, his daughter, who as Indira Gandhi governed India for nearly 20 years, as a young woman had noted with sadness that few Indians, including herself, were able "to enjoy [India's] loveliness and to make friends with our fellow countrymen who speak a tongue and think thoughts that are not our own."[2] Even more surprisingly, Mahatma Gandhi spoke of the difficulty of knowing the real Indians, living where "this cursed modern civilization has not reached. . . . Those in whose name we speak, we do not know, nor do they know us."[3] This sense of not knowing one's own people is surely an unusual note for nationalists to strike, but it indicates these Indian leaders' awareness, in the face of the almost overwhelming complexity of their society, of the urgent need to find a unifying center.

Defining "India" is all the more difficult because the complexity that seems to characterize Indian civilization is in a very real sense the product of modern interpretations by Westerners and Indians alike. In reading books about India written in the last two centuries, one encounters modern intellectual structures imposed by writers and scholars

---

Detailed reading lists appear at the end of the chapter.

1. Jawaharlal Nehru, *The Discovery of India*, ed. Robert Crane (New York: Anchor Books, 1960), p. 21.

2. Quoted in Pupul Jayakar, *Indira Gandhi: An Intimate Portrait* (New York: Pantheon, 1993), p. vii.

3. M.K. Gandhi, *Hind Swaraj, or Home Rule* (Ahmedabad: Navajivan, 1946), pp. 43–44.

attempting to make sense of an India that seemed to them elusive, perhaps even illusory. Some of the categories of particular relevance in reading about India are familiar ones: nation and its attendant ideas, nationality and nationalism; religion as a belief and behavioral system separable from other aspects of society; territorial sovereignty; social classes delineated in economic terms; and the possibility of social change through legislation. The inevitable use of such categories in books on India makes for a complexity that people living in premodern times would almost certainly not have seen as such.

One interpretation common among 19th-century British writers was that the term "India" did not correspond to any political reality. Such statements were made in explicit denial of the Indian nationalism just beginning to find expression in the Indian National Congress. India, this argument ran, had come into existence through the process of the British unification of the subcontinent under a single political authority for the first time in history, and it would resolve into its component quarrelsome fragments if British rule disappeared.

But this reading of Indian history and civilization should be balanced by another with a scarcely less privileged place in writing about India. This alternative reading exalts its enduring unity, both spiritual and political. Nineteenth-century German scholars emphasized spirituality as the defining characteristic of India through the ages. It was the great Indologist Max Muller's explicit message in his *India, What Can It Teach Us?*, and it infuses his editing of that great monument of 19th-century scholarship, *The Sacred Books of the East.* Scholars often coupled praise of Indian culture with a critical comparison with the West. Declared the philosopher Schopenhauer, "The fanatic crimes perpetrated in the name of religion are in reality attributable only to the adherents of monotheistic religions, that is to say, to Judaism and its two branches, Christianity and Islam. There is no question of anything resembling it among the Hindus and Buddhists."[4]

The view of India as an enduring political unity through the ages, which became a staple of Indian nationalist thought, drew heavily upon this German concept of the spirituality of Indian civilization. One of the most influential exponents of this idea was Radha Kumud

4. Quoted in Raymond Schwab, *The Oriental Renaissance: Europe's Discovery of India and the East, 1680–1880* (New York: Columbia University Press, 1984), p. 429.

Mookerji, a prolific author on many aspects of Indian history and civilization, whose books were widely used in colleges and universities. The title of his *Fundamental Unity of India* indicates his abiding concern to show that India indeed had existed, both as a nation and as a state, from the most ancient times.[5] For a nationalism seeking to define and legitimize itself, such articulations of the meaning of India were necessary correctives to imperialist interpretations.

This emphasis on the Indian nation's temporal and spatial continuity gained new importance in the 1980s, when what can best be identified as "Hindu nationalism" received widespread support, especially in northern India. Perhaps the most appealing aspect of the ideology of Hindu nationalism is its insistence that India is the land of the Hindus, whose culture is rooted in territory, as, its exponents argue, all true nations must be. This idea found its most potent expression in a pamphlet called *Hindutva: Who Is a Hindu?* written in 1922 by a famous radical nationalist, V.D. Savarkar; while in style and presentation this tract differs sharply from the scholarly work of Mookerji, Savarkar's view indicates an attitude toward India's past that anyone who seeks to understand modern India must take seriously.[6] As India became sovereign on August 15, 1947, Prime Minister Nehru summed up these memories of the past and asserted the unity of India through the ages by saying, "At the dawn of history India started on her unending quest, and trackless centuries are filled with her striving and the grandeur of her success and her failures."[7]

Aspects of those successes and failures are recounted in the books selected here from the vast literature about Indian civilization. I have divided them into categories that seem to reflect outsiders' interests, with the order given here following rather roughly the quantity of works produced. Ten categories, rather arbitrarily chosen, and with much overlapping and many exclusions, are as follows: accounts by travelers and journalists; general works on Indian religions; analyses of social structure; surveys of social and political history; art and architecture; classical literary genres; modern novels and short stories; biog-

---

5. Radha Kumud Mookerji, *The Fundamental Unity of India*, 2d ed. (Bombay: Bharatiya Vidya Bhavan, 1960).

6. V.D. Savarkar, *Hindutva: Who Is a Hindu?* (Bombay: Veer Savarkar Prakashan, 1969).

7. Jawaharlal Nehru, *Independence and After (1946–1949)* (Delhi: Publications Division, Government of India, 1949), pp. 3–4.

raphy and autobiography; a catchall subcategory, "India since independence"; and references and guides for travelers.

Purely academic books, that is, monographs written for a specialized audience and not really intended for readers outside that specialty, have been excluded. Omission here and elsewhere does not imply an unfavorable judgment. Those books selected have met the general criteria of accuracy, readability, and comprehensiveness. In a few cases, however, thoroughly unreliable works are included because their readability brought them undeserved attention. Books in the enumerated categories have been written in many Indian languages and in almost all other modern languages, but here only works written in or translated into English will be noted. I will begin, rather foolhardily, with a short list of what are probably the most useful books if one is beginning to read about India.

A Short List of "Most Useful Books"

While it is quite impossible to name one "best book" about India, one can suggest a half dozen or so general books covering broad topics that present a reasonable outline of what Nehru called India's "striving and the grandeur of her success and her failures." Perhaps the most useful of general books on Indian civilization is A.L. Basham's *The Wonder That Was India*, which is encyclopedic in scope, authoritative in scholarship, well written, and well organized. Basham's attitude toward Indian civilization, based on a good knowledge of other great civilizations of the ancient world, is summed up in his claim that India's people, "each finding a niche in a complex and slowly evolving social system, reached a higher level of kindliness and gentleness in their mutual relationships than any other nation of antiquity." *Sources of Indian Tradition*, a collection of annotated original materials by Indian thinkers and writers, provides an accessible guide to Indian intellectual and religious history. *The Art and Architecture of the Indian Subcontinent* by J.C. Harle is a comprehensive, reliable survey.

Few general histories of India have won wide critical acceptance from scholars, with the possible exception of *A History of India* by Romila Thapar and Percival Spear. There are dozens of useful books on Indian politics, but the serious reader will find *The Politics of India Since Independence* by Paul R. Brass a comprehensive guide to the dynamics of modern Indian life. And of the many illustrated books that take advantage of India as a uniquely photogenic land, it is hard to surpass Doranne Jacobson's *India: Land of Dreams and Fantasy*; it has a readable, scholarly text that places the photographs in their historical and cultural context.

Travelers and Journalists

Travel to India is a way of asking questions about one's culture and about oneself, for even the most casual travelers are forced, in one way or another, to assess their own values and the presuppositions of their society. Travelers to India may emphasize the bizarre and exotic simply to attract readers, but they are always saying something about their own culture as well. Milton Singer, the American anthropologist, in *When a Great Tradition Modernizes,* has suggested that when a writer reports on other cultures, a conversation is going on between two images: that of the author's society and that of the other.[8] Wilhelm Halbfass's *India and Europe: An Essay in Understanding* provides scholarly background for an exploration of this theme.

The many books by travelers and reporters can be roughly divided into three groups: books on their travels within India by people who lived and worked there; books by sightseers; and books by professional journalists. While these categories overlap, it is useful for understanding their books to place the authors in one of them.

The first Westerners to write accounts of their Asian travels were the Greeks, and like their successors for nearly 2,000 years they journeyed to India mainly for career reasons; as far as we know, few if any went because of an interest in Indian culture as such. While only fragments of the accounts of the earliest travelers have survived, for hundreds of years their stories of the wonders they had seen or heard about colored Western perceptions of India. Implicit always, and at times quite explicit, is the question that infuses so much of the reporting on India: Why are Indians so different from us? In the 19th and 20th centuries the question becomes, Why are we so much more much advanced than they are? Many travelers' reports can be found in R.C. Majumdar, *The Classical Accounts of India*, but the best introduction to the cultural impact of India on Europe is given in Donald F. Lach's *Asia in the Making of*

8. Milton Singer, *When a Great Tradition Modernizes* (Chicago: Midway, 1980), p. 12.

Europe. William Foster's *Early Travels in India* gives a good selection of European travel accounts.

Europeans were not the only travelers to leave early accounts of their visits to India. Chinese pilgrims in search of Buddhist texts made arduous journeys to India. Samuel Beal, who translated many of their accounts, claimed, "Never did more devoted pilgrims leave their native country to encounter the perils of travel in foreign and distant lands."[9] One of them, Fa-Hsien, has left a memorable account of his six-year stay in India at the beginning of the 5th century A.D., which pictures India as a prosperous land ruled by benevolent kings.

But the most remarkable account of India by any traveler comes from al-Biruni, who at the beginning of the 11th century arrived from Central Asia as a scholar-prisoner in the conquering armies of the great warrior Mahmud of Ghazni. He stressed the importance of firsthand observations, yet he knew that eyewitnesses were fallible guides unless they knew the languages of the people and the great literature of the past, a point travelers often missed. He also said that writers might give false accounts for a number reasons, and it is easy to fit much later reporting into his categories. Some people lie about other nations and praise their own expecting to gain from this at home. Others lie because the rulers of the visited country pay them to give a good report. Yet others misrepresent a country because something disagreeable happened to them there or because they are of a mean, depraved character. And most common of all, according to al-Biruni, are writers who blindly follow what others have reported.[10]

A few Europeans traveled to India in the Middle Ages, and some have left accounts, but none had much intellectual curiosity about the civilization; one suspects that life in Indian cities did not seem much different from their own. Then as trade increased, more Europeans wrote accounts of what they had experienced. François Bernier's sharp observations on the social and political life of India from 1658 to 1668, the height of the Mughal empire, make the Frenchman's account perhaps the most readable. Bernier's work, as he himself said, is "not absolutely correct, but merely less incorrect than others

9. Samuel Beal, trans., *Si-Yu-Ki: Buddhist Records of the Western World* (Delhi: Oriental Books, 1969), Vol. 1, p. ix.

10. Al-Biruni, *Alberuni's India*, trans. E.C. Sachau (Delhi: S. Chand, 1964), pp. 6–18. Sachau's translation is abridged in Ainslie T. Embree, *Alberuni's India* (New York: Norton, 1971).

I have seen."[11] He emphasized that the Mughal king owned all the land. Bernier attributed to this royal ownership the poverty of so many people and the stagnation of the economy, since the people had little incentive to accumulate capital and when they did, they hid it from the greedy eyes of rulers. "It is owing to this miserable system of government," he declared, "that most towns of Hindoustan are made up of earth, mud, and other wretched materials."[12] This reading of India as a land stricken by poverty and crushed by tyrannical rulers became common in the 19th century among Western writers.

Travelers in the late 18th and 19th centuries began to give more attention to Indian religion and the so-called manners and morals of the Hindus. Some writers lived in India as administrators or missionaries, but there was also a great increase in tourists. And, beginning with the uprisings of 1857–58, when the last important attempt to expel the British by military force was made, reporters from the *Times* of London and a few other papers made an appearance.

Out of the vast travel literature produced in the 19th century, much is harshly critical, although the very criticism made India interesting. There was a heavy emphasis on such practices as *sati,* child marriage, female infanticide, and *purdah. Nautch* girls (women dancers) receive frequent mention, as do so-called temple prostitutes, women dedicated to temple deities. It is astonishing when one lists these criticisms how many of them center on the allegedly degrading treatment of women, so much so that one is tempted to see in them prurient pornography. This literature was meant for foreign audiences, not for Indians, illustrating Singer's point that writing about another culture is in actuality a conversation between two cultures in which needs and fears are projected from one to the other.

One sometimes gets the impression that every British official who served in India wrote a book explaining his work for people at home. Two books of this genre from the first half of the 19th century are of enduring worth, both for what they say about India and as contributions to intercultural conversation. The first is a travel account by Bishop Heber, spiritual overseer of members of the Church of England living in India. His shrewd insights into Indian life and his sense of the

11. François Bernier, *Travels in the Mogul Empire,* A.D. 1656–1668 (Westminster: Archibald Constable, 1891), p. xv.

12. Ibid., p. 227.

unnaturalness of British rule combined with an unshakable self-assurance about his own odd role produce one of the more interesting documents of the Western encounter with India. The second, William Sleeman's account of his work and travels in India, *Rambles and Recollections of an Indian Official*, is unmatched for the picture it gives of how British "law and order" was imposed on a vast tract of northern India. Sleeman was famous for his suppression of the widespread banditry practiced by the roving bands known as "thags," an action that was continually cited as proof of the benefits of British rule.

In a new kind of travel literature that appeared in the early 19th century and is produced to the present day, the travelers themselves are center stage. Only the merest sampling of it can be given here, with an attempt to choose what is most representative and at the same time interesting and informative. This literature was almost wholly intended for Western readers. The Indian side offers virtually no response until very modern times.

Books by women travelers in the 19th century and the first half of the 20th are so numerous and so interesting that they deserve to be placed in a subcategory of travel literature. In regard to popular perceptions of India, a character in a period novel wonders "how much of the poisoning of the world's thinking comes from the idleness and ease of sheltered [Western] women, especially young women."[13] Many were wives or relatives of British officials, who found in writing about India an outlet for their energy and intelligence, giving them a role that might have been denied them in the West. A useful and entertaining analysis of this point is found in Pat Barr's *The Memsahibs: The Women of Victorian India.*

Two women from different social backgrounds wrote books in the early 19th century that are still interesting and informative on the conversation between cultures. Emily Eden, the sister of Lord Auckland, who was governor-general from 1838 to 1841, in *Up the Country* left a lighthearted and very readable account of Indian life as seen from her peculiar vantage. Like many aristocrats, she did not look down on other races; she much admired tall, handsome Indian soldiers. Fanny Parks was one of those intrepid women travelers the English produced in such profusion in the 19th century. Her husband was a minor official,

13. Edward Thompson, *An Indian Day,* quoted in David Rubin, *After the Raj* (Hanover, N.H.: University Press of New England, 1986), p. 286.

but she spent much of her time in India from 1822 to 1846 traveling, and the title of her book sums up her self-perception: *Wanderings of a Pilgrim in Search of the Picturesque.*

Two other women, Flora Annie Steel and Maud Diver, writing in the early 20th century, deserve special mention. Steel is especially interesting because she defends Indians against the slurs on their characters that were made almost automatically by many travelers, but like many women writers she criticized the treatment of women by Indian men. In her best-known book, *India*, this comes out in a rather odd context when she is describing the Taj Mahal. "Surely of all the blindingly contradictory things in the wide world," she exclaims, "is that in this land of . . . downtrodden womanhood, loveless marriages, polygamy, bestial couplings, this monument . . . should stand a record of a love given to a woman when her 13th child was born."[14]

Diver's well-written, popular books combine shrewd observations with facile generalizations about Indian character and history of the kind Steel deplored. Her books treat India in what can best be described as a proprietary manner, a sense that India is ours to nourish and protect. They are quite unself-conscious examples of popularized orientalism and worth reading for an insight into this important aspect of modern Western culture.

One of the most widely read books on India, *Mother India*, by an American, Katherine Mayo, has a special place in travel literature written by women. Published in 1927, it follows the well-trodden path of cataloguing alleged deficiencies and injustices in Indian society, attributing them to the malign influence of Hinduism; but the heart of the book, reflecting its title, is a denunciation of what Mayo believed were the monstrous wrongs visited on Indian women by men. Coupled with this was unstinting praise of British rule in India as the only hope for oppressed Indian women. The book evoked a hostile reaction from large sections of the Indian public, reflecting the self-consciousness and pride associated with the growth of Indian nationalism. The critics included Mahatma Gandhi, who called it a "drain inspector's report," but added with characteristic insight that while no Westerner should read it because it gave such a distorted picture of Indian life, every Indian should read it because the distortions represented realities of which they should be ashamed.

14. Flora Annie Steel, *India* (New York: Apt Books, 1983), p. 144.

Another book by a short-term traveler that had wide popularity, partly because its author was well known and partly because its tone, like Mayo's, reflected the long-standing Western evaluation of Indian culture, was Beverley Nichols's *Verdict on India*, which appeared in 1944. Unpleasant and nasty as the book is, it is important reading for anyone who wants to understand attitudes toward Indian culture on the eve of independence. Nichols's evaluation of Indian religion is summed up in his comment, "Of the many fine, truthful, unselfish Indians I met, hardly one was a sincere Hindu." Such attitudes have been carefully examined in *Scratches on Our Minds: American Views of China and India*, by the American scholar-journalist Harold Isaacs, but firsthand exposure to writers like Mayo and Nichols is useful.

An astonishing number of people from the second group of travelers, the genuine tourists, wrote accounts of what they had seen, or thought they had seen, after a short stay in India. Not surprisingly, few are of more than passing interest, but the modern reader can turn with delight to the sections on India in Mark Twain's *Following the Equator*. I find his book so insightful and thought-provoking that I will give it more than a fair share of comment. While Twain is self-consciously humorous, often with a mordant wit, he observes the contradictions and ambiguities of Indian life with surprising compassion. India was, he said, the land of dreams and romance, of fabulous wealth and fabulous poverty, of a hundred nations and a hundred tongues, of a thousand religions and two million gods, mother of history and grandmother of tradition, "the land that all men desire to see, and having seen once, by even a glimpse, would not give up that glimpse for all the shows of all the rest of the world combined."[15] But perhaps his reactions to India are best expressed in his comments on the Taj Mahal, the high point for all travelers in the 19th century, as for many in the present.

Other people's reaction to the Taj—and indeed to India in general—were in Twain's mind when he arrived in Agra. His question has occurred to many of us: Can one ever see the Taj—or India—through one's own eyes and not through someone else's? "When a thing is a wonder," Twain wrote, "it is a wonder not because of what we see in it, but because of what others have seen in it. We get almost all our wonders at secondhand. . . . These are not your enthusiasms and

15. Mark Twain, *Following the Equator* (New York: Dover, 1989), pp. 347–48.

emotions, they are the accumulated emotions and enthusiasms of a thousand fervid writers."[16] Then, he says, "you sober down, and you perceive that you have been drunk on the smell of somebody else's cork. . . . My Taj had been built by excitable literary people; it was solidly lodged in my head, and I could not blast it out."[17] Inescapably, we see much of India through images built by "excitable literary people." Images of Calcutta, for example, are at the opposite end of the scale from the Taj, but they derive from the process Twain describes.

Professional journalists comprise the third group of travelers, quite distinct from tourists or from those who lived and worked in India. Their motivations for going to India may not differ much from those others', but the purpose of their writing is generally not to put themselves on center stage, but rather to inform their home audience of what is happening in India, to interpret the meaning of events, to forecast future developments, and, almost always, to try to persuade their readers to accept their reading of India.

The first reporter in the modern sense was William Russell, who was sent out by the *Times* of London to report on the uprisings in 1857–58. His reporting, as edited in *My Indian Mutiny Diary,* is remarkably frank in commenting on the weaknesses of the British command as well as the excesses of the British troops and the racism rampant among them.

A special feature of reporting from India is the favored position enjoyed by Reuters. Its reporters were virtually press agents for the government of India; in return for access to news sources denied other journalists, they presented the government's point of view and often the information that it wanted disseminated in England and abroad. The most influential of its reporters was Sir Valentine Chirol, whose knighthood was a reward for his hard-hitting attack on the Indian nationalists at the turn of the century in his famous book *Indian Unrest.* It is still required reading for anyone who wishes to delve deeply into Indian political history at the beginning of the 20th century.

In contrast to the anti–Indian National Congress reporting of most of the British press, American reporters often sympathized with nationalist

16. Ibid., p. 507.
17. Ibid., pp. 508, 570.

aspirations, finding Gandhi an especially attractive figure. Louis Fischer's *Gandhi: His Life and Message for the World*, a warmly appreciative portrait, was the main introduction for a generation of Americans to the final struggle for Indian independence.

That V.S. Naipaul is the most widely read of all modern journalists-travelers is partly because he is a great literary stylist with an international reputation, but also because his books pick up and refine almost all of the contradictions and nuances of Western writers on India for the past 200 years, telling his readers in elegant prose what they already knew or suspected about Indian reality. Naipaul's *India, a Wounded Civilization*, however wrongheaded at times in the central thesis his title indicates, is in the mainstream of reporting on India.

After noting how often foreign travelers and reporters have harshly criticized India and its culture, it is a relief to conclude with an unpretentious, delightful account of one traveler's enjoyment of the Indian cultural mosaic, James Cameron's *An Indian Summer*. It is a good antidote to some other accounts, for unlike many travelers, Cameron is not interested in pointing out the weaknesses of Indian society or in changing it, but only in enjoying it and in reveling in its richness and variety. That his reactions to India are reminiscent of Twain's in *Following the Equator* indicates that India continues to cast a spell on travelers who give themselves to her.

General Works on Indian Religions

If one word is popularly associated with Indian civilization, both inside and outside India, it is "religion." The easy assumption that religion plays a peculiarly important role is, in many respects, a dubious reading of Indian culture, based largely on a failure to differentiate among belief systems, ritual observances, and cultural practices.

This belief that religion occupied a dominant place in India was widely accepted by both Indians and foreigners and was important for Indians' self-perception as well as for the way others perceived them. Swami Vivekananda, one of the most famous religious figures of modern India, speaking in Colombo in 1887, had this comment:

> If there is any land on earth that can lay claim to be the blessed *Puniya Bhumi*, to be the land to which . . . every soul that is wending its way

> Godward must come, the land where humanity has attained its highest towards gentleness, towards generosity, towards purity, towards calmness, above all the land of introspection and of spirituality—it is India.[18]

The widely respected philosopher Dr. Sarvepalli Radhakrishnan expressed the same sense, if less grandiosely, of the place of religion in India in *The Hindu View of Life.* It is essentially a restatement, using Western religious and philosophical categories, of an understanding of Hinduism that would be widely shared by Indian intellectuals.

While the view of the peculiar place of religion in Indian civilization should not be adopted without considerable reservations, for a long time it received almost universal acceptance through the work of 19th-century scholars, largely in Germany. They emphasized the study of the great religious and philosophical texts of the "high" or Sanskritic tradition, as noted in Halbfass's book cited above. Their work was immensely influential, not only in the West, but in India itself. At the same time, administrators and missionaries studied the "popular" expressions of religion. The result was an enormous amount of scholarly writing on Indian religions. The term "Indian religions" refers here to systems that originated in the Indian subcontinent, including not only Hinduism but also Buddhism, Jainism, and Sikhism. Expressions of imported religions also flourished, most notably Islam, but also Zoroastrianism, Christianity, and Judaism. Of these, only Islam will be noted here; references to the others can be found in the encyclopedias mentioned below.

The size of this corpus of writing and the varieties of religious experience that it describes make it difficult to select books that satisfy the criteria of accuracy, readability, and comprehensiveness. Little attempt will be made to distinguish between religious and philosophical works, for the distinction has little meaning except for specialists. Some of the more useful works that interpret the various forms of Indian religious experience will be listed, but I emphasize translations of texts that are highly regarded within Indian religious traditions and have earned the praise of foreign scholars for their literary and cultural importance.

One of the best brief introductions to Indian religion is found in

18. Swami Vivekananda, quoted in Ainslie T. Embree, *Utopias in Conflict: Essays on Indian History* (Berkeley: University of California Press, 1990), p. 159.

chapter 7 of Basham's *The Wonder That Was India*, listed above under the most useful books. Basham understands Indian religion as those varieties of religious experience that originated on the subcontinent and of which literary records remain. Encyclopedias are a readily accessible source of brief articles on Indian religion, but their reliability depends wholly upon the scholarly competence of the authors. Authoritative summaries of the Hindu tradition, however, written by such eminent scholars as J.A.B. Van Buitenen, Edward C. Dimock, and A.L. Basham, are found in the *Britannica* under such headings as "Hinduism," "history of Hindu mythology," "Hindu mysticism," and "Hindu sacred literature," while Arjun Appadurai's article on Hinduism in the *Encyclopedia of Asian History* is perhaps the best short summary available. The *Encyclopedia of Religion* has excellent articles on most aspects of Indian religions.

William Norman Brown's *Man in the Universe: Some Cultural Continuities in Indian Thought* succeeds better than most of the many attempts to demonstrate the relevance of Hinduism to Indian society through the ages. T.N. Madan in *Non-Renunciation: Themes and Interpretations of Hindu Culture* probes some of the same concepts, especially the complex issue of the role of asceticism. His edited volume *Religion in India* has studies on a number of aspects of the different religious traditions. Perhaps because of the sheer complexity of the subject, books on religion in modern India tend to concentrate on sectarian or reform movements, such as Kenneth Jones's *Socio-Religious Movements in British India*.

The many books by Wendy Doniger (under "Wendy Doniger O'Flaherty" in many listings) are in a class by themselves, as she is one of the few scholars of the classical Indian tradition to succeed in reaching an audience beyond specialists. She has explored with learning and wit such themes in the religious literature as the origins of evil, the nature of sexuality, the place of women in society, and the meanings of the great myths of the tradition. What Western tradition has termed "mythology," but is perhaps more accurately described as "sacred history"—the interactions of divine beings—is immense, and no single book can do it justice. But *Classical Hindu Mythology* by Cornelia Dimmitt and J.A.B. Van Buitenen covers a great deal. Doniger's and Heinrich Zimmer's books provide readable accounts, although Zimmer's interpretations have been criticized as being too imaginative and not securely enough based in a historical context. Diana Eck's

Darshan: Seeing the Divine Image in India examines the importance of images in Indian worship.

Islam as a form of religious expression in the subcontinent is not easy to disentangle from the history and politics of rulers who professed Islam, but Peter Hardy's article in *The Encyclopedia of Religion*, "Islam in South Asia," provides an authoritative and remarkably comprehensive survey. Annemarie Schimmel's *Islam in the Indian Subcontinent* examines a wide variety of religious beliefs and practices. Mohammad Mujeeb shows how Islamic beliefs adjusted to the political and cultural realities of India in *The Indian Muslims*. Richard Eaton's *Sufis of Bijapur, 1300–1700: Social Roles of Sufis in Medieval India* is a useful corrective to common interpretations of the hostility between Islam and Hinduism. Imtiaz Ahmad examines important aspects of Indian Muslim life in *Ritual and Religion Among Muslims in India*.

For Sikhism, two books by W.H. McLeod provide scholarly interpretations of the nature and origin of the faith and its practice: *The Evolution of the Sikh Community* and *Who Is a Sikh? The Problem of Sikh Identity.* While highly regarded by Western and many Indian scholars, McLeod's work has been the subject of bitter criticism by some guardians of the Sikh tradition, largely on the grounds that he unjustifiably applies modern critical methods to the Sikh scriptures.

The best insights for understanding Indian religions surely come from reading some of the immensely rich literature they have produced. *Sources of Indian Tradition*, on the "Most Useful Books" list, contains selected translations with introductory material on the major traditions—Hinduism, Buddhism, Jainism, Sikhism, and Islam. Many translations have been made of the *Bhagavad Gita*, the most famous Hindu religious text, but Barbara Stoler Miller's is at once scholarly and of high literary quality. Much of the great wealth of religious poetry comes from the *bhakti* or devotional tradition, which in its many forms has been the dominant mode of religious expression in India for many centuries. *The Sants: Studies in a Devotional Tradition of India*, edited by Karine Schomer and W.H. McLeod, while meant for scholars, is useful for anyone seeking to explore this important aspect of Indian culture. Excellent translations with scholarly introductions are found in John Stratton Hawley and Mark Juergensmeyer, editors, *Songs of the Saints of India*; A.K. Ramanujan, *Speaking of Shiva*; and Linda Hess and Sukhdev Singh, *The Bijak of Kabir*. P. Lal has made many translations, which he calls "transcreations," indicating that the translator transforms and changes the original; an example is his translation of some of the hymns of the Rig Veda.

Social Structure

From the 18th century on, Western writers almost invariably referred to what they called "the caste system" as closely related to religious beliefs, and indeed few aspects of Indian life have fascinated Westerners more. Most modern scholars, however, are careful to dissociate themselves from this interpretation, and while not denying the symbiotic relationships between social configurations and religious beliefs, point out that in fact "system" is a misleading term for amorphous and contradictory social practices. And yet no one familiar with Indian literature can doubt that Indian social structures and interpersonal relationships differ from those of areas outside the influence of Indian civilization. The issue is the subject of intense—often acrimonious—controversy. I can attempt only to note readings intended to help readers find their way through the complex analyses.

Works by three well-known Indian social scientists are especially rewarding as they give insider insights. M.N. Srinivas's *Caste in Modern India and Other Essays* has influenced the rethinking of the nature of social mobility in India. G.S. Ghurye's *Caste and Race in India*, as the title indicates, explores a much debated subject. T.N. Madan's essay "On the Nature of Caste in India" is a difficult but rewarding study. Surveys by two American social scientists discuss theories of origins, regional variations, and social utility: *Caste: The Emergence of the South Asian Social System* by Morton Klass, and *Caste in Contemporary India: Beyond Organic Solidarity* by Pauline Kolenda. As noted before, articles in reputable encyclopedias should not be overlooked, especially the one on caste in the *International Encyclopedia of the Social Sciences*. There are also excellent brief accounts in Basham's *The Wonder That Was India*, listed above, and Judith Brown's *Modern India: The Origins of an Asian Democracy*.

Generalizations and theories about Indian social structure find their reality in the Indian villages that guard and express social values. To the observer, Indian villages may appear isolated, but in fact villages over large areas are linked with complex familial and kin relationships, trading networks, and religious shrines. Village studies became a staple of anthropological and sociological fieldwork by social scientists from the 1950s on, but people who had worked closely with villagers had always been aware of this remarkable interdependence. One of the earliest and most interesting of village studies, *Behind Mud Walls: 1930–1960,* was done by an American missionary couple, the Wisers; few other books convey so well the day-to-day life of village India. *Village India*, edited by McKim Marriott, stresses the nature of the networks in Indian villages, demonstrating that a "village civilization" exists.

Surveys of Social and Political History

Teachers and writers about India are frequently asked this difficult question: What is a good one-volume survey of Indian history? The question assumes that the book named will meet the three requirements of accuracy, readability, and comprehensiveness. In fact, for a variety of reasons it is almost impossible to imagine a general book on Indian history that could meet them all. The subject is too vast and too complicated; and for many periods there are great gaps in scholarship. The books noted here give a reasonably coherent summary of social and political developments over long periods.

The two histories most widely used in American colleges are the two volumes of *A History of India* by Thapar and Spear, and Stanley Wolpert's *A New History of India.* Wolpert's readable book is a survey of Indian history and culture from the earliest beginnings to the present. The Thapar and Spear volumes were mentioned above under the rubric "Most Useful Books." Thapar's contribution on India up to the 13th century is a lucid and learned survey of a complex period of history. Much less readable than Wolpert but more comprehensive and based on assiduous attention to recent scholarship is *A History of India* by two German authors, Hermann Kulke and Dietmar Rothermund. For many years one of the most widely used texts, even in Indian schools, was *The Oxford History of India* by Vincent Smith, often cited as the chief example of history with a pronounced bias toward British imperialism. So deeply entrenched was this work that instead of abandoning it in the face of new scholarship and the transformation of views brought about by Indian independence, Oxford University Press had it revised, and much of it rewritten, by four distinguished British scholars. It is a dull but useful reference book. For modern India, that is, from the late 18th century to the present, the best survey is Judith Brown's *Modern India:*

The Origins of an Asian Democracy; her reference notes are a convenient guide to the scholarly literature.

The origin of civilization in the subcontinent has been much debated, and perhaps more than in any other country, ancient history has become involved with modern political discourse. Many Indian historians insist, for example, that the stress in older books on an invasion by "Aryan" people providing the basis for Indian civilization was a Western imperialist reading. B. Allchin and F.R. Allchin examine the archaeological and literary evidence for this and other issues in their comprehensive survey *The Rise of Civilization in India and Pakistan.*

Many volumes in *The New Cambridge History of India*, edited by Gordon Johnson, cover relatively short periods and special themes and are accessible to nonspecialists. A curious feature of this series is that it begins, without explanation, with the 16th century. P.J. Marshall's *Bengal: The British Bridgehead: Eastern India 1740–1828* succinctly describes the establishment of British power by the East India Company. John Richards' volume on the Mughal empire is a satisfying analysis of a crucial period in the history of the subcontinent.

Many of the numerous historical accounts of different periods by armchair historians are long on colorful incidents but short on accuracy. Some, however, are very good. Bamber Gascoigne gives a popular account of a period rich in dramatic incident in *The Great Moghuls*, which has excellent illustrations of the art and architecture of the period. Philip Mason (Philip Woodruff in some listings) provides a nostalgic and seductively sympathetic account of British rule in *The Men Who Ruled India.* Echoing Plato's *Republic*, the subtitles of its two volumes, "The Founders" and "The Guardians," remind the reader that many British officials saw themselves as extending the rule of law and order like the Greeks and Romans.

Three other interrelated topics have caught the imagination of popular writers on Indian history and have resulted in books that are both readable and accurate. The role of the army in founding and guarding the Indian empire is well told in *Armies of the Raj: From the Great Indian Mutiny to Independence, 1858–1947* by Byron Farwell. The exploration and acquisition of territories in the northwest, the rivalry with Russia, and the wars with the Afghans are satisfactorily summarized in Peter Hopkirk's *The Great Game: On Secret Service in High Asia.* And that centerpiece of 19th-century history, the great uprisings against British rule in parts of northern India in 1857–58, is recounted with zest and reasonable accuracy in Christopher Hibbert, *The Great Mutiny: India, 1857.*

Art and Architecture

Indian art and architecture have received little attention in comparison with the arts of China and Japan, and their importance has too often been underestimated. Partha Mitter describes the evaluation of the Indian plastic arts in a brilliant and very readable book with the evocative title, *Much Maligned Monsters: History of European Reactions to Indian Art.* A number of one-volume surveys of artistic and architectural achievements are available, but probably the most successful is J.C. Harle's *The Art and Architecture of the Indian Subcontinent.* It has an excellent bibliography. Benjamin Rowland's *The Art and Architecture of India* is much less detailed than Harle, but for this reason is somewhat more readable. *The Arts of India*, edited by Basil Gray, has interesting essays.

An older book, *Painting of India* by Douglas Barrett and Basil Gray, is still useful. Philip Rawson's *Erotic Art of India* is a good guide to a well-worn subject. Catalogues of museum collections and of special exhibitions are, however, the best and most authoritative guides. These include such beautifully illustrated volumes, with scholarly texts, as Stuart Cary Welch's *A Flower from Every Meadow: Indian Paintings from American Collections* and *India: Art and Culture, 1300–1900*, and Vishakha Desai's *Life at Court: Art for India's Rulers 16th–19th Centuries.* Vidya Dehejia's *Impossible Picturesqueness*, from an exhibit of Edward Lear's drawings, links 20th-century readers with 19th-century travelers.

Anyone visiting the most visible examples of Indian architecture should look at four books on architecture. Catherine Asher's *Architecture of Mughal India* easily fulfills our criteria of accuracy, readability, and comprehensiveness, as does Robert Grant Irving's *Indian Summer: Lutyens, Baker and Imperial Delhi. Fatehpur-Sikri: A Sourcebook*, edited by Michael Brand and Glenn D. Lowry, and *The Taj Mahal: The Illumined Tomb* by Wayne Begley and Z.A. Desai go beyond the romantic myths of the guide books.

Several good books on important, if often overlooked, aspects of India's artistic heritage deserve mention. Two, with self-explanatory titles, cover art forms that can truly be described as "ancient, indigenous, and creative": *Treasures of Indian Textiles*, from the famed Calico museum at Ahmedabad, and *Indian Folk Art* by Heinz Mode and Subash Chandra. In *Indian Film*, Erik Barnouw and S. Krishnaswamy relate the development of an extraordinary industry that has become an integral part of the life of modern India. *The Last Empire: Photography in British India*, edited by Clark Worswick for an exhibition at The Asia Society, brought to light a little-known chapter in the encounter of India with the West.

Music and dance, art forms that claim ubiquity in Indian culture, must be given short shrift in this essay on books, and the only defense is that these arts, above all others, must be experienced through performances. Furthermore, just as there is no such entity as "Indian cooking," but rather many regional and class variations, so with music and dance. For this reason, many elementary introductions to Indian music and dance seem peculiarly unsatisfactory, while specialized studies require considerable knowledge. A few can be recommended, however, in which specialists make an effort to communicate in simple language something of the creativity and variety of the forms of dance and music in India. Nazir Jairazbhoy has a good article entitled "Music" in *A Cultural History of India,* edited by A.L. Basham, and an older book, *The Music of India* by H.A. Popley, has been found helpful by many people. This novice found the useful article "Indian Music," in *The New Oxford Companion to Music,* intelligible. Recordings are, of course, the best introduction. For dance, two works by Kapila Vatsyayan are readable and informative: *Classical Indian Dance in Literature and the Arts* and *Indian Classical Dance.*

Music and dance are closely related to religion in India, and brief, authoritative articles on this important aspect of Indian culture can be found by consulting the index of *The Encyclopedia of Religion.* It should be noted that while music and dance are not as integral to Islamic religious practice in India as they are to Hinduism, both religions developed distinctive dance forms in the secular atmosphere of Islamic courts.

Classical Literary Genres

Works from the Indian religious tradition have been noted above, although the modern distinction between the sacred and profane is shadowy at best in Indian literature. This is not because the literature is "religious" in the modern sense, but because the world of the deities and the world of terrestrial beings are constantly interacting. This is strikingly so in the *Mahabharata*, the inexhaustible well of dramatic stories and didactic lessons from which Indian civilization has drawn for its art and political thought as well as for religious ideas. The size and complexity of the work are too forbidding to make the whole of it accessible to the nonspecialist. The general reader can make do with an abridged version, including those by William Buck, C.V. Narasimhan, and R.K. Narayan. Like foreigners, most Indian readers use translated summaries, but with the great difference that many of the stories are known to everyone.

The other great epic, the *Ramayana*, ascribed to the sage Valmiki, is the story of Rama and his consort, Sita. In this version Rama is a wondrous hero capable of supernatural marvels. The story spread throughout India and Southeast Asia, becoming the basis of much art and literature. The best English translation has been done by Robert Goldman and other scholars under his leadership. In later versions in Indian languages, most notably in Hindi by the great poet Tulsidas (ca. 1532–1632), Rama is pictured not just as a god, but as the greatest of all gods. In this form the story has played an extraordinary part in Indian life, especially in northern India, becoming a central element in the growth of Hindu nationalism. Besides English translations of Tulsidas's work, his interpretation is known through films, television, folk dramas, and dance performances, as well as through a pervasive tradition of storytelling.

Sanskrit is rich in sophisticated drama and lyrical poetry, and some of it, notably the work of Kalidasa (ca. 5th century A.D.), has been splendidly translated into modern, idiomatic English by talented American scholars, including Barbara Stoler Miller.

In Islamic culture in India, poetry written in both Persian and Urdu attained a high standard, and poetry writing was practiced widely by all the literate classes. Poetry is difficult to translate from any language, but this seems to be especially the case with the great poets of Indian Islamic culture. Nonetheless, a number of anthologies are successful in providing a sense of the richness of this genre. Ahmed Ali's translations of Urdu poetry in *The Golden Tradition* attain a high standard, as do Ralph Russell and Khurshidul Islam in their *Three Mughal Poets: Mir, Mir Hasan, and Sauda*.

Modern Novels and Short Stories

A long jump to the 20th century, passing over much great literature in many Indian languages, brings us to the modern novel, the literary form most accessible to foreign readers, and, arguably, the one that in the hands of a skilled novelist can give the sharpest sense of Indian reality. Novels fall into three distinct classes: novels by Indians written in English; novels in English translation; and novels about India by Westerners.

Novels in Indian languages made their first appearance in 19th-century Bengal, and while their authors were clearly influenced by their European contemporaries, they drew upon an ancient and continuous tradition of narrative discourse. The most famous such author was Bankim Chandra Chatterji (1838–94), whose influential novel *Anandamath*, a story of Hindu heroes and Muslim invaders, is seen by some as an anti-British allegory but by others, probably more correctly, as an early statement of fiery Hindu nationalism. Premchand (1880–1936), who wrote in Hindi and Urdu, provided a powerfully realistic picture of rural life in his most famous novel, *Godan*, and in his short stories. U.R. Anantha Murthy's *Samskara*, written in Kannada, has reached a wide audience in English translation as well as in a film version.

Hundreds of Indians have written novels in English. The first to achieve a major success in the West was R.K. Narayan with his many deceptively simple novels about a town called Malgudi, and it is hard to think of a better introduction to the inner life of modern India. Although he migrated to Pakistan, Ahmed Ali deserves a place in any list of Indian writers for his marvelous evocation of Islamic culture in Delhi on the eve of independence, *Twilight in Delhi*.

Recent Indian novelists, whose themes and characters are distinctively Indian, nevertheless clearly locate themselves in the mainstream of modern British and American writing—for example, Upamanyu Chatterjee, Anita Desai, Amitav Ghosh, Kamala Markandaya, Salman Rushdie, Nayantara Saghal, and Vikram Seth. The anguish and anxiety of alienation are common themes in the work of most of these writers.

English novels about India by foreigners, mainly British and American, run into the many hundreds, and it is not easy to make a representative selection, especially as the two most famous of the group, Rudyard Kipling and E.M. Forster, wrote essentially about the British in India, although in *Kim* Kipling conveys much of the color and drama of India that fascinated him as a young man. Intercultural encounters personified in Western and Indian characters tend to dominate Western fictional treatments of India. Of the Western novels set in India since 1947, the most famous are the four included by Paul Scott in *The Raj Quartet,* televised as *The Jewel in the Crown.* Many people, however, consider Scott's short novel *Staying On* a greater achievement. John Masters covers some similar terrain, but in *Bhowani Junction* he explores with great insight the life of the Anglo-Indian, or Eurasian, community, a group little noticed in fiction. Although Ruth Jhabvala is often classified as an Indian writer as she lived in India for many years, the sensibility of her beautifully crafted novels places her more easily with Western spectators who sympathize with India. Often her Westerners turn to India looking for alternatives to the West but find instead that India contains the West's worst features. Such was not the experience of American novelist David Rubin, who treats the interplay of foreigners with Indian culture with great sensitivity, especially in *The Greater Darkness.*

Biography and Autobiography

When a friend of Mahatma Gandhi heard that he was writing his autobiography, he voiced surprise that Gandhi had taken up such a Western form of expression, which had no real precedent in Indian literature. There was in fact remarkably little confessional, self-revelatory writing before Gandhi's book. While dozens of political figures have written autobiographies in recent years, they are generally reticent, compared to Western writers, in examining their motivations and their private lives.

As its subtitle, *My Experiments with Truth*, indicates, Gandhi's autobiography was intended partly as a didactic exercise to show his followers how he had ordered his own life. It remains one of the most readable books on India, providing an understanding of the complexity of Gandhi's life. Nehru's *Towards Freedom* is partly autobiographical but it focuses on explicating the nationalist movement, not Nehru's psyche. These books provide a unique insight into the lives of two remarkable men. A different kind of autobiography is Nirad Chaudhuri's *Autobiography of an Unknown Indian*, one of the most interesting literary productions of modern India, which in an idiosyncratic but arresting way probes the encounter of India with the West.

Most of India's political leaders have attracted biographers, but many of their productions are of a pedestrian quality. The exceptions to this are some of the many works on Mahatma Gandhi, Jawaharlal Nehru, and Indira Gandhi, although most lack the psychoanalytic approach and the probing analysis of personal life that Western readers have come to expect. For Gandhi, perhaps the best single volume is Judith Brown's sympathetic study, *Gandhi: Prisoner of Hope*. Nehru's career receives detailed, though readable, analysis in S. Gopal's multivolume study. B.R. Nanda has written carefully researched biographies of both Nehru and Gandhi. A.J. Akbar's readable one-volume study of Nehru has been faulted by some Indian critics as lacking in critical analysis of Nehru's policies, but the general reader will find it a useful summary of a complex career. Indira Gandhi has attracted both sycophantic biographers and virulent critics, but two books, while generally sympathetic, provide material for making one's own judgment of this puzzling and controversial figure. One is by her close friend Pupul Jayakar, and the other by a journalist, Inder Malhotra. The books listed in the section below on contemporary India also make frequent reference to the work of these and other leaders.

India Since Independence

Almost all the books noted in the various sections above are relevant to an understanding of contemporary India, that is, India since independence in 1947; while the transfer of political power from British to Indian leaders was obviously of enormous significance, in no area, not even in political administration, was there any abrupt break with the past. Even the three great goals enshrined in the Indian Constitution—socialism, secularism, and democracy—could be linked with India's heritage, which largely explains the relative political stability India enjoys.

Contemporary India's politics, economy, society, and arts are explored in The Asia Society's *India Briefing* series, in which this is the eighth volume. Another collection of authoritative essays that range widely over contemporary Indian culture and society is the Fall 1989 issue of *Daedalus*, "Another India." Numerous well-edited, thoughtful journals follow current events, of which the most accessible is *India Today*. Other excellent journals of opinion, although not found so easily outside India, are *Frontline*, *Seminar*, and *Economic and Political*

Weekly. Lead articles in the major English daily newspapers, including the *Times of India*, the *Statesman*, the *Hindu*, the *Pioneer*, and *Asian Age*, are of a high standard.

Political and economic issues greatly interested both Indian and foreign scholars, especially from 1947 to the early 1980s. While they produced works of major importance, only a few cover a fairly wide range of time and subject matter and are accessible to the nonspecialist. Paul Brass in *The Politics of India Since Independence* provides an overview of politics, but with considerable attention to political economy and social change. Lloyd and Susanne Rudolph's *In Pursuit of Laksmi: The Political Economy of the Indian State* and Francine Frankel's *India's Political Economy: 1947–1977* are much more detailed on the economy but show the close relationships between political and economic decisions the governments made during the period. Jagdish Bhagwati in *India in Transition: Freeing the Economy* brings the viewpoint of a professional economist to a critical analysis of those decisions.

Rajni Kothari's *Caste in Indian Politics* is an early, and fairly optimistic, report on the effect of caste on the democratic polity to which India is committed. In a more recent work, *State Against Democracy: In Search of Humane Governance*, he is more pessimistic about the management of Indian politics by the elites. Myron Weiner's *The Child and the State in India* deals with child labor, an issue of great concern in contemporary India. The position of women is depicted with great compassion by Anees Jung in *Seven Sisters: Among the Women of South Asia*.

India has been fortunate in having many writers, including journalists and people in public life, who have written perceptively about current issues. Books in this category are by nature ephemeral, and often polemical, but many provide shrewd assessments of contemporary India. The insurrectionist movements in Punjab and Kashmir have naturally received a great deal of attention. Among the more useful books on Punjab are *Punjab: The Fatal Miscalculation*, edited by Patwant Singh and Harji Malik, and *Punjab in Indian Politics*, edited by Amrik Singh. On Kashmir, A.G. Noorani, *The Kashmir Question*; M.J. Akbar, *India: The Siege Within*; and Ajit Bhattacharjea, *Kashmir: The Wounded Valley* provide insights from different points of view. Of the many books on the vexed question of Hindu-Muslim relations, three give useful overviews: Saeed Naqvi, *Reflections of an Indian*

Muslim; Rasheeduddin Khan, *Bewildered India: Identity, Pluralism, Discord*; and the volume edited by S. Gopal, *Ayodhya and the Rise of Communal Politics in India*, on the controversy over the destruction of the Babri mosque in Ayodhya in 1992.

Two foreign correspondents have summarized their impressions of contemporary India in interesting personal accounts. In the early 1990s *New York Times* reporter Barbara Crossette became a controversial figure in India, especially among government officials, for what they regarded as her biased reporting on human rights abuses in Punjab and Kashmir by the Indian army and the police. Her *India: Facing the 21st Century* carried on this emphasis but added to it much criticism of the Indian elites for what she regards as their unresponsiveness to the need for social justice.

Mark Tully was undoubtedly the best known—and many would argue the best—foreign reporter in the years after independence, marking a change in the nature of the media, since he was primarily identified with the BBC's radio and television coverage of the subcontinent. His book with Satish Jacob, *Amritsar: Mrs. Gandhi's Last Battle*, which covers the uprisings in Punjab and Indira Gandhi's assassination, has been widely accepted as the most authoritative statement on the events of the period. Tully's analysis of contemporary politics and society, using a quasi-autobiographical approach, has the intriguing title *No Full Stops in India*.

References and Guides

A book that defies classification but has delighted and fascinated generations of people interested in India is the oddly named *Hobson-Jobson*, written by Henry Yule and A.C. Burnell. A work of immense erudition, with articles on all manner of words related to India, it provides an introduction to many aspects of Indian society. *Hanklyn-Janklin* by Nigel Hankin is a useful attempt to follow the same pattern for contemporary India.

Anyone seeking information on South Asian geography should start with Spate and Learmouth's *India and Pakistan*, which is at once authoritative and readable. The most detailed combination of maps and historical material is *A Historical Atlas of South Asia*, edited by Joseph Schwartzberg. It should be available in libraries, as will be the most complete bibliography of books on India, *South Asian Civilizations: A*

Bibliographic Synthesis, edited by Maureen Patterson.

On a different level are actual travel guides, of which many are available in India, although not abroad. Occupying pride of place is the venerable *Murray's Guide,* which has gone through many editions in the last hundred years. Indispensable to the serious visitor who wants information on the principal monuments and layouts of major towns, it is the closest thing India has to the *Guides Bleus* of Europe. For comfortable places to stay as well as brief, sensible descriptions of sites, the most reliable guide is Louise Nicholson's *India Companion*. *India: A Travel Survival Kit* is fine for the young and adventuresome.

Conclusion

As far as a comprehensive account of India's history and culture is concerned, there is no "best" book. One writer, however, succeeds marvelously, better than any other I know, in permitting us to get to know India. In his most recent book, *The Grandmother's Tale and Selected Stories,* R.K. Narayan brings to readers a sense of intimacy and a depth of understanding with a world that is not our own but in which we feel welcome. This quality led Graham Greene to say that Narayan had "offered him a second home. Without him I could never have known what it is like to be an Indian."[19] All the books mentioned here in some fashion offer us—Indians and Westerners alike—a second home through the life of the mind.

Many years ago I wrote to Narayan about his Malgudi, the fictional town where so many of his novels are set. He wrote back that it was not "his" Malgudi:

> I am only a town-planner of Malgudi, that is all, neither its owner nor its creator. It was always there, flourishing perhaps in Pallava period; left alone during Muslim invasions; and suffering neglect under British rule. Sometime in the third decade of the 20th century, we rehabilitated its citizens and tidied up the city and its environs. The process still goes on. I can't say when it will stop.[20]

All of the writers—travelers, novelists, poets, scholars—who through the centuries have been engaged in reading India have contributed to

19. Graham Greene, jacket comment on *The Financial Expert* (Chicago: University of Chicago Press, 1952).

20. Private letter, July 11, 1961.

that process of planning, building, and rehabilitating. But the process does not concern just India, for understanding India helps us to understand better the larger story into which it fits, the story of humanity.

Suggested Readings

Many of these books have been published in several editions; the editors have chosen editions according to the likelihood of their being readily available in the United States.

A Short List of "Most Useful Books"

Basham, A.L. *The Wonder That Was India*. 2d ed. (Calcutta: Rupa, 1989).

Brass, Paul R. *The Politics of India Since Independence. The New Cambridge History of India.* 2d ed. Part 4, Vol. 1 (Cambridge: Cambridge University Press, 1994).

Embree, Ainslie T., and Stephen Hay, eds. *Sources of Indian Tradition* (New York: Columbia University Press, 1988). 2 vols.

Harle, J.C. *The Art and Architecture of the Indian Subcontinent* (Harmondsworth: Penguin Books, 1987). Reprinted with corrections.

Jacobson, Doranne. *India: Land of Dreams and Fantasy* (New York: Todtri, 1992).

Thapar, Romila, and Percival Spear. *A History of India* (Harmondsworth: Penguin Books, 1966). 2 vols.

Travelers and Journalists

Al-Biruni. *Alberuni's India.* Trans. E.C. Sachau (Delhi: S. Chand, 1964). Sachau's translation is abridged in Ainslie T. Embree, *Alberuni's India* (New York: Norton, 1971).

Barr, Pat. *The Memsahibs: The Women of Victorian India* (Bombay: Allied Publishers, 1976).

Bernier, François. *Travels in the Mogul Empire,* A.D. 1656–1668 (Westminster: Archibald Constable, 1989). Reprint.

Cameron, James. *An Indian Summer* (New York: McGraw-Hill, 1974).

Chirol, Valentine. *Indian Unrest* (London: Macmillan, 1910).

Diver, Maud. *Royal India* (New York: Appleton, 1942).

Eden, Emily. *Up the Country: Letters Written to the Sister from the Upper Provinces of India.* New introduction by Elizabeth Claridge; notes by Edward Thompson (London: Virago Press, 1983).

Fischer, Louis. *Gandhi: His Life and Message for the World* (London: Granada, 1982).

Foster, William. *Early Travels in India* (New Delhi: Munshi Ram, 1985).

Halbfass, Wilhelm. *India and Europe: An Essay in Understanding* (Albany: SUNY Press, 1988).

Heber, Reginald. "Bishop Heber in Northern India." In *Selections from Heber's Journal.* Ed. M.A. Laird (London: Cambridge University Press, 1971).

Herodotus. *History.* Trans. David Grene (Chicago: University of Chicago Press, 1988).

Isaacs, Harold. *Scratches on Our Minds: American Views of China and India* (Armonk, N.Y.: M.E. Sharpe, 1980).

Lach, Donald F., ed. *Asia in the Making of Europe* (Chicago: University of Chicago Press, 1993). Vol. 1, books 1 and 2. Reprint.

Majumdar, R.C. *The Classical Accounts of India* (Calcutta: Mukhopadhyay, 1960).

Mason, Philip (a.k.a. Philip Woodruff). *The Men Who Ruled India* (New York: Norton, 1985). 2 vols.

Mayo, Katherine. *Mother India* (London: Jonathan Cape, 1927).

Naipaul, V.S. *An Area of Darkness* (New York: Random House, 1981).

———. *India: A Wounded Civilization* (New York: Random House, 1977).

Nichols, Beverley. *Verdict on India* (London: Jonathan Cape, 1944).

Parks, Fanny. *Wanderings of a Pilgrim in Search of the Picturesque* (Karachi: Oxford University Press, 1975). Reprint of 1900 ed. 2 vols.

Russell, William. *My Indian Mutiny Dairy* (London: Cassell, 1957).

Si-Yu-Ki: Buddhist Records of the Western World. Trans. Samuel Beal (Delhi: Oriental Books, 1969). 2 vols. in 1.

Sleeman, William. *Rambles and Recollections of an Indian Official* (London: Oxford University Press, 1973). Revised and annotated.

Steel, Flora Annie. *India* (New York: Apt Books, 1983).

Twain, Mark. *Following the Equator* (New York: Dover, 1989).

General Works on Indian Religions

Ahmad, Imtiaz. *Ritual and Religion Among Muslims in India* (Columbia, Mo.: South Asia Books, 1982).

Brown, William Norman. *Man in the Universe: Some Cultural Continuities in Indian Thought* (Berkeley: University of California Press, 1970).

Dimmitt, Cornelia, and J.A.B. Van Buitenen, eds. and trans. *Classical Hindu Mythology* (Philadelphia: Temple University Press, 1978).

Doniger, Wendy. See O'Flaherty.

Eaton, Richard. *Sufis of Bijapur, 1300–1700: Social Roles of Sufis in Medieval India* (Princeton: Princeton University Press, 1978).

Eck, Diana. *Darshan: Seeing the Divine Image in India* (Chambersburg, Pa.: Anima Books, 1985).

Embree, Ainslie T. *Utopias in Conflict: Essays on Indian History* (Berkeley: University of California Press, 1990).

Encyclopedia Britannica. 14th ed. (Chicago: University of Chicago Press, 1981).

Encyclopedia of Asian History (New York: Charles Scribner's Sons, 1988).

Encyclopedia of Religion (New York: Macmillan, 1987).

Hawley, John Stratton, and Mark Juergensmeyer, eds. *Songs of the Saints of India* (New York: Oxford University Press, 1988).

Hess, Linda, and Sukhdev Singh. *The Bijak of Kabir* (Delhi: Motilal Banarsidas, 1986).

Jones, Kenneth. *Socio-Religious Movements in British India. The New Cambridge History of India*. 2d ed. Part 3, Vol. 1 (Cambridge: Cambridge University Press, 1989).

Lal, Purushottama. *The Golden Womb of the Sun: Rig Vedic Songs* (Calcutta: Writers Workshop, 1965).

McLeod, W.H. *The Evolution of the Sikh Community* (New York: Oxford University Press, 1976).

———. *Who Is a Sikh? The Problem of Sikh Identity* (New York: Oxford University Press, 1989).

Madan, T.N. *Non-Renunciation: Themes and Interpretations of Hindu Culture* (New York: Oxford University Press, 1988).

———, ed. *Religion in India* (New York: Oxford University Press, 1992).

Miller, Barbara Stoler. *The Love Song of the Dark Lord* (New York: Columbia University Press, 1977).

———, trans. *Bhagavad Gita* (New York: Bantam, 1986).

Mujeeb, Mohammad. *The Indian Muslims* (London: Allen and Unwin, 1967).

Muller, Max. *The Sacred Books of the East.* Reprint of 1879–1910 ed. (Delhi: Motilal Banarsidas, 1962–66). 50 vols.

O'Flaherty, Wendy Doniger. *The Origins of Evil in Hindu Mythology* (Berkeley: University of California Press, 1977).

———. *Siva, the Erotic Ascetic* (New York: Oxford University Press, 1981).

Radhakrishnan, Sarvepalli. *The Hindu View of Life* (New York: Macmillan, 1927).

Ramanujan, A.K. *Speaking of Shiva* (New York: Penguin, 1973).

Schimmel, Annemarie. *Islam in the Indian Subcontinent* (Leiden: E.J. Brill, 1980).

Schomer, Karine, and W.H. McLeod. *The Sants: Studies in a Devotional Tradition of India* (New Delhi: Motilal Banarsidas, 1987).

Zimmer, Heinrich. *Myths and Symbols in Indian Art and Civilization* (Princeton: Princeton University Press, 1972).

Social Structure

Brown, Judith. *Modern India: The Origins of an Asian Democracy*. 2d ed. (New York: Oxford University Press, 1994).

Ghurye, G.S. *Caste and Race in India* (Bombay: Popular Prakashan, 1986).

International Encyclopedia of the Social Sciences (New York: Macmillan, 1968).

Klass, Morton. *Caste: The Emergence of the South Asian Social System* (Philadelphia: ISHI, 1980).

Kolenda, Pauline. *Caste in Contemporary India: Beyond Organic Solidarity* (Prospect Heights: Waveland Press, 1985).

Madan, T.N. "On the Nature of Caste in India." *Contributions to Indian Sociology*, no. 5, 1971.

Marriott, McKim, ed. *Village India* (Chicago: University of Chicago Press, 1955).

Srinivas, M.N. *Caste in Modern India and Other Essays* (Bombay: Asia Publishing House, 1962).

Wiser, C.M., and W.H. Wiser. *Behind Mud Walls: 1930–1960* (Berkeley: University of California Press, 1989).

Surveys of Social and Political History

Allchin, B., and F.R. Allchin. *The Rise of Civilization in India and Pakistan* (Cambridge: Cambridge University Press, 1982).

Brown, Judith. *Modern India: The Origins of an Asian Democracy.* 2d ed. (New York: Oxford University Press, 1994).

Farwell, Byron. *Armies of the Raj: From the Great Indian Mutiny to Independence, 1858–1947* (New York: Norton, 1991).

Gascoigne, Bamber. *The Great Moghuls* (London: Cape, 1971).

Hibbert, Christopher. *The Great Mutiny: India, 1857* (Harmondsworth: Penguin Books, 1980).

Hopkirk, Peter. *The Great Game: On Secret Service in High Asia* (London: Murray, 1990).

Johnson, Gordon, ed. *The New Cambridge History of India* (Cambridge: Cambridge University Press, 1987—). Published as a series of individual volumes.

Kulke, Hermann, and Dietmar Rothermund. *A History of India* (New York: Routledge, 1990).

Marshall, P.J. *Bengal: The British Bridgehead: Eastern India 1740–1828* (Cambridge: Cambridge University Press, 1987).

Mason, Philip (a.k.a. Philip Woodruff). *The Men Who Ruled India* (London: Jonathan Cape, 1954). 2 vols.

Richards, John. *The Mughal Empire. The New Cambridge History of India.* Part 1, Vol. 5 (Cambridge: Cambridge University Press, 1993).

Smith, Vincent. *The Oxford History of India.* 4th ed. Ed. Percival Spear (Oxford: Clarendon Press, 1981).

Thapar, Romila, and Percival Spear. *A History of India* (Harmondsworth: Penguin Books, 1966). 2 vols.

Wolpert, Stanley. *A New History of India*. 4th ed. (New York: Oxford University Press, 1992).

Art and Architecture

Asher, Catherine B. *Architecture of Mughal India. The New Cambridge History of India.* Part 1, Vol. 4 (Cambridge: Cambridge University Press, 1992).

Barnouw, Erik, and S. Krishnaswamy. *Indian Film*. 2d ed. (New York: Oxford University Press, 1980).

Barrett, Douglas, and Basil Gray. *Painting of India* (Geneva: Skira, 1963).

Begley, Wayne, and Z.A. Desai. *The Taj Mahal: The Illumined Tomb* (Seattle: University of Washington Press, 1990).

Brand, Michael, and Glenn D. Lowry, eds. *Fatehpur-Sikri: A Sourcebook* (Bombay: Marg Publications, 1987).

Dehejia, Vidya. *Impossible Picturesqueness: Edward Lear's Watercolors, 1873–1875* (New York: Columbia University Press, 1989).

Desai, Vishakha. *Life at Court: Art for India's Rulers 16th–19th Centuries* (Boston: Museum of Fine Arts, 1986).

Gray, Basil, ed. *The Arts of India* (Ithaca: Cornell University Press, 1981).

Harle, J.C. *The Art and Architecture of the Indian Subcontinent* (Harmondsworth: Penguin Books, 1987).

Irving, Robert Grant. *Indian Summer: Lutyens, Baker and Imperial Delhi* (New Haven: Yale University Press, 1981).

Jairazbhoy, Nazir. "Music." In *A Cultural History of India*. Ed. A.L. Basham (Oxford: Oxford University Press, 1975).

Mitter, Partha. *Much Maligned Monsters: History of European Reactions to Indian Art* (Oxford: Clarendon Press, 1977).

Mode, Heinz, and Subash Chandra. *Indian Folk Art* (Bombay: Taraporevala, 1985).

The New Oxford Companion to Music (Oxford: Oxford University Press, 1984).

Popley, H.A. *The Music of India* (New Delhi: YMCA Publishing House, 1966).

Rawson, Philip. *Erotic Art of India* (New York: Universe Books, 1977).

Rowland, Benjamin. *The Art and Architecture of India: Buddhist-Hindu-Jain* (New York: Viking Penguin, 1971).

Treasures of Indian Textiles: Calico Museum, Ahmedabad (Bombay: Marg Publications, 1980).

Vatsyayan, Kapila. *Classical Indian Dance in Literature and the Arts* (New Delhi: Sangeet Natak Akademi, 1968).

———. *Indian Classical Dance* (New Delhi: Publications Division, Ministry of Information and Broadcasting, 1974).

Welch, Stuart Cary. *A Flower from Every Meadow: Indian Paintings from American Collections* (New York: The Asia Society, 1973).

———. *India: Art and Culture, 1300–1900* (New York: Metropolitan Museum, 1985).

Worswick, Clark, ed. *The Last Empire: Photography in British India* (Millertown, N.Y.: Aperture, 1976).

Classical Literary Genres

Ali, Ahmed, ed. and trans. *The Golden Tradition: An Anthology of Urdu Poetry* (New York: Columbia University Press, 1973).

Jayadeva. *Gitagovinda.* Trans. Barbara Stoler Miller as *Love Song of the Dark Lord* (New York: Columbia University Press, 1977).

Kalidasa. "Shakuntala." In *The Theater of Memory: Three Plays of Kalidasa.* Ed. Barbara Stoler Miller (New York: Columbia University Press, 1984).

Mahabharata. (Selections) Ed. William Buck (Berkeley: University of California Press, 1973); C.V. Narasimhan (New York: Columbia University Press, 1965); and R.K. Narayan as *Gods, Demons, and Others* (New York: Bantam, 1986).

Russell, Ralph, and Khurshidul Islam. *Three Mughal Poets: Mir, Mir Hasan, and Sauda* (New York: Oxford University Press, 1992).

Tulsidas. *Ramacaritamanas.* Trans. W.D.P. Hill as *The Holy Lake of the Acts of Rama* (Bombay: Oxford University Press, 1971).

Valmiki. *Ramayana.* Trans. Robert Goldman et al. (Princeton: Princeton University Press, 1990).

———. Abridgment by William Buck (Berkeley: University of California Press, 1976).

Modern Novels and Short Stories

Ali, Ahmed. *Twilight in Delhi* (Bombay: Oxford University Press, 1966).

Anantha Murthy, U.R. *Samskara.* Trans. A.K. Ramanujan (Delhi: Oxford University Press, 1976).

Chatterjee, Upamanyu. *English, August: An Indian Story* (Boston: Faber and Faber, 1988).

Chatterji, Bankim Chandra. *Anandamath.* Trans. and adapted by Basanta Koomar Roy (New Delhi: Vision Books, 1992).

Desai, Anita. *Fire on the Mountain* (New Delhi: Penguin, 1983).

———. *Baumgartner's Bombay* (New York: Viking Penguin, 1990).

Forster, E.M. *Passage to India* (New York: Harcourt, 1924).

Ghosh, Amitav. *The Circle of Reason* (London: Granta Books, with Penguin, 1994).

Jhabvala, Ruth. *Heat and Dust* (London: Murray, 1975).

———. *Travelers* (or *A New Dominion*) (New York: Harper and Row, 1973).

Kipling, Rudyard. *Kim* (New York: Doubleday, 1924).

Markandaya, Kamala. *Nectar in a Sieve* (New York: New American Library, 1982).

Masters, John. *Bhowani Junction* (New York: Viking, 1954).

Narayan, R.K. *The Financial Expert* (Chicago: University of Chicago Press, 1952).

———. *The Guide* (New York: Penguin, 1958).

———. *The Man Eater of Malgudi* (New York: Viking Penguin, 1983).

———. *The Grandmother's Tale and Selected Stories* (New York: Penguin, 1994).

Premchand. *Godan*. Trans. G.C. Roadarmel as *The Gift of a Cow* (Bloomington: University of Indiana Press, 1968).

———. *The World of Premchand* [short stories]. Trans. David Rubin (Bloomington: University of Indiana Press, 1969).

Rubin, David. *The Greater Darkness: A Novel of India* (New York: Farrar, Strauss, 1964).

Rushdie, Salman. *Midnight's Children* (New York: Penguin, 1991).

Sahgal, Nayantara. *Rich Like Us* (New York: New Directions, 1988).

Scott, Paul. *The Raj Quartet* (New York: Morrow, 1976). Includes the following five novels, also published separately:

———. *The Jewel in the Crown* (New York: Morrow, 1966).

———. *The Day of the Scorpion* (New York: Morrow, 1968).

———. *The Towers of Silence* (New York: Morrow, 1972).

———. *A Division of the Spoils* (New York: Morrow, 1975).

———. *Staying On* (New York: Avon, 1979).

Seth, Vikram. *A Suitable Boy* (New Delhi: Viking, 1993).

Biography and Autobiography

Akbar, A.J. *Nehru: The Making of India* (New York: Viking, 1988).

Brown, Judith. *Gandhi: Prisoner of Hope* (New Haven: Yale University Press, 1990).

Chaudhuri, Nirad. *Autobiography of an Unknown Indian* (Reading, Mass.: Addison-Wesley, 1989).

Gandhi, M.K. *Autobiography: My Experiments with Truth* (New York: Dover, 1983).

Gopal, S. *The Story of Jawaharlal Nehru* (Cambridge: Harvard University Press, 1976, 1980, 1984). 3 vols.

Jayakar, Pupul. *Indira Gandhi: An Intimate Biography* (New York: Pantheon, 1993).

Malhotra, Inder. *Indira Gandhi: A Personal and Political Biography* (Boston: Northeastern Press, 1991).

Nanda, B.R. *Gandhi and His Critics* (New York: Oxford University Press, 1985).

———. *Gandhi: Pan-Islamism, Imperialism, and Nationalism* (New York: Oxford University Press, 1989).

Nehru, Jawaharlal. *Towards Freedom* (New York: Oxford University Press, 1989).

India Since Independence

Newspapers, Journals, and Series

"Another India." Daedalus. Vol. 11 (Fall 1989).

Asian Age, daily, Delhi.

Economic and Political Weekly, Bombay.

Frontline, biweekly, Madras.

Hindu, daily, Madras and other cities.

India Briefing (Boulder, Colo.: Westview, 1987–93). Ed. Marshall M. Bouton, 1987; ed. Marshall M. Bouton and Philip Oldenburg, 1988–90; ed. Philip Oldenburg, 1991, 1993; ed. Leonard A. Gordon and Philip Oldenburg, 1992.

India Today, biweekly, New Delhi; North American special ed. available in the United States.

Pioneer, daily, Delhi.

Seminar, monthly, New Delhi.

Statesman, daily, Calcutta and other cities.

Times of India, daily, Bombay and other cities.

Books

Akbar, M.J. *India: The Siege Within* (London: Viking, 1985).

Bhagwati, Jagdish. *India in Transition: Freeing the Economy* (Oxford: Clarendon Press, 1993).

Bhattacharjea, Ajit. *Kashmir: The Wounded Valley* (Delhi: UBS, 1994).

Brass, Paul R. *The Politics of India Since Independence. The New Cambridge History of India.* 2d ed. Part 4, Vol. 1 (Cambridge: Cambridge University Press, 1994).

Crossette, Barbara. *India: Facing the 21st Century* (Bloomington: Indiana University Press, 1993).

Frankel, Francine. *India's Political Economy, 1947–1977: The Gradual Revolution* (Princeton: Princeton University Press, 1978).

Gopal, S., ed. *Ayodhya and the Rise of Communal Politics in India* (London: Second Press, 1992).

Jung, Anees. *Seven Sisters: Among the Women of South Asia* (New Delhi: Penguin, 1994).

Khan, Rasheeduddin. *Bewildered India: Identity, Pluralism, Discord* (New Delhi: Har-Anand, 1994).

Kothari, Rajni, ed. *Caste in Indian Politics* (New York: Gordon and Breach, 1986).

———. *State Against Democracy: In Search of Humane Governance* (New York: New Horizons, 1989).

Naqvi, Saeed. *Reflections of an Indian Muslim* (New Delhi: Har-Anand, 1993).

Noorani, A.G. *The Kashmir Question* (Bombay: P.C. Manaktalas, 1964).

Rudolph, Lloyd, and Susanne Rudolph. *In Pursuit of Lakshmi: The Political Economy of the Indian State* (Chicago: University of Chicago Press, 1987).

Singh, Amrik, ed. *Punjab in Indian Politics* (Columbia, Mo.: South Asia Books, 1986).

Singh, Patwant and Harji Malik, eds. *Punjab: The Fatal Miscalculation* (New Delhi: Patwant Singh, 1984).

Tully, Mark. *No Full Stops in India* (New Delhi: Penguin, 1991). Published in the United States as *The Defeat of a Congressman: And Other Parables of Modern India* (New York: Knopf, 1992).

Tully, Mark, and Satish Jacob. *Amritsar: Mrs. Gandhi's Last Battle* (New Delhi: Rupa, 1985).

Weiner, Myron. *The Child and the State in India* (Princeton: Princeton University Press, 1991).

References and Guides

Hankin, Nigel. *Hanklyn-Janklin* (New Delhi: Banyan Books, 1991).

India: A Travel Survival Kit (Oakland, Calif.: Lonely Planet Publications, 1993).

Murray's Guide to India: A Handbook for Travellers in India, Pakistan, Nepal, Bangladesh, and Sri Lanka (London: Murray, 1975).

Nicholson, Louise. *India Companion* (London: Century, 1991).

Patterson, Maureen L.P. *South Asian Civilizations: A Bibliographic Synthesis* (Chicago: University of Chicago Press, 1981).

Schwartzberg, Joseph, with the collaboration of Shiva Bajpai and others. *A Historical Atlas of South Asia*. 2d impression. (New York: Oxford University Press, 1992).

Spate, O.H.K., and A.T.A. Learmouth. *India and Pakistan: A General and Regional Geography* (London: Methuen, 1967).

Yule, Henry, and A.C. Burnell. *Hobson-Jobson: A Glossary of Anglo-Indian Words and Phrases* (London: Routledge and Kegan Paul, 1968).

1993 & 1994: A Chronology

Kanchan Chandra

January 1993

4 At least two people are reported killed and scores wounded when Bangladesh security forces fire on some of the 50,000 Muslim demonstrators attempting to cross the border from Bangladesh to India in protest against the proposed building of a Hindu temple at Ayodhya.

5 **Intense communal violence triggered by the destruction of the mosque at Ayodhya flares up in Bombay and Ahmedabad.**

6 **More than 60 people are killed in the town of Sopore after the Border Security Force troops shoot indiscriminately and set fire to buildings in retaliation against an attack by Kashmiri militants.**

7 **President Shankar Dayal Sharma promulgates an ordinance with immediate effect, acquiring the land in and around the Babri mosque/Ram temple complex at Ayodhya, including the disputed site on which the demolished structure had stood, in an attempt to end all conflicting claims to ownership.**

10 **Eighty people die in communal violence in Bombay, bringing the city to a standstill. Arson and looting continue despite the deployment of security forces with orders to shoot on sight.**

Minister for Civil Aviation Madhav Rao Scindia resigns, taking "moral responsibility" after a chartered Uzbek Airways Tu–154 aircraft, leased to Indian Airlines when the domestic carrier's pilots went on strike in December, crashed the previous day in dense fog at New Delhi airport. All 163 passengers and crew survived.

Six leaders of the Bharatiya Janata Party (BJP), including L.K. Advani and Murli Manohar Joshi, are released unconditionally after being arrested in December on charges of inciting "communal hatred."

11 **The combined death toll in six days of communal violence in Bombay and Ahmedabad rises to 215. Army units later consolidate their control of Bombay. Over 1,700 people are arrested and 2,000 placed in preventive detention.**

16 Four senior executives of the U.S. bank Citibank, implicated in the Bombay securities scandal that erupted in May 1992, resign. The resignations are expected to prompt renewed demands for an investigation of the bank by the Joint Parliamentary Committee (JPC) appointed to inquire into the scandal.

17 Prime Minister P.V. Narasimha Rao carries out his first major government reshuffle, making four appointments at cabinet level and bringing in ten junior ministers.

23 United Kingdom Prime Minister John Major arrives on a five-day official visit to India.

28 During a three-day state visit, Russian President Boris Yeltsin and Prime Minister Narasimha Rao sign a new Indo-Russian Treaty of Peace, Friendship and Cooperation that replaces the 1971 Soviet-Indian treaty. They also sign a ruble-rupee agreement, according to which India's outstanding debt of Rs.380 billion to the former

Soviet Union would be based on exchange rates that would reduce the total amount by one-third over a period of 45 years, and a military accord that stipulates the promotion of bilateral defense relations and cooperation.

February

3 The Bombay High Court orders the seizure of 77 audio-cassettes purporting to show that the police had supported Hindu attacks on Muslims during communal riots in the city in January.

4 An interior power struggle in the Home Affairs Ministry appears to have been resolved when Minister of State for Home Affairs Rajesh Pilot assumes control of the key departments of internal security, Jammu and Kashmir, and Punjab, reportedly against the wishes of Home Affairs Minister S.B. Chavan.

7 The Central Bureau of Investigation (CBI) identifies at least 400 people who had participated in the demolition of the Babri mosque at Ayodhya on December 6 and announces its plan to issue charges against them. The CBI observes that a majority of those who took part in the demolition were from Maharashtra, Uttar Pradesh, and Gujarat.

8 The World Bank approves a loan worth \$3.2 billion to India, including concessional assistance of \$1.3 billion from the International Development Association. It also approves a request for an annual \$2.5 billion in exceptional financing over the next three years.

9 The Congress Working Committee meeting concludes with the unanimous decision that the one-man one-party-post principle does not apply to the prime minister, thus rejecting the demand of some senior Congress Party leaders for Narasimha Rao's resignation as party president.

12 **The government bans a widely publicized mass rally planned by the BJP in the capital for February 25.** Citing the events in Ayodhya, Home Minister Chavan notes that there is no guarantee that the rally would be conducted peacefully. The BJP calls the ban "arbitrary" and "counterproductive" and declares its decision to hold the rally nevertheless.

19 **The Congress Party is returned to power in state elections in Meghalaya and Nagaland,** with over 100 companies of paramilitary forces looking on. Elections scheduled simultaneously in Tripura were postponed after the Election Commission declared the state's law-and-order situation to be unsuitable for free polls.

On an official visit, German Federal Chancellor Helmut Kohl urges India to accede to the Nuclear Nonproliferation Treaty. Kohl notes that India is "emerging as the largest market in the Southeast Asian region" and states his conviction that the liberalization process initiated by the Rao government is "irreversible."

20 A Memorandum of Settlement aimed at ending the six-year agitation for a separate homeland for the Bodo tribe is signed between the Assam state government, the central government, and representatives from the All-Bodo Students' Union and the Bodo People's Action Committee. The agreement, which falls short of acceding to demands for a separate Bodo state, envisages the creation of a 40-member Bodoland Autonomous Council, with separate legislative and executive branches. The BAC will have control over 38 subjects dealing with the socioeconomic and cultural development of the area.

21 The Naxalite People's War Group (PWG) in Andhra Pradesh releases Congress Party member of the legislative assembly P. Balaraju and a second remaining hostage, ending a 22-day crisis precipitated by the kidnapping in late January.

22 The Congress Party Chief Minister of Maharashtra, Sudhakarrao Naik, resigns, ending a long controversy over his continuation in office. Naik's resignation is widely interpreted as a victory for his chief political rival, Defense Minister Sharad Pawar.

24 The central government releases a White Paper absolving itself of responsibility for the demolition of the Babri mosque at Ayodhya and blaming the Uttar Pradesh state government for failing to protect the site. Human Resources Development Minister Arjun Singh had earlier resigned from the three-member cabinet subcommittee entrusted with the task of drafting the paper, saying that he thought it would be a "whitewash."

25 **The government employs massive security measures to thwart the planned BJP rally in New Delhi.** BJP activists attempting to hold the rally are *lathi*-charged (beaten back with bamboo staves) and tear-gassed, BJP President Murli Manohar Joshi is injured in a clash with the police, and party leaders L.K. Advani and Atal Behari Vajpayee are arrested. Over 1,000 persons are taken into custody in the capital, and preventive arrests are also made in other states. About 500 companies of the Punjab police, the Haryana police, the Railway Police Force, the Border Security Force, and the Central Reserve Police Force are deployed in the city.

27 **The finance minister announces the government's budget proposals for 1993–94.** The highlights of the budget, which is aimed primarily at raising export earnings, are the full convertibility of the rupee on current account, substantial reductions in tariffs and import duties, and tax relief for foreign investors and export-oriented industries.

March

3 Former Defense Minister Sharad Pawar is appointed chief minister of Maharashtra.

12 **More than 250 people are killed and at least 1,200 injured in Bombay when a synchronized chain of car bombs destroys the city's stock exchange, gutting the offices of the country's international airline and ripping through a crowded marketplace, a bus stand, hotels, and hospitals.** Home Minister S.B. Chavan claims that the bombings are part of "an international conspiracy" against India. After sporadic Hindu-Muslim violence in several parts of Bombay soon after the blasts, the city quickly recovers and remains calm. On March 18, police in Bombay claim that arrests related to the explosions had yielded "clinching evidence" showing that they were the work of criminal gangs loyal to Ibrahim Abdul Razak Memon, a notorious Bombay-based narcotics and gold smuggler.

Former army chief General K.V. Krishna Rao is appointed governor of Kashmir, replacing Girish Saksena. Rao had previously served as governor of the state in 1988–90.

16 **Another 86 people die and 70 are injured after a bomb explosion destroys a crowded trade and residential district in Calcutta.**

18 Nearly one million employees of state-run banks stage a nationwide strike demanding higher wages.

29 A bill passed by both houses of parliament on March 29 grants permission to the government to acquire land around the demolished mosque at Ayodhya.

30 **The government asks for the cancellation of remaining loans by the World Bank worth $170 million for the half-finished Narmada river project, saying that it will "be going ahead with the project on [its] own."** The cancellation is requested after the bank was accused of "passing on" to India protests by environmental groups that had questioned the environmental

impact of the project and opposed the resettlement of some 300,000 people, mostly tribespeople. The bank had temporarily suspended funding for the project, totaling $3 billion, after pressure from the environmental groups.

April

5 Pakistani troops prevent several hundred marchers from crossing the Line of Actual Control separating Pakistan and Kashmir.

The all-India Muslim personal law board meets the prime minister to urge him to fulfill his promise of rebuilding the mosque destroyed at Ayodhya at the same site.

6 Results for the state assembly elections in Tripura are announced. The Congress Party loses power in a landslide to the CPM-led left front.

10 Large-scale violence hits Srinagar as the Hizbul Mujahideen call a general strike to mourn the death of its second-in-command, Maqbool Illahi, in a clash with the army. Shops and houses are gutted and 20 people are killed.

11 The seventh SAARC (South Asian Association for Regional Cooperation) summit concludes in Dhaka with the unanimous adoption of the 63-point Dhaka declaration, which seeks to "provide a dynamic impetus to activities in the core areas of economic, social and cultural cooperation in the SAARC region." The summit also reaches agreement on the South Asian Preferential Trade Agreement seeking to reduce trade barriers between member countries.

16 The Supreme Court suspends the reinstatement of the BJP Madhya Pradesh government, thereby quashing a

ruling of the Madhya Pradesh High Court that the dismissal of the state government in December 1992 had been "invalid" and "beyond the scope of the constitution."

The Joint Parliamentary Committee set up by Prime Minister Rao to investigate the 1992 stock market scandal criticizes the Finance Ministry and government nominees on the boards of nationalized banks for having failed to check serious irregularities in the banking sector that led to the scandal.

19 Film star Sanjay Dutt is arrested under the Terrorist and Disruptive Activities (Prevention) Act (TADA) after he confessed to possessing an AK-56 assault rifle. The Bombay police accuse him of smuggling and distributing explosives and firearms during the March bomb blasts.

The 35-day-old Jharkhand agitation is called off after a meeting with Prime Minister Narasimha Rao and the leaders of the Jharkhand Mukti Morcha.

The Finance Ministry agrees to provide funds equivalent to $170 million for the execution of the controversial Sardar Sarovar Project, ending doubts regarding the completion of the project on schedule after India refused the equivalent credit of $170 million from the World Bank.

24 A man claiming to be a member of the Hizbul Mujahideen hijacks an Indian Airlines Delhi-Srinagar flight. He is killed after being captured by Indian commandos, who free all 141 passengers at Amritsar airport.

28 The army is called in Srinagar to end the strike by the Jammu and Kashmir police. More than 3,500 policemen belonging to all wings of the Jammu and Kashmir police were protesting the death of a colleague in custody, alleging that the paramilitary forces and some In-

dian Police Service officials are responsible. The agitating policemen lay down their arms peacefully.

30 The United States designates India as a priority country for immediate punitive action under the "Super 301" provision of the 1988 U.S. Omnibus Trade and Competitiveness Act unless it improves its enforcement of intellectual property rights.

May

1 **Sri Lankan President Ranasinghe Premadasa is assassinated by a suicide bomber believed to be a member of the Liberation Tigers of Tamil Eelam (LTTE).**

7 The final report of the Reserve Bank of India (RBI) committee, appointed to inquire into the 1992 securities scandal and headed by RBI Deputy Governor R. Janakiraman, finds that the main source of funds for the irregular transactions was the corporate sector, particularly the public sector units.

12 President's Rule is extended for six months in Uttar Pradesh, Madhya Pradesh, Rajasthan, and Himachal Pradesh. All four states had been placed under President's Rule in the aftermath of the communal violence that followed the demolition of the Babri mosque at Ayodhya in December 1992.

14 Justice V. Ramaswami resigns as Supreme Court judge. Three days before, a motion to impeach the former chief justice of the Punjab and Haryana high court on corruption charges was defeated in the Lok Sabha when the Congress Party abstained from the vote.

17 India and Israel sign a memorandum of understanding in New Delhi on economic cooperation in areas including trade, agriculture, solar energy, natural resources, tourism, research and development, and setting up joint ventures.

19 Asim Mahato, leader of the separatist Jharkhand Mukti Morcha in Bihar, is assassinated near Jamshedpur.

22 The Congress Party suffers reverses in the by-elections to 2 Lok Sabha seats and 16 assembly seats, conceding 2 assembly seats to the Telugu Desam in Andhra Pradesh, 2 to the BJP in Gujarat, and 1 to the Samajwadi Janata Party (SJP) in Haryana. The by-elections are marred by widespread violence.

23 Prime Minister Rao embarks on a five-day official visit to the Central Asian republics of Uzbekistan and Kazakhstan.

27 Vishwa Hindu Parishad (VHP) leader Ashok Singhal reiterates the call for the "liberation" of the Mathura and Varanasi shrines.

June

3 Lal Krishan Advani is elected unopposed as president of the BJP, replacing Murli Manohar Joshi, whose two-year term had been marked by internal party disputes.

8 The Bahri tribunal rules that there is no evidence that the demolition of the Babri mosque at Ayodhya was preplanned by the leaders of the Rashtriya Swayamsevak Sangh (RSS), the VHP, or the Bajrang Dal. Justice P.K. Bahri notes, "Even the white paper prepared by the central government does not support this theory of preplanning for destruction of the disputed structure by these organizations."

11 Removing a significant obstacle in trade relations between the two countries, Russian Prime Minister Victor Chernomyrdin agrees to convert most of India's debt to Russia from rubles to rupees and to calculate all future trade credits in rupees.

12 The 11th test firing of the medium-range surface-to-surface Prithvi missile is carried out, after which the missile is handed over to the army for further evaluation. Capable of a 1,000 kg. payload, the missile is designed to target military bases, airfields, and industrial facilities such as oil depots.

15 Manmohan Singh, leader of India's delegation at the second world human rights conference in Vienna, rejects external intervention on the issue of safeguarding human rights on Indian territory, saying "we do not need outside goading" on this issue.

16 **Prime Minister P.V. Narasimha Rao is accused of accepting an undeclared campaign contribution worth Rs.10 million ($320,000) from the Bombay stockbroker Harshad Mehta, who faces charges relating to the banking and securities scandal that erupted in May 1992.** Mehta alleges that the payment was made to secure political patronage and government support. Mehta's allegations are flatly denied by Rao and senior Congress Party figures. The opposition, led by the BJP, calls for Rao's immediate resignation.

22 **The Joint Parliamentary Committee appointed in August 1992 to investigate the Bombay securities scandal releases a draft report criticizing the finance minister, Dr. Manmohan Singh, and the Reserve Bank of India and the Finance Ministry for failing to introduce an effective system of inspection.**

28 The sixth round of Sino-Indian talks held in New Delhi ends with the opening of an additional border post in Shipkilah in Himachal Pradesh and agreement on further confidence-building measures, including increased transparency about the location of military positions.

29 A joint report by Asia Watch and Physicians for Human Rights accuses security forces in Kashmir of "summa-

rily executing detainees and killing civilians in reprisal attacks." The report also criticizes rebel groups for violating human rights "by engaging in summary executions, rape, kidnappings, threats and assaults against civilians."

July

2 The Aid-India consortium meeting in Paris pledges $7.4 billion in assistance for 1993–94; the amount represents a $200 million increase over the previous year's pledges. The pledge is made one day after India announces a special package for the speedy utilization of external assistance, including prefinancing and lending on the same terms to projects and discontinuation of mediation by the central government for foreign borrowing by public sector undertakings, in response to concerns by Western donors at India's failure to utilize the existing aid commitments of more than $18.5 billion piled up over the years.

6 In an escalation of violence, three senior district officers of Baramulla district are abducted by a group of unidentified militants, while 39 people are killed and 16 militants captured. Security officials are able to rescue the abducted officials one day later.

France announces that it will suspend the supply of low-enriched uranium for the Tarapur atomic power station from October, after the Indian government refuses to accept comprehensive safeguards required by the International Atomic Energy Agency.

8 The BJP declares its decision to oppose "tooth and nail" a bill proposed by the Rao government delinking religion from politics to be introduced in the next session of the Lok Sabha.

12 In a second major offensive against the multinational Cargill Seeds company within a year, about 100 activ-

ists of the Karnataka Rajya Raitha Sangha ransack and partially damage the company's factory building at Siravara.

14 Amnesty International reveals that the Indian government has refused to agree to a proposed visit by its team to Bombay from July 18 to July 24 to discuss matters relating to police behavior and training in view of the allegations that some policemen had failed to act impartially during the riots in December 1992 and January 1993.

17 Reacting to the Russian government's decision to suspend a $350 million contract to supply cryogenic space rockets and technology to India, an official spokesman for the External Affairs Ministry accused Russia of having "yielded blatantly to U.S. pressure" and stated that India would continue to develop the required technology indigenously.

20 The Swiss Supreme Court orders the release of information on Swiss bank accounts relating to the 1986 Bofors armaments deal. In September 1992 the Indian Supreme Court had facilitated access to the documents by the Central Bureau of Investigation.

21 Tamil Nadu Chief Minister Jayaram Jayalalitha ends her four-day fast to demand the equitable sharing of Cauvery River waters with Karnataka, after an assurance is given by Water Resources Minister V.C. Shukla that the interim order of the Cauvery tribunal will be implemented.

28 **The government of Prime Minister P.V. Narasimha Rao survives by 265 to 251 votes a no-confidence motion brought against it by opposition parties.** The opposition motion claims that the government was tainted by accusations of Rao's involvement in the Bombay financial scandal; that it failed to check the

communal violence that followed the destruction of the Ayodhya mosque in December; and that its program of economic liberalization had left the country's poor worse off. Sponsored by the CPM with the support of the BJP, the National Front–Left Front groupings and the AIADMK, it marked the third attempt to oust the Rao government since it came to office in June 1991.

29 Amid protests from several opposition parties led by the BJP, the government introduces two bills in the Lok Sabha seeking to remove religion from politics and to empower the election commission to bar political parties with religious names from contesting elections.

Minister of State for Home Affairs Rajesh Pilot informs parliament that there is "solid proof" of Dubai-based Dawood Ibrahim's involvement in the Bombay bomb blasts.

August

1 A nationwide strike to secure the abolition of octroi and road taxes called by the All-India Motor Transport Congress begins. The strike ends after six days with an agreement by the government to abolish road and interstate taxes in the states of Bihar, Gujarat, Haryana, Madhya Pradesh, Orissa, Punjab, Rajasthan, and Uttar Pradesh.

2 **In an unprecedented action, the Election Commission issues an order indefinitely suspending biennial parliamentary and legislative elections and by-elections in all states. Election Commissioner T.N. Seshan justifies the order on the grounds that the commission's constitutional powers to control civil and state officers deployed for electoral duties were being obstructed by the government.** He notes that it is "absolutely imperative that the constitutional position of the commission, particularly in regard to its constitu-

tional prerogative of securing the assistance of necessary staff, is unequivocally and clearly accepted by the government of India." The central government proposes to move a public interest litigation in the Bombay high court in response.

6 A mass rally to protest against the Narmada River project is called off after the government pledges to review the scheme, encompassing a network of about 30 dams across the states of Gujarat, Madhya Pradesh, and Maharashtra; the review is expected to be completed within three months and its findings made public within a month of their submission. The decision follows a robust campaign organized by environmental activists, led by Medha Patkar, who had threatened to commit *samarpan* (self-sacrifice) by drowning themselves in protest against the dam, which they claimed would displace thousands of farmers.

9 Nine people are killed and five injured in a bomb explosion at the headquarters of the RSS, in Madras. BJP General Secretary M. Venkiah Naidu blames "fundamentalist forces" for the bombing.

10 The constitutional quarrel involving the Election Commission and the government is resolved after the chief election commissioner, T.N. Seshan, rescinds his August 2 order suspending by-elections.

15 Speaking from the Red Fort on Independence Day, Prime Minister Narasimha Rao declares that the Babri mosque structure will be reconstructed, calling its demolition a "black spot" on the secular face of India. He warns Pakistan that Kashmir is an integral part of India and openly criticizes Pakistan for supporting insurgency in the valley. Rao asserts also that Punjab has successfully returned from 12 years of violence to normalcy.

22 Janata Dal leader and former prime minister V.P. Singh begins a self-imposed exile from the capital and the Lok

Sabha, vowing not to return to the capital until the central government implements job reservations for backward classes in government services.

24 **The government is embarrassed by being forced to defer the bill banning political parties from using religious appeals in their campaigns after it cannot muster a two-thirds majority in the face of BJP and Janata Dal opposition.**

26 Crisis grips the ruling Congress Party in Karnataka as Chief Minister Veerappa Moily suspends eight of his party members for "unruly behavior" in the legislature.

28 The Lok Sabha approves the extension of President's Rule in Jammu and Kashmir for another six months, with the central government ruling out early elections, saying that it will take "some time" to create the congenial atmosphere necessary for elections in the state.

September

2 More than one million employees of banks and insurance companies go on a one-day strike, paralyzing business and financial institutions across the country. The strike had been called by the joint action committee of unions and federations in banks, insurance companies, and other financial institutions, in support of demands for wage revisions, pensions, and payment of bonus.

6 More than 1,000 tribal guerrillas belonging to the All-Tripura Tribal Force surrender to the state government in accordance with a peace settlement concluded in late August. About 350 people have died in clashes since 1990, since local tribespeople first claimed that they were threatened by an influx of Muslim immigrants from Bangladesh.

7 **In a significant measure aimed at settling the 31-year border dispute between India and China, the**

two countries sign an agreement on troop reductions during a visit to Beijing by Indian Prime Minister Narasimha Rao. Both sides agree to respect and observe the Line of Actual Control and undertake not to use force against each other. Signed after talks between Rao and Chinese Premier Li Peng, the agreement makes no mention of each country's conflicting claims to thousands of square kilometers of territory. The agreement was hailed by both sides as a landmark in bilateral relations.

8 The central government issues a notification to implement the Mandal Commission's recommendation to reserve 27 percent of jobs in the central government for persons from the "backward" classes.

9 At least 3,000 people are arrested during a one-day general strike called by left-wing trade unions. The strike was the latest in a series mounted against the government's economic reforms.

11 Ten people are killed and 34 others injured when two powerful bombs go off outside the New Delhi offices of the All-India Youth Congress. About 150 people are arrested in Punjab after several Sikh extremist groups claim responsibility for the explosion.

13 Nearly 1,500 troops are airlifted to Manipur to quell renewed ethnic violence between Naga and Kuki tribespeople. Fighting had flared after the banned National Socialist Council of Nagaland issued Kuki residents with an ultimatum to leave the predominantly Naga region so that a separate Naga homeland could be established.

20 The first developmental flight of the Polar Satellite Launch Vehicle (PSLV) fails in its attempt to put the Indian remote sensing satellite, IRS-IE, into the specified orbit. The failure of the mission does not affect the continuation of the PSLV program.

29 The government announces plans to establish a National Human Rights Commission. On October 7, Home Minister S.B. Chavan says that allegations of "excesses" by the security forces would definitely fall within its purview.

30 **A powerful earthquake, measuring 6.5 on the Richter scale, devastates around 30 villages in the states of Maharashtra, Karnataka, and Andhra Pradesh, with a death toll of 10,000.** The epicenter of the earthquake lay at a point where Maharashtra, Karnataka, and Andhra Pradesh converge near Latur. Within days, the central government pledges Rs.500 million (about $16 million) in relief assistance to earthquake victims and says that it will welcome foreign donations. Offers of rescue and relief come from several Western countries.

October

5 The government files charges against the leaders of the BJP and Shiv Sena, including L.K. Advani and Bal Thackeray, for "criminal conspiracy" in the December demolition of the Ayodhya mosque.

12 The CBI drops its inquiries into allegations that Prime Minister Narasimha Rao had accepted undeclared campaign contributions from Harshad Mehta on grounds of insufficient evidence.

13 Nekhlun Kuki, chief of the rebel Kuki National Army involved with clashes with the Naga tribespeople in Manipur, is killed in a gun battle with security forces.

16 Indian security forces lay siege to the Hazratbal shrine in Srinagar, where Kashmiri separatists have taken refuge. The 17th-century shrine, said to hold a strand of hair belonging to the Prophet Mohammad, is regarded by Kashmiri Muslims as one of Islam's holiest sites.

21 Amid international tension over the standoff between security forces and the militants, and threats by Jamaat-i-Islami leader Syed Alishah Geelani to organize processions from various parts of the valley to the Hazratbal shrine, the Jammu and Kashmir government makes a conditional offer to free militants entrenched in the shrine.

22 Seventeen people are killed and more than 40 injured when security forces open fire on demonstrators demanding an end to the Hazratbal siege. Jamaat-i-Islami leader Alishah Geelani is arrested, and negotiations between the administration and the militants stall.

25 India and Pakistan agree to end their year-long impasse and begin bilateral talks on all issues. The reopening of dialogue comes one week after Benazir Bhutto is re-elected prime minister of Pakistan.

28 India announces its resolve not to accept the Dunkel proposals, which aim to reduce government subsidies in agriculture, one day before the visit of the GATT director-general, Peter Sutherland, to New Delhi.

29 Tension in relations with the United States mounts over remarks made in Washington by U.S. Assistant Secretary of State for South Asian Affairs Robin Raphel that question the accession of Kashmir to India in October 1947.

November

4 A Finance Ministry report shows that the country's external debts, which in March 1986 had stood at $37 billion, had risen to $85 billion in March 1993, largely because of an increase in loans from multilateral lending agencies.

6 **State elections, a "mini-general election," begin with the poll for the newly constituted 70-member legisla-**

tive assembly in Delhi. Polls are held in Himachal Pradesh on November 9, Rajasthan on November 11, Uttar Pradesh on November 17, and Madhya Pradesh on November 24. This schedule permits security arrangements that prevent almost all violence and much fraud.

10 In a reversal of its earlier stand, the BJP announces that if it comes to power, it will welcome investment by U.S. multinationals in the consumer goods sector.

14 A landmine planted by the outlawed guerrilla People's War Group explodes in Mahboobnagar, Andhra Pradesh, killing ten people. On November 4, the PWG bombed two government buildings in Hyderabad in retaliation for a police campaign against its members.

15 The Indo-U.K. extradition treaty, approved in January 1992 and ratified by the British parliament in September 1993, comes into force. The instruments of ratification also cover the confiscation of assets of people involved in terrorist activity.

16 **The Hazratbal crisis in Srinagar ends peacefully as the armed Kashmiri separatists, besieged by Indian security forces at the Hazratbal mosque since mid-October, surrender. The end of the siege comes after weeks of intensive negotiations during which the government sought the help of Muslim clergymen, promilitant politicians, and family members close to the militants.** Almost 60 people died during demonstrations triggered by the siege.

18 In a major step toward further liberalization of the Indian financial sector, the Reserve Bank of India permits foreign equity participation in private sector Indian banks.

19 The Supreme Court clears Sharad Pawar, the chief minister of Maharashtra, who had appealed against

the March 1993 finding of the Bombay High Court that he was guilty of corrupt electoral practices.

22 India and South Africa reestablish diplomatic relations, 49 years after India withdrew its ambassador to protest apartheid.

30 **Early results of elections to state assemblies in Uttar Pradesh, Himachal Pradesh, Rajasthan, and Delhi are announced. As the results are declared in the following days, it becomes clear that the BJP has suffered a setback, losing power in Uttar Pradesh, Himachal Pradesh, and Madhya Pradesh, while scoring a close victory in Rajasthan and a thumping one in Delhi. The Bahujan Samaj Party (BSP) and Samajwadi Party (SP) alliance does unexpectedly well in Uttar Pradesh, winning 176 seats, a total equaled by the BJP, while Congress is routed with only 28 seats. In Himachal Pradesh, the Congress Party wins a two-thirds majority, with 52 of the 68 seats, and the BJP wins 8. In Rajasthan, the BJP emerges as the single largest party with 95 seats while the Congress Party secures 76 and the Janata Dal 6 of the 199 seats. In Delhi, however, the BJP wins a clear majority, with 48 of the 70 member seats. In Madhya Pradesh, the Congress Party wins handily, taking 173 of the 316 seats, while the BJP (which had held 220 seats) wins only 114.**

The Joint Parliamentary Committee investigating the stocks and securities scandal decides not to examine the prime minister regarding the alleged Rs.10 million payoff by Harshad Mehta.

Polling begins for Mizoram's 40-member state assembly.

December

2 Twenty-four persons, including four Border Security Force personnel and 14 militants are killed in the Kashmir

valley, while 134 militants are arrested. The town of Sopore, considered to be a safe haven for militants and their accomplices, is cordoned off by security forces.

3 A Congress Party government headed by Chief Minister Vir Bhadra Singh assumes office in Himachal Pradesh.

A coalition ministry headed by SP leader Mulayam Singh Yadav is sworn in in Uttar Pradesh. On the same day, the BJP's Bhairon Singh Shekhawat is invited to become the chief minister of Rajasthan for the third time, with his government's majority dependent on the support of ten independent deputies.

5 Congress Party governments are confirmed in both Madhya Pradesh and Mizoram, headed by Digvijay Singh and Lal Thanwala respectively. In Delhi, M.L. Khurana of the BJP becomes the first chief minister since Delhi became a union territory in 1956.

6 The first anniversary of the destruction of the Babri mosque at Ayodhya is marked by bomb explosions aimed at four Delhi-bound trains, which kill two passengers and injure more than 20 others.

8 The Maharashtra state government signs an agreement with the U.S. company Enron Power to buy electric power from an Enron gas-fired plant to be built at Dhabol. The successful completion of talks was considered vital to the Indian government's efforts to attract foreign investment.

10 A four-day nationwide strike by postal employees is called off following discussions between the three principal postal federations and the government. The demands of the striking employees included the regularization of over 300,000 "extradepartmental" employees and the revision of pay scales.

11 At the opening session of the G-15 session in New Delhi, External Affairs Minister Dinesh Singh urges the group of 15 developing countries to focus attention on terrorism as the greatest threat to human rights, especially when aided and abetted from across national borders.

15 Amnesty International issues a report alleging that disappearances in Kashmir and Punjab have become "systematic" and pointing to the deliberate and unlawful suppression of information by the army and security forces. The government criticizes the report as "substantially incorrect," "ill-advised," and "ill-timed."

16 **Commerce Minister Pranab Mukherjee announces India's accession to the GATT treaty, as opposition members accuse the government of having surrendered the country's economic sovereignty.** Mukherjee says that India has more to gain by signing the trade agreement than by pursuing any alternative course of action, and expects that Indian exports should go up by about $2 billion annually following the trade deal.

18 **The Lok Sabha adopts the Protection of Human Rights Bill, which provides for the setting up of a National Human Rights Commission and is expected to apply to the actions of the armed forces.** Concluding the debate on the bill, Home Minister S.B. Chavan notes that it will foil the designs of some countries to malign India at the United Nations and in other international forums.

20 India and the European Community sign an agreement granting each other Most Favored Nation status and agree to intensify cooperation in agriculture, transport, communication, banking, and technology.

21 **The Joint Parliamentary Committee issues its report on the May 1992 Bombay Securities scandal. The**

report indicts the Reserve Bank of India and criticizes the Finance Ministry for failing to supervise the stock exchange and ignoring signs of fraudulent activity. It also recommends suspending the licenses of four foreign banks (Bank of America, Citibank, ANZ Grindlays, and Standard Chartered Bank) that in its view had been "the originators" and "the biggest players" in the scandal. While the report falls short of openly criticizing Finance Minister Manmohan Singh, it holds him responsible for his ministry's shortcomings.

30 Prime Minister Rao rejects Finance Minister Manmohan Singh's resignation, submitted on December 24, under pressure from cabinet colleagues who argued that Singh's departure would threaten India's moves toward a market economy. Addressing parliament following a two-day debate, Singh acknowledges "full constitutional responsibility" in the stocks and securities scandal and announces that financial sector reform is under way.

Congress obtains an absolute majority in parliament as 10 of the 13 members of the Janata Dal(A), including its leader Ajit Singh, join the Congress Party, raising its strength from 256 to 266.

31 President's Rule is imposed in Manipur following a renewed outbreak of intertribal fighting.

January 1994

2 The seventh round of talks between India and Pakistan on Kashmir and other bilateral issues begins in Islamabad. The countries are represented by their respective foreign secretaries, J.N. Dixit and Shaharyar Khan.

The Gorkha National Liberation Front obtains a landslide victory in the elections for the 28-member Gorkha Hill Council.

14 Maharashtra Chief Minister Sharad Pawar announces the official renaming of the Marathwada University in Aurangabad as the Dr. Babasaheb Ambedkar Marathwada University. Justified by Pawar as a mark of respect to Dr. Ambedkar, the renaming was regarded by some observers as a ploy to win the support of the lower castes. Several days of rioting, violence, and riots follow. A strike called by the Shiv Sena on January 21 in opposition to the decision paralyzes Bombay and triggers widespread commercial violence.

19 Seven Kuki women are killed by armed militants in Manipur. Official figures released in mid-January showed that 410 local militants and 87 security personnel had died in armed encounters in Manipur during 1993. Another 316 people had died in clashes between Naga and Kuki ethnic groups.

The trial of 26 Indian and Sri Lankan nationals, all Tamils, charged with the assassination in May 1991 of Rajiv Gandhi opens at the high security Poonamalle prison in Madras.

20 All-India Radio reports that Russia has agreed to supply seven cryogenic rockets worth $220 million to India to offset the consequences of Russia's refusal to honor its earlier commitment.

27 Twenty-six people are reported to have died in secessionist-related violence in Kupwara, Kashmir, according to the Press Trust of India. A *bandh* called by militants in protest the next day paralyzes life in the valley.

February

1 Speaking to a gathering of global leaders of industry and finance in Davos, Switzerland, at a symposium organized by the World Economic Forum, Prime Minister

Narasimha Rao declares that India's economic reforms are "irreversible." At the same time, he defends the concept of a mixed economy. The rejection of the command system, according to Rao, does not mean the total acceptance of the market economy: India has been saved from "political submission and economic dependence" because it has followed a middle path between the two. Both Rao and Commerce Minister Pranab Mukherjee emphasize that they welcome foreign investment, but on India's terms.

3 Addressing the 50th session of the U.N. Human Rights Commission, Finance Minister Manmohan Singh seeks the support of the international community against the disruptive forces of Pakistan state-sponsored terrorism. He says that the accession of Kashmir to India not only enjoys "perfect legal validity" but was also "sanctified by popular will."

Border talks with China under the terms of the September 1993 Sino-Indian agreement are held in New Delhi.

8 In special *dharam sansads* (religious parliaments) held in various parts of the country, the banned VHP and its allied organizations resolve to oppose the rebuilding of the Babri mosque anywhere in India. They also announce plans to begin the construction of a Ram temple at Ayodhya in October.

11 **The Indian government reacts strongly to a statement made by U.S. Assistant Secretary of State Robin Raphel equating the situation in Kashmir with the civil war in Pakistan, saying that such references by U.S. officials were "unhelpful and hindered the resumption of the democratic political process."**

17 Chief Minister of Gujarat Chimanbhai Patel dies following a heart attack; he is replaced on an acting basis by the state finance minister, Chhabildas Mehta.

The biennial partial elections to the Rajya Sabha are held by the state assemblies of Bihar, Karnataka, Sikkim, and West Bengal. Congress wins all four seats in Karnataka, while the Left Front wins all five seats in West Bengal. Out of eight seats in Bihar, Congress wins two, the Janata Dal four, and the CPI and BJP one each. The single seat in Sikkim goes to the Sikkim Sangram Parishad. Elections in Gujarat are postponed on account of the chief minister's death.

19 The third test launch of India's Agni intermediate-range ballistic missile, originally scheduled for March 1993 and delayed again in January 1994, is successfully completed in Chandipur, near Balasore, Orissa.

24 The 1994–95 railway budget is unveiled. It provides for a 6 percent rise in upper-class passenger fares, a marginal increase in other fares, and an adjustment in goods rates to raise revenue by an additional Rs.99,700 million.

The government publishes its annual economic survey, which estimates that the economy will grow by only 3.8 percent in the 1993–94 financial year, well short of the target of between 5 and 5.5 percent in the original 1993–94 budget. Agricultural output declined slightly, while industrial production, growing by 1 percent in the first seven months of 1993–94, recovered more slowly than anticipated. There is, however, "striking evidence of progress" in the country's export performance, after a marked decline in 1992–93.

28 **The government's budget proposals for the 1994–95 financial year are announced by Finance Minister Manmohan Singh.** They underline the government's continuing commitment to growth despite worries over the rise in public borrowing to beyond target levels. Convertibility of the rupee on current account, increase in foreign currency retention for exporters, lowering of

interest rates, and a package of measures to boost industrial investment and capital goods production are the highlights of the budget. In a further boost to its program of economic expansion launched in mid-1991, the government cuts the maximum rate of customs duty from 85 percent to 65 percent; lowers the maximum rate of corporate tax including surcharges from 65 to 55 percent; and reduces the minimum lending rate by 1 percentage point to 14 percent.

March

4 The ruling Congress Party suffers a serious setback in elections held in Gujarat for four Rajya Sabha seats. It wins only two seats, instead of the expected three, with the other two going to the opposition BJP. Massive cross-voting by Congress deputies in favor of the BJP is said to have influenced the outcome.

8 The 27-member All-Parties Hurriyat Conference calls a *bandh* in Kashmir to attract the attention of a team of ambassadors from ten countries, including Venezuela, Turkey, Indonesia, Nigeria and Mexico, who are in Kashmir to survey the human rights situation in the state.

9 After several days of diplomatic maneuvering, Pakistan withdraws its resolution on human rights in Kashmir at the session of the U.N. Human Rights Commission in Geneva. The withdrawal comes after as many as 45 of the 53 members of the commission, including the United States, inform Pakistan of their decision to abstain from voting.

11 **The Supreme Court, in a landmark judgment, unanimously upholds the dismissal of the state governments of Himachal Pradesh, Madhya Pradesh, and Rajasthan following the demolition of the Babri mosque in Ayodhya.** In its verdict, the panel of nine

justices notes that no political party could simultaneously be a "religious party" and that any state government that pursued "unsecular policies" did so in breach of the constitution. In a separate ruling, a majority of the panel declared unconstitutional the dismissal of the state governments of Karnataka and Meghalaya in April 1989 and October 1991 respectively.

Professor Rajendra Singh, formerly the joint general secretary, succeeds Balasaheb Deoras as *Sarsanghchalak* (Supreme Head) of the RSS; Deoras resigns on grounds of ill health.

16 A 48-hour "Jharkhand *bandh*" jointly called by the All-Jharkhand Students' Union and the Jharkhand People's Party begins in southern Bihar. Police and paramilitary forces keep a close watch on the agitators, who demand the introduction of a bill for a formation of a separate Jharkhand state during the current session of parliament.

18 The Supreme Court strikes down the government order of December 1992 banning the Muslim religious party Jamaat-e-Islami, saying that it is unjustified.

20 Pakistan closes its consulate in Bombay. A spokesman for the Pakistani government attributes the decision to the supposed refusal of India to honor its commitment to lease the Jinnah House in Bombay for the use of the consulate general.

26 "Frank and friendly" talks with visiting Assistant Secretary of State Robin Raphel, who arrived in India on March 22, conclude.

28 The G-15 summit begins in New Delhi with a call from Prime Minister Narasimha Rao to mobilize world opinion against terrorism, fundamentalism, and separatism, which, according to him, "undermine the nation-state system upon which the international order rests."

30 During a special sitting of the Lok Sabha to discuss the "Dunkel draft" GATT proposals, the opposition warned that Dunkel would have deleterious consequences for India's farming interests, drug industry, and public procurement and distribution system. Finance Minister Manmohan Singh defends the agreement as an imperfect but positive step in an international system characterized by "inequalities of economic and political power."

April

1 The World Bank announces a $246 million loan to India to support the Maharashtra government's rehabilitation program for the victims of last September's earthquake in Latur.

4 **The Supreme Court criticizes Chief Election Commissioner T.N. Seshan for attempting to "usurp" the powers of various organs of states including the judiciary, and orders him to "mend his ways," warning that it would be forced to carry out the "painful duty of summoning him and setting him right" if he did not do so.** The court also issues an injunction barring Seshan from unilaterally enforcing a nonstatutory "model code of conduct" for the forthcoming parliamentary by-elections. This is the second such ruling aimed at restricting the powers of the chief election commissioner since August 1993.

6 U.S. Deputy Secretary of State Strobe Talbott arrives in New Delhi on the first leg of his tour of India and Pakistan. The visit, designed to improve recently strained relations between India and the United States, is dominated by issues of regional disarmament and the prospects of India's accession to the Nuclear Nonproliferation Treaty.

8 The leaders of the All-Parties Hurriyat Conference, Maulvi Abbas Ansari, Professor Abdul Ghani, G.M.

Bhat, and Bahauddin Farouqi, announce during a visit to New Delhi that they are ready for talks "without reservation and without prejudice" with people from all levels for solving the Kashmir issue.

Thirty-six senior leaders of the BJP meet at Sariska to formulate the party's stand on the three issues of Hindutva, Swadeshi, and caste-based politics. Attended also by RSS General Secretary H.V. Seshadri and the Joint General Secretary K. Sudershan, the meeting concludes with a decision to take a hard Hindutva line, including a commitment to Swadeshi.

19 The government is forced by opposition parties to debate India's accession to the Final Act of the Uruguay Round of the General Agreement on Tariffs and Trade, which was formally adopted in Marrakesh, Morocco, on April 15. While the GATT Final Act is not subject to parliamentary ratification, opposition parties had urged fuller discussion on the grounds that the government's action amounted to "surrendering the country's economic sovereignty." Responding to the charge amid scenes of uproar in both houses of parliament, Prime Minister Narasimha Rao claims that the government's decision is necessary for "the Indian economy to be integrated into the world economy."

22 Interim Chief Minister Chhabildas Mehta is formally sworn in as chief minister of Gujarat, ending a two-month-long intraparty struggle over the selection of former chief minister Chimanbhai Patel's successor.

23 **The Central Panchayati Raj Act comes into effect after it is ratified by the states. The 73rd Amendment of the Indian Constitution, passed on April 24, 1993, had required all states to legislate afresh or amend their existing *panchayat* acts to bring them into conformity with the central act within a year.**

27 Ambassadors from 11 countries with diplomatic representation in India, including 8 Muslim countries, visit Kashmir at the invitation of the government.

28 Minister of State for External Affairs R.L. Bhatia confirms that unpublicized official-level talks between India and the United States on nuclear nonproliferation are under way in London.

May

2 Six leading Akali Dal factions dissolve to form a new political party, the Shrimoni Akali Dal, in Amritsar. At a public rally inside the Golden Temple complex, leaders of the new party read out a declaration demanding the formation of a separate "area" for the Sikhs.

3 The Indo-U.S. nuclear nonproliferation talks end in London without any agreement. Prime Minister Narasimha Rao asks parliament not to attach significance to the talks and announces the revival of the National Security Council to address issues relating to defense and national security. The U.S. Department of State confirms that the talks were "preliminary in nature and came to no conclusions."

4 India successfully launches the Augmented Satellite Launch Vehicle from Sriharikota, near Madras.

12 The Clinton administration announces the nomination of Frank Wisner, the current undersecretary of defense policy, as the next U.S. ambassador to India. Wisner is nominated after Clinton decided against the nomination of former congressman Stephen Solarz to the post, anticipating opposition from Congress.

13 The government's monopoly on providing basic telephone services is officially ended with the announcement of a new national telecommunications policy in

parliament that allows private companies, including those with foreign collaborators, to operate telephone services.

14 The World Bank approves loans totaling $6.5 billion to India over the next three years. The loans are less than the $9 billion approved for the previous three-year period and are aimed at financing specific economic projects, no longer at propping up India's currency reserves.

18 **Prime Minister Narasimha Rao addresses a joint session of the U.S. Congress during his visit to the United States.** Speaking on nuclear disarmament, Rao rejects nonproliferation proposals restricted to South Asia and calls for a "nuclear no-first-use" agreement to outlaw nuclear weapons, and the simultaneous launching of multilateral negotiations for nuclear disarmament. On human rights, Rao notes that while India was taking "scrupulous care" to punish human rights violations, the most dangerous threat to the violation of human rights came from "the bullets of terrorists." On economic reforms, Rao observes that American firms are in the forefront of taking advantage of the vast investment opportunities created by the reforms and calls for the establishment of a new economic relationship between India and the United States.

26 Russian deputy foreign minister Anatoly Adamishin announces that Russia will supply seven cryogenic engines used in rocket launching to India beginning in 1996, but that the technology for the engines will not be transferred.

By-elections are held for seven Lok Sabha seats in Maharashtra, Andhra Pradesh, Orissa, West Bengal, Bihar, and Madhya Pradesh; and ten assembly seats in Himachal Pradesh, Tamil Nadu, Punjab, Rajasthan, Kerala, West Bengal, and Nagaland.

Congress wins four of the seven Lok Sabha seats and five of the ten assembly seats.

31 **Violence marks the second round of by-elections in six assembly constituencies in Uttar Pradesh and one constituency in Punjab.** In Uttar Pradesh, the SP and BSP share four seats and the BJP wins two; in Punjab, the Akali Dal(B) defeats the Congress Party, its closest rival, for the Ajnala seat.

June

4 The short-range surface-to-surface missile Prithvi is successfully test-fired from a mobile launcher inside the Interim Test Range at Chandipur. A second test-firing is carried out on June 6, during which the missile is tested to its full range of 250 km. The United States once again appeals against the deployment of the missile.

7 Two British citizens are abducted at Aroo, near Pahalgam, in southern Kashmir.

9 Swami Dhirendra Brahmachari is killed in an airplane crash along with the pilot of his private plane in Udhampur district in Jammu and Kashmir. Brahmachari had first shot into prominence for his association with Prime Minister Indira Gandhi during the Emergency.

10 A two-day session of the All-India Congress Committee opens in New Delhi. As its three main tasks, the Congress Party identifies the fight against the BJP's brand of communalism; the formulation of a politico-economic program with which to combat "caste-ist" parties; and the resolution of the situation in Jammu and Kashmir without alienating the people.

The National Council of the Bharatiya Janata Party meets in Baroda and declares that the party is committed to the Hindutva agenda. Arguing that the BJP is the principal opposition in an emerging two-party system, party president Advani notes that "the BJP will ensure that the spirit of India, epitomized by Hindutva, prevails over draconian, undemocratic laws."

13 A special session of parliament is stalled by demands from the BJP and other opposition parties for the resignation of Food Minister Kalpnath Rai for his role in the sugar scandal that erupted in early June. Rai, who accused bureaucrats in his and other departments of being responsible for the decisions, was stripped of his power over sugar policies by the prime minister on June 7.

14 **Defeating the purpose for which the special four-day session of parliament had been convened, the central government fails to introduce the much-debated Constitution (83rd) Amendment Bill, which had aimed to create a multimember election commission.** The bill could not be introduced for want of the requisite two-thirds majority. The main point of disagreement was over the demand by opposition parties that the selection panel for chief election commissioner include the leader of the opposition, a demand that the government did not concede because of the fear that it would add a "political element" to the mode of appointing a constitutional functionary. The government also defers consideration of the linked Representation of People Act (Second Amendment), which proposed the deregistration of political parties bearing religious names.

17 A government-sponsored *bandh* in Tamil Nadu is held seeking the central government's intervention to get early presidential assent for the bill passed by the Tamil Nadu Assembly for the continuation of the 69 percent reservation quota in educational institutions and government jobs. The Supreme Court had earlier ordered that the reservation percentage should not exceed 50.

21 The Janata Dal splits again, as 14 members of the 40-member parliamentary party led by socialist leaders George Fernandes and Rabi Ray declare their intention to elect a new leader.

23 The two British nationals held hostage by the Harkat-ul-Ansar are released unconditionally in Anantnag.

30 India and Russia sign a declaration during Prime Minister Rao's visit to Moscow recognizing the growing threat from aggressive nationalism and religious and political extremism to the unity of pluralistic states, and urging the international community to respect the integrity of such states.

July

9 The governor of Punjab Surendra Nath and nine members of his family are killed in an airplane crash over Himachal Pradesh. Allegations of massive corruption later surface against Nath, as large amounts of cash, gold, and gems are reported to have been recovered from the governor's residence after his death.

13 The central government and the major opposition parties reach a broad consensus on allowing Tamil Nadu to continue with a 69 percent reservation for Scheduled Castes and "backward" classes in educational institutions and jobs. The agreement between parties extends beyond Tamil Nadu to respecting the status quo on the levels of reservation in all states. Home Minister S.B. Chavan announces that the Tamil Nadu bill, pending for six months, will be forwarded to the president for his immediate assent.

17 Prime Minister Narasimha Rao entrusts former comptroller and auditor general Gian Prakash with conducting an inquiry into the sugar scandal. The Public Accounts Committee, initially responsible for the task,

had been asked to put off its investigation on the grounds that it was outside its jurisdiction.

18 During a visit by Chinese Vice Premier and Foreign Minister Qian Qichen, China supports the Indian stand that the Kashmir issue should be solved by bilateral Indo-Pakistan negotiations. Qian maintains, however, that China's sale of arms to Islamabad does not undermine regional security.

23 The situation in Assam deteriorates further as Bodo militants massacre 60 Muslim inmates at a relief camp in Bansbari Barpeta district.

26 In an action-taken report tabled in parliament in response to the charges made by the Joint Parliamentary Committee investigating the Bombay securities scandal, the government defends Finance Minister Manmohan Singh, Petroleum Minister B. Shankaranand, then-minister of state for finance Rameshwar Thakur, the ministries of railways and civil aviation, and former RBI governor R. Venkitaramanan, all of whom had been indicted by the JPC. A united and enraged opposition demands the withdrawal of the report.

August

5 One of the main conspirators in the Bombay blasts of March, Yakub Abdul Razak Memon, is arrested by the CBI at the New Delhi railway station. He blames Pakistan and his elder brother, "Tiger" Memon, the main accused, for the blasts. Home Minister S.B. Chavan asserts that evidence gathered following Yakub Memon's arrest confirms Pakistan's complicity in the blasts "beyond an iota of doubt."

The Hazratbal crisis in Kashmir comes to an end as the government announces that all 14 security bunkers will be removed from the complex, and the

Muslim Auqaf Trust agrees to take control of the shrine. Trust spokespersons say that both they and the leaders of the All-Party Hurriyat Conference are satisfied that the holy relic enshrined in the mosque is "safe." Two days later, 21 people are killed and 60 wounded in separate incidents in the Kashmir Valley, even as the leaders of the Muslim Auqaf Trust and the All-Parties Hurriyat Conference lead devotees in the purification of the Hazratbal mosque.

10 Two policemen are killed in a grenade attack as the annual Amarnath Pilgrimage begins in Kashmir. The Hurriyat Conference, the Hizb-ul-Mujahideen, and other organizations appeal to the Harkat-ul-Ansar to end its threat to disrupt the pilgrimage. Heavily protected by army, Border Security Force, and Central Reserve Police Force battalions, the pilgrimage ends peacefully.

15 Kashmir forms the centerpiece of Prime Minister Rao's speech from the Red Fort on Independence Day. Rao attacks Pakistan for sponsoring terrorism in Kashmir and threatens not only never to part with Kashmir, but to move toward winning back "Pakistan Occupied Kashmir" as well: "If there is an unfinished task before India it is to get Pakistan to vacate that part of Kashmir it continues to occupy."

Four persons are killed and 86 injured in police firing as BJP activists make repeated attempts to hoist the tricolor at the disputed Idgah Maidan in Hubli, Karnataka.

17 The two-week-long clash over the action-taken report between the opposition and the government ends as the government agrees to revise and modify the report and the opposition parties end their boycott of parliament.

23 **Pakistan's former prime minister Nawaz Sharif declares at a public rally, "I can confirm that Pakistan possesses an atomic bomb." While the government**

of Pakistan immediately denies Sharif's claim, the Indian External Affairs Ministry notes that Sharif's claim must be taken seriously and accuses Pakistan of confronting India with a nuclear threat to settle its outstanding bilateral differences.

September

2 Thousands of students gather at Srinagar in the Garhwal region of Uttar Pradesh, under the banner of the Uttarkhand Chattra Sangharsh Samiti, to demand the formation of a separate Uttarkhand state comprising the eight hill districts of Kumaon and Garhwal. Concerned about the escalating violence in the hill region, where three people were killed and over 100 injured in police firing in another agitation on September 1, Prime Minister Rao invites Mulayam Singh Yadav to a meeting with the central government and requests him to find a solution through negotiations.

13 A government-sponsored pro-reservation *bandh* in Uttar Pradesh results in the death of three persons and injuries to over 250. More than 500 persons are arrested for their involvement in the violence. Mulayam Singh had earlier rejected the advice of the central government to cancel the *bandh*. The state unit of the Congress Party, meanwhile, recommends that the Congress withdraw support from the SP-BSP government over the issue.

15 The Maharashtra government confirms that 36 cases of suspected plague have been reported from Mamala village in the Marathwada region.

20 The Congress-Party-led Karnataka legislative assembly passes a bill providing for 73 percent reservations for the Other Backward Classes and Scheduled Castes and Scheduled Tribes, in spite of a boycott by members of the two main opposition parties, the Janata Dal and the BJP.

22 **The Gujarat government confirms that 17 people have died of pneumonic plague in Surat. Large numbers of families begin an exodus from the city as rumors spread that the city's water supply has been poisoned. The Gujarat government declares the city "disease affected" and attempts to seal all exit points. As the death toll in Surat rises, suspected cases of plague are reported in Ahmedabad, Baroda, Bhuj, Cambay, Gandhinagar, and Palanpur. Cases of bubonic plague are reported from Beed district in Maharashtra.**

23 Hundreds of Muslims in Bombay receive letters from the police asking them to prove their Indian nationality before they can be issued identity cards to vote in the next elections. Muslim leaders declare the letters offensive, and Police Commissioner Satish Sahney criticizes the move as "a wrong thing," insisting that that he had "no idea how this happened."

27 The central government and the Bihar government sign the long-awaited agreement on the formation of the Jharkhand autonomous council, which will cover 18 districts of the Jharkhand area in Bihar.

28 The Maharashtra government declares that the plague situation in the state, where the total number of cases of suspected bubonic plague stands at 500, is stable. A single case of pneumonic plague is also reported in the state.

29 The Delhi chief minister declares all Delhi schools and cinema halls closed as a precautionary measure to prevent the spread of plague; 18 confirmed cases and 43 suspected cases are reported from the capital. Citizens are also advised to avoid crowded places. At the same time, Sri Lanka, Bangladesh, the United Arab Emirates, Saudi Arabia, Kuwait, Bahrain, Oman, Qatar, and Pakistan suspend air services to and from India.

October

4 The United States announces its decision not to invoke any part of the U.S. trade law "Super 301" against India for its alleged restrictions on imports of American textiles. The Clinton administration says that it will seek to lower the restrictions on American imports through negotiations rather than by resorting to penalizing provisions.

West Bengal Chief Minister Jyoti Basu announces in a new industrial development policy that the state government "welcomes foreign technology and investment as may be appropriate or mutually advantageous." The new policy signals a significant departure from the Left Front's attitude toward foreign investment.

5 Former comptroller and auditor general Gian Prakash submits his report on the sugar scandal to the prime minister's office. The report holds that the sugar crisis was the result of the mismanagement of available surplus stock, delay in the decision to import sugar, delay in the implementation of the decision to import, and poor coordination. It holds the Cabinet Committee on Prices, the food minister, the civil supplies minister, and the cabinet secretary responsible for not bringing the matter to the notice of the prime minister.

7 Violence breaks out in Bangalore as pro-Kannada activists protest the telecast of the Urdu news bulletin introduced on October 2 on Doordarshan. On October 14, criticizing the telecast of the Urdu news bulletin by the Bangalore Doordarshan Kendra as a violation of its code of conduct for political parties, the Election Commission suspends the telecast until the completion of assembly elections in the state.

15 The Polar Satellite Launch Vehicle is successfully launched at Sriharikota. Considered to be the most tech-

nologically challenging endeavor taken up by the Indian Space Research Organisation, the PSLV launch demonstrates India's capability to launch 1,000-kg. satellites into orbit by means of a fully indigenous launch vehicle technology.

The formation of a nine-member apolitical trust for the construction of a Ram temple at Ayodhya is announced by several Shankaracharyas, who say that they will ask the government to hand over the undisputed land around the Babri mosque site to initiate the process of temple construction. The VHP, which has sponsored its own trust, promptly declares that the "government-sponsored trust" will be a nonstarter. The CPM and Babri mosque Movement Coordination Committee condemn the trust as "a challenge to the Indian constitution and secular values" and ask that the government publicly dissociate itself from it.

16 The central government announces an economic package and administrative changes for Jammu and Kashmir in an effort to restore normalcy to the state. Rs.750 crores are allotted to the state, and the central government expects to earmark additional funds for infrastructural projects.

18 Chief Election Commissioner T.N. Seshan threatens to withdraw recognition from political parties that fail to hold inner party elections within four months. The BJP and Janata Dal(G) welcome the order while the CPM and CPI criticize it as "untenable." The Congress asks for time to study the order and understand its implications.

21 The government raises the ceiling of election expenses for a candidate in assembly elections from Rs.50,000 to Rs.150,000 in response to a recommendation made by the Election Commission in September.

24 **In a unanimous judgment, the Supreme Court declines to answer the presidential reference seeking its opinion on whether a temple existed at the site of the demolished mosque at Ayodhya.** At the same time, the court upholds by a 3:2 majority the validity of the acquisition of land in the disputed area. The central government, however, is not allowed to assume ownership of the disputed land but is to act as a "receiver of the property" until the pending suits of title on the property are disposed of. **In a separate decision, the Supreme Court also convicts former Uttar Pradesh Chief Minister Kalyan Singh of the "grossest contempt of court" in allowing construction of a concrete platform near the disputed site in Ayodhya in July 1992 and sentences him to one day's symbolic imprisonment and a fine of Rs.2,000.**

30 The Congress Party releases a 15-page manifesto as a forerunner to separate state manifestos for the forthcoming assembly elections in Andhra Pradesh, Karnataka, Goa, and Sikkim. The manifesto highlights the economic achievements of the central government.

November

1 Prime Minister Rao relieves the Home Ministry of all political affairs relating to Jammu and Kashmir and takes charge himself.

8 The Bharatiya Janata Party and the Shiv Sena reach an understanding on seat adjustments in the Maharashtra assembly elections after months of bitter negotiations. The two parties together will contest all 288 seats, with the Shiv Sena contesting 171 seats and the BJP 117.

11 The Supreme Court stays the implementation of the bill passed by a special session of the Karnataka legislative assembly in September increasing reservations for ap-

pointments in the civil service to 73 percent, saying it will not permit any reservations beyond the 50 percent limit set by the court.

16 **Assembly elections are held in Goa and Sikkim.** The counting of the votes will begin on December 9, after Andhra Pradesh and Karnataka go to the polls.

17 The Election Commission declares Welfare Minister Sitaram Kesri and Food Minister Kalpnath Rai guilty of violating the code of conduct laid down by the commission for elections and recommends that the Congress Party "purge itself of elements which bring such disrepute to the system."

24 Agitating in Nagpur for inclusion in the list of tribes entitled to reservations in matters of employment and education, 113 Gowari tribals are killed in a stampede during a *lathi* charge. Maharashtra Tribal Welfare Minister Madhukar Pichad resigns, accepting moral responsibility for the deaths. Opposition parties call a statewide *bandh* to protest the tragedy and demand the resignation of the Pawar government.

28 Maharashtra Chief Minister Sharad Pawar announces reservations to Gowar and other tribes in proportion to their population. With the extension of the reservations, the state exceeds the ceiling of 50 percent imposed by the Supreme Court. Pawar says that Maharashtra will follow the example of Tamil Nadu in overcoming this hurdle. At the same time, the opposition-sponsored no-confidence motion against the Pawar government is defeated by 152 votes to 80.

30 Chief Election Commissioner T.N. Seshan extends the deadline for the issue of photo-identity cards to voters from November 30 to January 15 to enable the states of Maharashtra, Manipur, Bihar, Orissa, Gujarat, and Arunachal Pradesh, which will be going to the polls by March 1995, to comply with the order.

December

1 Elections for the legislative assemblies of Andhra Pradesh and Karnataka begin.

A major case of alleged espionage involving the Indian Space Research Organisation scientists, a representative of the Russian space agency Glavkosmos, and two Maldivian women is discovered.

5 Former prime minister and Janata Dal leader V.P. Singh resigns from the Lok Sabha, saying that he will focus on his campaign for "social justice and a cleaner public life."

10 **As the results of the assembly elections in Andhra Pradesh, Karnataka, Sikkim, and Goa come in, it is clear that the Congress Party, previously in power in all of these states, has suffered a crushing defeat.**

11 **The full results of the assembly elections are declared.** In Andhra Pradesh, the Telugu Desam Party led by N.T. Rama Rao secures 214 out of 292 seats, the Congress Party secures 26 seats, and the BJP 3. In Karnataka, the Janata Dal wins 115 seats in the 224-member Assembly, capturing power in the state for the third time in 11 years, and the BJP wins 40 seats, the highest number it has won in any southern state. A hung assembly emerges in Goa: the Congress Party, with 18 seats, stakes its claim to form a government; the Maharashtrawadi Gomantak Party wins 12 seats, the United Goans Democratic Party 3 seats, the BJP 2 seats, and independents 3 seats. In Sikkim, the Sikkim Democratic Front led by Pawan Kumar Chamling wins a majority of 19 out of 32 Sikkim assembly seats, and the Congress wins 2. N.T. Rama Rao, Deve Gowda, Pawan Kumar Chamling, and Pratapsing Rane are subsequently sworn in as chief ministers of Andhra Pradesh, Karnataka, Sikkim, and Goa respectively.

12 Home Minister S.B. Chavan rules out the construction of either a temple or a mosque at the disputed site in Ayodhya until all suits pending before the high court are decided.

14 Civil Supplies Minister A.K. Antony resigns following adverse observations about him in the Gian Prakash report on the sugar scandal.

16 The Gian Prakash report is not tabled in parliament but kept in the parliamentary library for perusal by its members under an agreement between the government and the opposition. The report accuses Food Minister Kalpnath Rai of being "fully responsible" for the crisis. The State Trading Corporation is also blamed for "professional incompetence."

22 In a sudden cabinet reshuffle, Prime Minister Rao drops Food Minister Kalpnath Rai, Minister of State for Rural Development Rameshwar Thakur, and Health and Family Welfare Minister B. Shankaranand from his council of ministers. While Rai had been criticized for his role in the sugar scandal, the other two ministers had been indicted by the JPC for their role in the securities scam.

24 **Minister for Human Resources Arjun Singh resigns from the cabinet.** In a seven-page resignation letter, he notes that Rao has failed to provide adequate leadership to the party. Paying tribute to Rajiv Gandhi at a press conference, he notes that the Congress Party will benefit if Sonia Gandhi decides to play an active role in its affairs. Maharashtra Chief Minister Sharad Pawar criticizes the resignation, saying that it is improper to resign on the verge of assembly elections in five states.

25 Former president Giani Zail Singh dies of complications from injuries in a road accident.

26 Pakistan asks India to close down its consulate in Karachi immediately. Pakistan Prime Minister Benazir Bhutto accuses India of spreading terrorism in Karachi.

Glossary

Some Common Abbreviations

AIADMK: All-India Anna Dravida Munnetra Kazhagam
AGP: Asom Gana Parishad
BJP: Bharatiya Janata Party
BSP: Bahujan Samaj Party
CBI: Central Bureau of Investigation
CPI: Communist Party of India
CPM: Communist Party of India–Marxist
DMK: Dravida Munnetra Kazhagam
JKLF: Jammu and Kashmir Liberation Front
JPC: Joint Parliamentary Committee
LTTE: Liberation Tigers of Tamil Eelam
NRI: Nonresident Indian
OBC: Other Backward Classes
PWG: People's War Group
RBI: Reserve Bank of India
RSS: Rashtriya Swayamsevak Sangh
SAARC: South Asian Association for Regional Cooperation
SC/ST: Scheduled Castes and Scheduled Tribes
SJP: Samajwadi Janata Party
SP: Samajwadi Party
TADA: Terrorist and Disruptive Activities (Prevention) Act
VHP: Vishwa Hindu Parishad

Advani, Lal Krishan. Leader of the Bharatiya Janata Party in the Lok Sabha. Usually seen as the leader of the "moderate" group within the party.

Akali Dal. The major party of the Sikhs, it governed the state of Punjab until May 1987 when President's Rule was imposed. Its several factions boycotted the February 1992 Punjab elections.

All-India Anna Dravida Munnetra Kazhagam (AIADMK). Ruling party in the state of Tamil Nadu, led by Jayalalitha, one of the most powerful women in Indian politics.

Ayodhya. Small city in east-central Uttar Pradesh; the city of Ram (or Rama), the god-king who is the hero of the Ramayana, and site of the disputed Babri mosque/Ram temple shrine, which was demolished on December 6, 1992, provoking widespread rioting and a major political crisis.

Babri mosque/Ram temple (Babri Masjid/Ramjanmabhoomi). Literally, "Mosque of Babur/Birthground of Ram." Ram (or Rama), an avatar of the god Vishnu and the hero of the Ramayana, one of the two great epics of Hinduism, is believed to have been born in Ayodhya on a particular spot of ground, on which a mosque was believed to have been built by the Mughal emperor Babur. The mosque was demolished on December 6, 1992, and a shrine to Ram was installed on the site.

Backward Classes (BCs). Classes recognized by the Indian Constitution as disadvantaged and allowed remedial treatment. In practice, "backward" classes have been defined in terms of caste membership. Composed of Scheduled Castes, Scheduled Tribes, and Other Backward Classes.

Bahujan Samaj Party (BSP). Literally "party of society's majority," which first contested in the 1989 parliamentary election and is part of the coalition that won the 1993 Uttar Pradesh elections. Led by Kanshi Ram, it attracts support not only from scheduled-caste voters, but also from other "oppressed" groups: Muslims, backward castes, and others.

Bajrang Dal. Militant youth organization, associated with the VHP.

Bhakti. The devotional tradition of Hinduism, originating as a movement in southern India in the 6th century and proceeding northward and lasting in full force until the 16th century. Contrasting with Vedic-origin, Sanskritic Hinduism, the poet-saints of this tradition emphasize personal devotion to God.

Bandh. Protest through general strike or closure of shops and offices.

Bharatiya Janata Party (BJP). Party formed from the Janata Party by elements of the Jana Sangh, with support mainly in northern India.

It favors a Hindu nationalist ideology, and expects to emerge as the single largest party in the next parliamentary election. In the November 1993 elections it was defeated in Uttar Pradesh, Madhya Pradesh, and Himachal Pradesh, states where it had ruled prior to the Ayodhya crisis, but returned to power in Rajasthan and in the newly formed Delhi state government. In the 1994–95 state elections, it won in Gujarat and (with the Shiv Sena) in Maharashtra, but lost in Bihar, Orissa, Andhra Pradesh, and Karnataka.

Bofors. Swedish armaments company that allegedly paid commissions to middlemen connected with the Congress Party and Rajiv Gandhi, in violation of its agreement with the government of India, to secure a Rs.1.1 billion contract to supply 155 mm howitzer field guns. In the 1989 election particularly, "Bofors" became a code word for corruption in high places. As late as April 1995, the investigation had not yet managed to get documents revealing the names of the holders of the relevant Swiss bank accounts from the Swiss courts.

Booth Capturing. The practice of forcing polling station officials to acquiesce in voting irregularities such as ballot box stuffing.

Chandra Shekhar. Prime minister of India from November 1990 until the May 1991 elections.

Communal. Refers to ethnic communities, most commonly Hindu and Muslim; a "communalist" is what opponents call those whose political identity is bound up with their ethnic or religious identity and who allegedly put their community "above" the nation.

Communist Party of India (CPI). The less influential of the two major Communist parties; at present a part of the Left Front in parliament.

Communist Party of India–Marxist (CPM). The stronger segment of the Communist Party of India after the split of 1964. The CPM has run the government of the state of West Bengal since 1977 and competes with the Congress Party for power in Kerala.

Congress Party. The dominant Indian national party since independence, it formed the government after the 1991 elections. Led by Prime Minister P.V. Narasimha Rao, who is also party president, it is virtually shut out of power in the major states. It won power in

Madhya Pradesh and Himachal Pradesh in November 1993 and in Orissa in February–March 1995, but lost in all the other states that went to the polls then. Also known as the Congress(I), the name of the faction created by a party split in 1977 and initially led by Indira Gandhi (the "I" stands for Indira).

Crore. Ten million (10,000,000).

Dalit. Literally, "oppressed" or "ground down," the term for Scheduled Caste persons preferred by militant and educated ex-untouchables and by many of those who sympathize with their aspirations.

Dravida Munnetra Kazhagam (DMK). Tamil nationalist party, led by M. Karunanidhi, who served as chief minister of Tamil Nadu from 1969 to 1976 and 1989–90.

Doordarshan. The monopoly television network owned and run by the government. It now competes with satellite-broadcast services.

Emergency. Declared by the Indira Gandhi government in June 1975, it lasted 21 months; opposition leaders were jailed, press censorship imposed, and the constitution amended to restrict the judiciary. Ended with the defeat of Indira Gandhi in the 1977 election.

Five-Year Plans. Formulated by the Planning Commission and approved by parliament, these analyze the economic situation of the country and set out broad goals and specific guidelines for investment and other economic policy, for both public and private sectors. The First Five-Year Plan covered the 1951–56 period. The current plan, covering 1991–96, is the eighth.

Gandhi, Indira. Daughter of Jawaharlal Nehru and prime minister from 1966 to 1977 and from 1980 to 1984, when she was assassinated by her own Sikh bodyguards.

Gandhi, Mohandas K. The preeminent leader of India's fight against British colonial rule from 1919 until independence. He was assassinated in January 1948 by a Hindu nationalist fanatic. Also known as Mahatma Gandhi.

Gandhi, Rajiv. Son of Indira Gandhi and prime minister from 1984 to 1989 when the Congress Party lost the parliamentary election. Assassinated on May 21, 1991, while campaigning in Tamil Nadu.

Green Revolution. The transformation of agriculture beginning in the mid-1960s based on the development of high-yielding varieties of wheat and rice, and the adoption of necessary modern practices of irrigation, and of fertilizer and pesticide use.

Harijan. Literally, "people of God," the name Mohandas K. Gandhi used for the Scheduled Castes. See also Dalit.

Hindi Heartland. The belt of states in which Hindi is the major language spoken: from west to east, Rajasthan, Haryana, Delhi, Madhya Pradesh, Uttar Pradesh, and Bihar.

Hindutva. Literally, "Hindu-ness," the term was used as the title of a book written in 1922 by Hindu nationalist leader V.D. Savarkar to argue that Hindus were a nation. It is now used as the equivalent of "Hindu nationalism."

Jammu and Kashmir Liberation Front (JKLF). Militant group fighting for the independence of Kashmir.

Janata Dal. Party formed from the Jan Morcha, the Janata Party, factions of the Lok Dal, and a Congress splinter known as the Congress(S), it had 141 of the 144 seats held by the National Front in the Lok Sabha elected in 1989 that formed the government led by V.P. Singh. The party split in November 1990, but defeated an incumbent Congress government in Karnataka in November 1994, and, led by chief minister Laloo Prasad Yadav, won reelection in Bihar in March 1995. The Janata Dal Orissa government was defeated in the March 1995 election.

Jati. Caste or subcaste that defines acceptable interactions in marriage, dining, and other caste-related practices.

Jharkhand. The region of east-central India (covering parts of the states of Madhya Pradesh, Andhra Pradesh, Orissa, and West Bengal, but mainly the southern segment of Bihar) in which various tribal people live. Name given to the state or autonomous region sought by those people.

Kashmir Valley. Also the Vale of Kashmir. The spectacularly beautiful valley of the river Jhelum, a part of the Indian state of Jammu and Kashmir (the other major regions being Buddhist-dominated Ladakh and Hindu-dominated Jammu, with other areas claimed by

India now controlled by Pakistan and China), which is populated almost entirely by Muslims. The political heartland of the state.

Khalistan. Name given to the sovereign state demanded by Sikh militants in Punjab.

Lakh. One hundred thousand (100,000).

Liberation Tigers of Tamil Eelam (LTTE). Leading Sri Lankan Tamil militant group, which seeks a separate state for Sri Lankan Tamils in the northern and eastern sections of the island.

Lok Sabha. Lower house of India's bicameral parliament. Equivalent to the British House of Commons, its 542 members are directly elected from district constituencies for a five-year maximum term.

Mahabharata. One of two major epics of India, it describes the internecine warfare that results from a feud of succession involving descendants of the legendary king Bharata.

Mandal Commission. The common name—from its chairman, B.P. Mandal—of the Backward Classes Commission, which in its report (published in 1980) proposed far-reaching governmental regulations to increase the employment of "backward" classes.

National Front. An electoral alliance composed of the Janata Dal, DMK, Telugu Desam, and AGP, it formed the government headed by V. P. Singh after the 1989 election.

Naxalite. A revolutionary or radical activist ready to adopt violent means. The name comes from participants in a rebellion in Naxalbari, West Bengal, in 1967.

Nehru, Jawaharlal. Nationalist leader who served as prime minister from 1947 until his death in 1964.

Nonresident Indians (NRIs). Persons of Indian origin living abroad, including those holding citizenship elsewhere. Allowed certain privileges denied to other foreigners with respect to owning real property, investment, and travel, among other things, in an effort to keep them attached to India and to attract their foreign exchange.

Other Backward Classes (OBCs). "Backward" classes other than the Scheduled Castes and Scheduled Tribes. Typically defined in caste terms, to mean the non-elite, non-untouchable *jatis*.

Panchayat. Literally, a council of five. A village or *jati* council. Panchayati raj is the system of rural local government introduced in 1959 and changed significantly since, with variations from state to state. A new, standardized system that will give greater political and economic power to the *panchayats* has been entrenched in the constitution; enabling legislation in the states was passed by the beginning of 1995.

Planning Commission. Government body that prepares five-year plans, which provide a broad framework for public and private economic goals.

President. In India, the equivalent of a constitutional monarch, who gives formal assent to bills but whose powers are severely restricted. Elected by members of parliament and the state legislatures for a five-year term. Currently the president is Shankar Dayal Sharma, elected unopposed in July 1992. The vice president, elected in August 1992, is K.R. Narayanan, the first Harijan to hold either office, who had a distinguished career in the foreign service and then entered politics as a member of the Congress Party.

President's Rule. Suspension of a state's assembly and direct rule of the state by the central government through the centrally appointed governor, typically when the state government loses its majority or is deemed unable to govern due to a "disturbed" political situation. It has sometimes been used by the center to topple opposition-controlled state governments.

"Quit India." The slogan of the 1942 movement reflecting the Congress demand for immediate independence. Instantly and largely successfully suppressed by jailing large numbers of Congress leaders.

Rajya Sabha. Upper house of India's bicameral parliament. All but 6 of its 256 members are elected by the legislatures of the states for staggered 6-year terms. Roughly equivalent in power to Britain's House of Lords.

Ramayana. One of two major epics of India, it describes the adventures of Rama, a warrior-king and the incarnation of the god Vishnu.

Rashtriya Swayamsevak Sangh (RSS). Militant Hindu organization founded in 1925 and associated with the Bharatiya Janata Party, the

Vishwa Hindu Parishad, and the Bajrang Dal—the members of the "Sangh parivar" (RSS family). The RSS draws its membership mainly from urban and lower–middle classes and seeks the consolidation of a Hindu nation.

Reservation. The provision for quotas in legislative bodies, civil services, educational institutions, and other public institutions, typically in proportion to the percentage in the population, for qualified members of Scheduled Castes and Scheduled Tribes, and, in some places, for Other Backward Classes.

Sabha. Literally an "assembly," it also is extended to mean "association."

Samiti. Literally a "committee," it usually refers to an organization, typically a voluntary organization.

Sati. A widow who immolates herself on the funeral pyre of her husband; by extension, the practice. Outlawed since the 19th century, there are still, very rarely, cases of *sati*.

Satyagraha. Literally, "truth-force." A term coined by Mohandas K. Gandhi for civil disobedience, especially courting arrest.

Scheduled Castes and Scheduled Tribes (SC/STs). List of untouchable, or Harijan, castes and tribes drawn up under the 1935 Government of India Act and subsequently revised. Legislative seats as well as government posts and places in educational institutions are reserved for members of these castes and tribes.

Shankaracharya. The head of a *math* (monastery) founded by the 8th–9th century philosopher-saint Shankara. There are four Shankaracharyas, and from time to time they have individually played significant roles in national politics, as defenders of orthodox Hinduism.

Shiv Sena. Militant nativist communal organization, it was founded in Bombay in 1966 to agitate against South Indian immigrants to the state of Maharashtra. Alleged to have played a major part in the riots in December 1992 and January 1993 in Bombay, following the demolition of the Babri mosque. In alliance with the BJP, it won the March 1995 elections in Maharashtra.

Sikh, Sikhism. The religion of Sikhism was founded in the 16th century by the first guru, Nanak, drawing on Hindu devotionalism and

Islam. Persecuted by the later Mughal emperors, Sikhs developed into a martial community, led by the tenth and last guru, Gobind Singh; a Sikh kingdom in central Punjab was defeated by the British in the mid-19th century.

South Asian Association for Regional Cooperation (SAARC). Organization formed in 1985 to enhance regional cooperation in social, economic, and cultural development. The SAARC members are Bangladesh, Bhutan, India, the Maldives, Nepal, Pakistan, and Sri Lanka. The eighth SAARC summit was held in India in May 1995.

"Super 301" provision. Section 301 of the 1988 U.S. Omnibus Trade and Competitiveness Act designed to discourage unfair trading. Countries found to be trading unfairly or discriminating against American goods may have preferences for their goods canceled and restrictions such as special duties imposed by way of retaliation.

Swadeshi. Literally, "[one's] own country." A nationalist slogan in the early 20th century that asked Indians to boycott foreign goods, especially cloth, in favor of Indian manufactures. More recently used to indicate an ideology of economic self-reliance.

Terrorism and Disruptive Activities (Prevention) Act (TADA). Intended for use in Punjab in the mid-1980s and allowed to lapse in May 1995, this law permitted extended preventive detention and secret testimony (to protect witnesses under threat from terrorists) and required those charged of certain crimes to prove their innocence, among other provisions. Extended to almost all states, it was widely abused by police and state governments and strongly criticized by both Indian and foreign human rights organizations, including the chair of the Indian Human Rights Commission.

Vishwa Hindu Parishad (VHP). A movement seeking to reinvigorate Hinduism. Leader of Hindu sentiment and organizer of actions regarding the Babri mosque/Ram temple controversy, although precisely what its responsibility was for the demolition of the mosque is not clear.

Yadav. An agrarian (cowherd) caste of the Gangetic plain, it forms a substantial bloc within the "backward" castes; leaders of the community have governed as chief ministers of Uttar Pradesh and Bihar.

About the Contributors

Kanchan Chandra is a Ph.D. candidate in the Department of Government at Harvard University.

Meghnad Desai, Professor of Economics at the London School of Economics and Political Science, is currently Director of the Centre for the Study of Global Governance, LSE. He was educated at the University of Bombay and secured his Ph.D. from the University of Pennsylvania. From 1984 to 1991 he was co-editor of the *Journal of Applied Econometrics.* Desai was Chair (1986–92) and is currently President of Islington South and Finsbury Constituency Labour Party in London. He was made a peer in April 1991.

Ainslie T. Embree is Professor Emeritus of History at Columbia University, where he was Chairman of the History Department (1982–85), Associate Dean of the School of International and Public Affairs (1972–78), and Director of the Southern Asian Institute. He served in the U.S. Embassy in Delhi as Cultural Counselor (1978–80) and as Special Consultant to the Ambassador (1994–95). Embree edited the *Encyclopedia of Asian History,* and his most recent books are *Imagining India* and *Utopias in Conflict: Regionalism and Nationalism in India.*

James Manor is Director of the Institute of Commonwealth Studies at the University of London's School of Advanced Study, and Professional Fellow at the Institute of Development Studies, University of Sussex. He has previously taught at Yale, Harvard, and Leicester universities. His works include *Nehru to the Nineties: The Changing Office of Prime Minister in India* (as editor); *Power, Poverty, and Poison: Disaster and Response in an Indian City; The Expedient Utopian: Bandaranaike and Ceylon; Rethinking Third World Politics* (as editor); and *States or Markets? Neo-Liberalism and the Development Policy Debate* (as co-editor). Manor is also the co-author, with Richard Crook, of a forthcoming book, *Participation and Performance: Democratic Decentralisation in South Asia and West Africa.*

Philip Oldenburg is an independent scholar who teaches at Columbia University. He has published on topics of domestic and foreign policy in South Asia, including work on Indian electoral politics, rural development, and municipal government. His current research project is on the grass-roots foundations of state legitimacy in India.

E. A. Ramaswamy is a sociologist who teaches industrial relations and human resource management as Visiting Professor at the Institute of Social Sciences, The Hague, and the Institute of Management, Bangalore. He also freelances as a management consultant. He has previously taught at the Delhi School of Economics, University of Delhi, and Administrative Staff College, Hyderabad. Ramaswamy has researched trade unions, industrial relations, and human resource management in India for the past three decades and published extensively on these subjects, mostly with the Oxford University Press, New Delhi. He also writes a column on labor for *Business India*, a popular business biweekly. His recent work *The Rayon Spinners: The Strategic Management of Industrial Relations* (Delhi: Oxford University Press, 1994) was shortlisted for the Booker Prize in 1994.

John R. Wood is Associate Professor of Political Science at the University of British Columbia. He is the Chair of the Centre for South Asian Research, UBC, and Associate Editor (South Asia) of *Pacific Affairs*. His research and publications have focused on Indian federal and state politics including, recently, interstate conflicts over river water allocation as exemplified in the Narmada and Cauvery River disputes (see *Asian Survey,* October 1993). Wood has served twice in New Delhi as Resident Director of the Shastri Indo-Canadian Institute and is its President for 1994–96.

Index